Träd, Gräs och Stenar:
A Collective History

Håkan Agnsäter
Mats Eriksson Dunér
Jakob Sjöholm
Jonas Stål

Translation by Linda McAllister

Originally published in 2022 in Sweden as *Träd, Gräs
och Stenar, Pärson Sound, International Harvester:
En kollektiv berättelse* by Dokument Press
This edition published by Anthology Editions, 2023

87 Guernsey Street
Brooklyn, NY 11222

anthologyeditions.com

Creative Directors: Jesse Pollock, Keith Abrahamsson
Translator: Linda McAllister
Editor: Mark Iosifescu
Editorial Assistant: Donna Allen
Original Design: Jon Edergren
Cover Design and Interior Layout: Martha Ormiston
Sales and Marketing: Casey Whalen

The cost of this translation was supported by a subsidy
from the Swedish Arts Council. Their support is gratefully
acknowledged.

First English Edition
ARC 124
Printed in China

ISBN: 978-1-944860-58-5

Contents

In memory of
Torbjörn Abelli,
Thomas Mera Gartz,
and Urban Yman

Foreword

Pärson Sound, International Harvester, and Träd,
Gräs och Stenar's history is a collective story of
musical pioneering spirit and its liberating force,
of the individuals behind the music and the people
surrounding it, of ideas and ideals, friendship
and friction, of community and alienation, of soil
and crops, happiness and sorrow, life and death,
all woven together by music that has evolved since
Pärson Sound's first show in April of 1967 to their
current iteration as Träden, over half a century
later—music that has impacted generations of
people, in Sweden and beyond. Our book tells the
group's story from the bandmembers' and their
friends' perspectives. In the spirit of the band,
the book has come together through a thoroughly
collective effort.

Bo Anders wrote once that sounds become
music if we listen to them, and by listening people
show their love for life and matter. Pärson Sound,
International Harvester, and Träd, Gräs och Stenar
were nothing without their audience. The audience
members, the listeners, are those who make the
group's repetitive soundscape into music and, in the
end, into a collective declaration of love to life.

Håkan Agnsäter, Mats Eriksson Dunér, Jakob
Sjöholm, and Jonas Stål

PROLOGUE

Sheep with Antennae

Jon Jefferson Klingberg

I've been told a story of a mother who parked her baby stroller in the middle of the cacophony at a rock concert. Someone came up to the woman and pointed out how inappropriate it was to expose the child to music of this kind: "The child will be overwhelmed by anxiety." The child in the stroller was me, and one of the musicians was my father, Bo Anders Persson. Both music and anxiety have characterized my life. Music as a form of expression and source of power and togetherness. Anxiety as a color defending its spot on the human palette of feelings.

Today, my job is supporting people with psychosocial difficulties. What role early exposure to International Harvester and Träd, Gräs och Stenar plays in all this is unclear. When I hear about people who work within the arts coming from backgrounds where their parents spent their time on things other than books, art, and music, I sometimes feel a pang of jealousy—that they are talented and driven enough to have made it to where they are today, regardless of their upbringing. As if they were touched by an inexplicable divine hand. That is not what it's been like for me.

Early on in my life, music seemed to be something important, judging by how many adults in my life were involved with it. My earliest memories are of musicians in the commune in Djursholm, where I lived together with my mother, Margareta, and the members of the band Blå Tåget when I was five years old. I have two clear memories from that time. The first is of nice conversations with Mats G. Bengtsson, the pianist in Blå Tåget. The other is a big living room full of electric guitars. As I remember it, one of them was covered in leopard skin. Still to this day, I can't understand what Blå Tåget was going to do with that many guitars. Let alone picture someone in the band with a Fender Stratocaster covered in leopard skin.

In the years that have passed, things have been compartmentalized into brackets and boxes where they weren't initially. Especially the music. What I later in life learned to identify as Arbete & Fritid, International Harvester, Träd, Gräs och Stenar, and Hot Boys, as I kid I just saw as "the adult's music." How the various projects differed from and related to each other was something I wasn't able to reflect on until way later. If a child cares about the lineup of their parents' rock band it's probably time to call a therapist.

At the beginning of the 1980s, my dad and I lived in Björkhöjden. A place located one mile from the village Borgvattnet in the county of Jämtland, which is known mostly for stories of its clergy house being haunted, something that the local shop owner Erik Brännholm used, with limited success, in his branding. Brännholm, a creative businessman, had prominence in the area. Among other things, he is said to have managed to get rid of a lot of unreasonably small suits made in Asia by including ties in the price. The previous owners of our house had come straight from Christiania [an intentional community] in Copenhagen. They had painted everything inside the house bright red and yellow, an act we assumed had to do with their Christiania background and that garish psychedelic aesthetic. One of the first things we did when we moved in was to tear down all that colorful Masonite. Room was needed to let the discreet charm of the shifting landscape outside into the house. The work was conducted to music. When the Masonite was being torn down, the choice was the Sex Pistols' *Never Mind the Bollocks*. Peter, a friend of the family who was present that day, pointed out that it was "good wrecking music." I remember the adult camp of the household expressing pleasant surprise that the infamous Englishmen were a decent classic rock 'n' roll band after all.

We acquired about half a dozen sheep, a stock that in a few years grew to about ninety animals. Two outhouses were moved to their pasture to house them. The arrival of the sheep meant that ideals were put to the test. The method of marking them by cutting their ears seemed cruel. So, to temporarily

keep track of their origins, the sheep were marked with green spray paint. Just writing letters and numbers on them was considered impersonal. Instead, a code system of circles, dots, and lines was invented. After being marked, each one of the stressed-out sheep ran back into the flock, where newly painted fleeces rubbed up against each other, making the mysterious symbols even harder to decipher.

Corralling them was another problem. Anyone who has tried to carry rolls of sheep fencing knows why. They are extremely heavy and finding a simpler way of utilizing the surrounding areas' potential as pasture became a top priority. The question of why sheep couldn't, like horses and cows, be fenced in using an easily installed electrical fence needed to be explored. To teach sheep to respect electrical fences would be to find a sheep farmer's answer to an alchemist's philosopher's stone. Could the issue be tackled pedagogically? The idea was tested in a kind of schooling pasture for the lambs, where the electrical wires were strung closely together like the lines in sheet music. The lambs wiggled through anyway. Was the problem that their thick fleece protected them from electricity? A number of adult sheep were fitted with DIY conductive collars connected to vertical antennas, which were supposed to give the sheep an electric shock on contact with the fence. The antennae were made from welding wire with the ends bent into loops so that the sheep wouldn't poke one another in

Above: Jon Klingberg tilling in the sunset. Photo: Private.

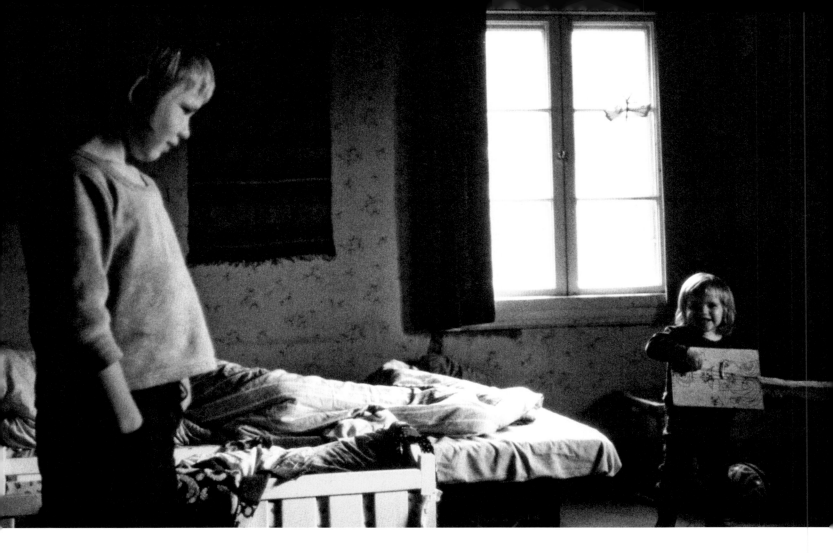

the eye. There, somewhere, is when the line between ingenuity and animal cruelty was crossed. In defense of my usually very animal-rights-conscientious father, I have to add that the experiment was immediately terminated when the first sheep got stuck with its antenna loop in the electric fence. I haven't seen sheep with antennae since.

These animals, together with Bo Anders's assignment as cantor in Borgvattnet's church, became crucial to the social connections in the community.

Especially after we herded them into Borgvattnet, where they were allowed to graze on lusher meadows than what Björkhöjden had to offer. They frequently escaped, and our phone rang often. The cause: fallen down electrical fencing.

Gusten was a person of vital importance to our existence in Björkhöjden. He showed up to watch the sheep for a week but stayed for three years. He was evading the Swedish justice system and became my educator and psychedelic governess when

Bo Anders was at his job as a music teacher in Hammerdal. Gusten was always crafting or repairing something. He was in the habit of disassembling things that he didn't always reassemble. That's how a pair of bongos were transformed into firewood, for example. He liked marijuana and could eat fire. Probably not the type of babysitter that would have a high ranking on Nanny. com. One dark evening when I had some friends over, Gusten, who had been smoking some marijuana, scared us by turning

Above: Jon Klingberg listens as his little sister Klara plays her homemade guitar. Photo: Bo Anders Persson.

the house's main switch off, climbing up on the roof, and howling like a wolf. When we ran out into the snow, he played a fanfare on a dented post horn as he sat on the chimney, before a fire-eating show ensued.

Others came and went. Some had psychological problems. One guy had worked as a dealer in Amsterdam. One ended up going to jail later for a tragic act of violence, another had a trunk full of the very first issue of *Galago* [a satire comic series first published in 1979]. Our home was, despite its isolated location, a place for high social influx. When it came to cultivation at Björkhöjden, I only remember two crops: potatoes and turnips. Our mailbox was located in the closest village—Fullsjön, which was three kilometers away. This became character-building when I started ordering fanzines and punk singles and had to bike to the mailbox regardless of the season.

One day I brought a note home from school on the dangers of drug use. Everyone in our class got it and was to return it to school signed by a guardian. I left it on the kitchen table and later found it with unmistakable traces of having been used to protect the table while packing a bowl with weed. It took a while for me to shake the worry that the school was going to send all the collected notes to some kind of lab for analysis, which would expose what was going on in our home.

At our house, there was always a tape recorder ready to record songs from P3 [Swedish public radio]. The show *Ny Våg* aired for fifteen minutes three days a week, and I listened to it with one hand constantly on the tape deck's pause button. The deck's counter was indispensable for what came next. Every song was recorded and the counter reset. If I didn't like a song after one minute, I stopped the tape and pressed "Rewind" until the counter again displayed 000.

That is how I discovered Missbrukarna, Blitzen, Pizzoar, Dom Dummaste, Sven Unos Kanoner, P-Nissarna, and Ståålfågel, as well as the Residents, Suicide, Chron Gen, Sham 69, and a bunch of other bands connected to punk and new wave. One cassette tape was also devoted to a live broadcast of Docent Död's show at Rock Palais in Stockholm in 1980— something that would later end up having some significance in my life.

The boredom of life in Sweden's concrete-heavy "Million program" [public housing] areas featured in the punk bands' lyrics became both a menacing and alluring fairytale. A Nangijala [fictional land of the dead from Astrid Lindgren's children's book *The Brothers Lionheart*] with a particular attraction for those who didn't have access to it. When a friend came back from a trip to Uppsala, he told me of the night he had seen the band Ebba Grön. The place had become surrounded by

members of the "raggare" subculture and he had been forced to flee for his life. The story made me cry with envy over not having been there.

Here and there in the vast landscape around our house there were remains of torn-down houses, often buried under soil and vegetation. We dug out an intact concrete foundation which ended up being fully functional for skateboarding. It was on a little hill, and if I positioned myself just right I could sail through the air on my skateboard before plunging again toward the grassy reality.

A visiting acquaintance named Kryddan ["the Spice"] made himself unpopular by stealing a pair of jeans in one of Brännholm's stores. After that, the shop ladies in Borgvattnet started observing Gusten with a new kind of suspicion. Kryddan contested his mistake and reframed the act as a "liberation" of the jeans. Incidentally, Kryddan was one of many adults in my life who liked to talk about the harmful effects of watching TV, something he compared to drug addiction, stating that "the only difference is that a TV viewer changes the channel and a drug addict changes the needle." We didn't have a TV. But once in a while, we visited our friends at the Skogsnäs commune to watch shows like *How the West Was Won*. Skogsnäs was a five mile drive away. I remember very few occasions when something from SVT [Swedish public television]'s listing was

considered unmissable. The exception was when SVT would show Swedish punk. One time it was a gig with Ebba Grön. We visited some friends whose TV displayed static while we listened for barely decipherable musical fragments in the TV's crackling noise. The other time it was this gala with, among others, Incest Brothers, a band whose claim to fame was that the guitarist Johnny Essing, later part of Bob Hund, was part of the lineup. That time, we went to our neighbor Valter, a retired accordion player that lived alone with his elderly mother and had a fully function-ing TV. The musical elements of the show were intercut with audience interviews. "What are your views on society?" the host asked a young punk rocker in the audience. "Shit," was the answer he got. Despite the cocky punk attitude, people in the audience seemed to shy away from the TV cameras and the interviewer's attempts to strike up a conversation, until a progg-looking man unabashedly walked up to the hosts' micro-phone and declared, "We want a society for humans, not for machines," and the audience burst into cheers.

The eighties had just begun. My father's old friend Per Odeltorp—better known as Stig Vig in the band Dag Vag—had printed these futuristically designed stickers that said

"WITH DAG VAG INTO THE EIGHTIES." It was both an elegant and challenging slogan that was met with amused admiration in our household. Eventually, even the reunited version of Träd, Gräs och Stenar would print stickers. However, the band name changed to T.GåS since it was feared that Träd, Gräs och Stenar would be too difficult to pronounce for a stressed eighties person. The stickers included a drawing of a goose rocking out with an electric guitar: a comedic kind of imagery very different from the romantic depictions of nature and dystopian elements that characterized the band's early graphic design and a clear indication of the will to find new expressions.

Around this time an anti-nuclear-power gala was arranged at Konstfack—University of Arts, Crafts and Design. The lineup included everything from Lill Lindfors to Ebba Grön and a reunited Träd, Gräs och Stenar. Ebba Grön's short, chaotic gig was one of the most intense stage performances I have experienced. Träd, Gräs och Stenar's gig was recorded on a tape that was later listened to in the kitchen at home on Björkhöjden. Between two songs, the band members engaged in lengthy banter about how it's time to perform an old song that's still relevant, to

which Einar Heckscher from the audience loudly retorted, "It would be damn great to hear that song now."

The reunited band eventually booked a tour in Norrland [the northernmost region of Sweden] with Arbete & Fritid and I came along for part of it. The show in Örnsköldsvik began with Thomas Gartz sitting down at the drums and explaining to the audience that it was time to "cook everything down in the same pot," which meant that both bands performed together. Then the intimate venue was filled with the sound of a self-oscillating modulation effect while Gartz delivered an impromptu monologue about space mopeds. The listeners who had come to hear true-to-original versions of "Sommarlåten" and "Sannin-gens silverflod" were probably disappointed.

When the tour reached Umeå, it had become my job to introduce the band. I was encouraged to do it in a way that was similar to roasting— a concept that would become popular on the comedy scene many years later—by castigating the band. I took on the task with great enthusiasm and without much preparation. No one in the audience seemed to take offense. The band went on after me, and beak boots stomped to the beat.

Left: Klara, Jon, and Bo Anders on an evening walk with the cat. Totjärnsberg, 1974. Photo: Private.

When the Lingonberries Ripen

When the Lingonberries Ripen

Thomas Mera Gartz:

I was born in the attic of a granary outside Linköping in the spring of 1944. As a kid, I played a lot with sound. I made sounds with my mouth and would bang and thump with my hands. Mom gave me a little rubber-skin drum and there would be many more drums to come in my life after that.

Bo Anders Persson:

We lived on Ringvägen in Stockholm. The streets were empty when one went outside during the Second World War. A car was a big event. In 1942 or '43 we moved from Ringvägen to Tallkrogen, an area of small single-family homes south of town, where my dad had managed to build a house for us. There was a social idea behind it all. This was during World War II, so materials were somewhat scarce. But my parents managed to qualify for it. At first, they made too little to get a mortgage, then they made too much. They used to make fun of that.

Anyway, they passed through the eye of that needle and started building the place. I grew up there, from about five years old. There was a bit of settler's spirit through-out the area, since everyone was building at the same time. The paved road stopped just outside the area and a gravel road continued out into the countryside.

At the end of the war, the atmosphere changed and a bunch of practical stuff took over. That's when bananas arrived, which was a big deal, a sign of the times. Those goddamn bananas! Rather undeservedly, they acquired an almost mythical status.

Previous spread: Bo Anders Persson on his motorcycle, late 1950s. Photo: Private.
Left: Thomas Mera Gartz drumming in the basement at Bagarmossen, late 1950s. Photo: Private.

Arne Ericsson:

We had a forceful piano at home. My mom and sisters sang quite a bit. Dad, who claimed he was tone-deaf, was actually pretty skilled at playing the mandolin. When I was six or seven years old, I took lessons with a piano teacher, a cantor. He was a strict old man. He rested a pencil on my hand and demanded that it not fall off while I was playing for him. As a kind of protest, I demanded that my parents give me blank sheet music paper and I wrote a song. When we had company over, I performed the piece and it was a success. At ten years old, I moved from Alfta to Bollnäs. I went to high school there and started participating in a few musical ensembles. I was a part of Bollnäs's youth marching band for a year. I would pick up on instruments that were missing in the band. I played alto horn, and flute, and tried to learn the clarinet, but that was too much of a hassle. We were a group of youngsters that played with a band leader named Birger Näslund. He was very nice and actually, not a typical strict marching-band type. Later, when I was seventeen or eighteen, I had the urge to play the cello, and Birger got one for me. I was in a few small jazz bands, one of which included guys on baritone sax, guitar, and drums, and me on piano. We had a few gigs at the youth center and at school. Our idols were mainly Charlie Parker and Gerry Mulligan, and later it was John Coltrane and Miles Davis. There are songs still stuck in my head from that time that sometimes resurface. Then came rock 'n' roll in the '50s and we were of course trying to imitate Elvis, Tommy Steele, and Bill Haley.

Bo Anders Persson:

My parents were part of a Baptist congregation, and there was quite a bit of music at home. My mom was in the choir. During the church service—which I sat through— I was confronted with organ music that accompanied the songs and the four-part harmonies. I thought about how it all fits together. Of course, it had an impact on me. I remember being amazed at how the bass moved in the psalms.

Thomas Mera Gartz:

My mom played piano at home and I used to stand next to her, singing in my high-pitched boy's voice. Beautiful notes, big and strong. Then she started asking me to sing and play the violin at gatherings with her friends, "the sewing meetings." I would get five krona for it. It felt strange to be coaxed, lured, and shown off like that. It was a new kind of exploitation and was probably carried out to get my sister— who played piano—and I to play concerts together. We played for Mom's friends and a bunch of visibly moved old ladies in Hammarbyhöjden's school auditorium. I went to the Saturday matinées and listened to the symphony at Stockholm Concert Hall. I had to wear a cap that I thought was pretty silly. Some ridiculous old guy joked with us young boys and girls in the audience. But all these strings moving up and down and the conductor's back and arms and all the vibrating vibrato hands and body movements—this incredible sound filled the hall, disappeared, and came back and vanished again with the music—the sound was the same as the music. Wonderful!

Bo Anders Persson:

I have had very good piano teachers in my life. The first one was a talented Jewish lady who really saw me as the worried and sensitive boy that I was. I was about ten, actually a bit late considering when you should start playing, but I had a hard time concentrating. I can't practice and I can't learn anything by heart. I don't know if it's some kind of physical lack of talent or just a fixation I have? I was too tense about life and I was convinced that this was going to

be difficult. Not just the playing in itself but everything in life. Life was something I didn't really feel like I could manage. I had a hard time in school. I didn't feel at home there. A lot of people moved to Stockholm in the 1950s, after the war. Suburbs kept popping up, but everyone felt like hicks even though they wanted to be Stockholmers. It wasn't a good social climate to be in.

Thomas Mera Gartz:

I was eight when my mom put me in violin school. After learning to play solo, trio, quartet, and orchestra, and performing in numerous school concerts, I stopped playing at sixteen, the same time I graduated from school. By that time, Black music had saved me. Little Richard, Fats Domino, the Coasters, Louie "Ludde"

Above: Bo Anders Persson and his sister Kerstin outside their childhood home on Lemmings Väg in Tallkrogen, Stockholm, late 1960s. Photo: Private.

Armstrong, Dizzy Gillespie, Max Roach, and Thelonious Monk. It was swinging, hot, and you could feel it, it was direct. I had started practicing on my pieced-together drum kit, which had gone from a collection of metal cans to actual drums. At fourteen, I started taking lessons with an old 1930s drummer and kept going there for a few years. I had my first gigs at sixteen: corporate parties and a tour of Gotland [Sweden's largest island]'s summer dance pavilions with a traveling carnival, an accordion player, and a guitarist.

Bo Anders Persson:

My dad had an antiquarian bookshop and was often out looking for or selling books. My mom worked in a school. She was really the one that supported the family. Conditions were tough. I remember those years as pretty hard. When I started realskolan [secondary school] at the beginning of the 1950s, the concept of the Dixieland band emerged. It was the great music of the youth at that time and in my school by the Skanstull bridge in Stockholm, a Dixieland band was formed. I managed to get in! To me, this band was a kind of renaissance orchestra. We had a very talented guy in the band who would later become a psychiatrist. He was a star lute player and played clarinet in the band. The Dixieland band brought me in contact with music from New Orleans pretty early on, when I was thirteen or fourteen years old.

Unfortunately, I probably had psychosocial problems, because I did badly in school and wasn't really making any progress when it came to playing the piano. But my piano teacher had taught me a few chords, so I was able to decipher the songs on the albums. This made my status among my classmates increase significantly.

Barbara

Dagens Nyheter, March 24, 1962

Medborgarhuset's large hall was filled with some peculiar sounds this Friday evening. Sixteen school bands entered Södra Latin's band competition, but despite that, almost all of them played so loud that it made ears flutter. It was impossible to hear them clearly. The audience was so interested that hardly a single note could pass without comment.... The winning band in the modern category: Christer Lundvall's Quartet with Stig Dahlgren, trumpet, Jonny Jönsson, drums, Urban Yman, bass and band leader.

Urban Yman:

I have roots in jazz music. I had a fundamental pursuit for freedom that I found an outlet for in jazz, which probably characterizes all kinds of youth music. This pursuit was conditioned by the times: authoritarian education, disciplining, and an authoritative way of thinking. Growing up, school was discipline. Rock music and the Flower Power movement that emerged had their own distinctive roots in the Beat movement—Jack Kerouac's *On the Road* and Jean-Paul Sartre—which inspired travels, to places such as Paris. All this was part of the culture that created the countermovement that I was inspired by, a movement that defied all norms in society. I was inspired by existentialism and Zen Buddhism in an attempt to liberate myself from the rigid, authoritative times I grew up in.

Torbjörn Abelli:

I attended Adolf Fredrik [a junior high school for music], and had all that so-called "serious music" in my backbone. There was a lot of music and choir singing at home. My parents also played. I was mildly successful at playing the violin, but my parents kept pushing me. I started playing piano when I was seven or eight years old. There was no musical instrument education at school, but there was a lot of choir singing and musical theory in addition to what was taught in

"We pulled out all the stops and played with our forearms, and feet, letting all hell loose in the church. It was so satisfying to play flipped-out, all-encompassing music."

Torbjörn Abelli

all schools. My classmate's mother knew Karl-Erik Welin, who at the time was a guru when it came to the interpretation of piano and older organ music. He was a very special man, very expressive in many ways. My classmate dragged the whole class to Moderna Museet [art museum]; Karl-Erik Welin was having a concert. Some thought it was a little weird, but I was so taken by it that I stayed. I was no older than sixteen. Sometime around 1963 or '64, a dark night around midnight, I was with a small group that snuck into Gustav Vasa church—one of Stockholm's largest—and played some very avant-garde Karl-Erik Welin–inspired organ music. We pulled out all the stops and played with our forearms, and feet, letting all hell loose in the church. It was so satisfying to play flipped-out, all-encompassing music. I didn't really know what I wanted to be when I grew up. So after high school, when my classmates went to university, I ended up in an old Volkswagen bus driving all over the country. In the years between graduating high school in 1964 and starting to play in the band, I studied aimlessly at university. Music research, art history, and the most trendy subject of all—sociology. I was piecing together a bachelor's degree with these ingredients as well as folk studies, ethnology, and anthropology, subjects that were popular among friends and that I had been thinking about. But I didn't have a clue what I was going to do with it.

Thomas Mera Gartz:

Some jazz guys came over to my place. [Bengt] **Frippe** [Nordström], a strange guy, played *Natural Music* on a white plastic alto saxophone, just like Ornette Coleman. I had the same one. Frippe played saxophone while I played drums in the basement. When my friends and I played music at home we had "sound play" sessions, we were no strangers to music sounding in any

and all ways. We put a clarinet mouthpiece on the trombone and vice versa. We played and experimented with all the mechanisms. We heard a piece of classical music on the radio and we immediately started playing and sounding like it. I was definitely a jazz lover and Gyllene Cirkeln [a historic jazz club] was my watering hole. I was at Gyllene Cirkeln and heard Cecil Taylor play and saw everyone that was there. Black jazz at that time was very free and revolutionary in its expression. They played freely and almost over one another to an almost nonexistent rhythm, which went *kschhhhaaa*.

Arne Ericsson:

When I was nineteen, I left home for Framnäs Folkhögskola [a school for adult education]. I attended a music education program there for four years. That's when I started enjoying writing music and doing quite a bit of it. From the beginning, I had no idea what I wanted to write, but I just felt that I wanted to compose. I had heard about the twelve-tone technique, and wrote a little in that style. When I later showed it to my teacher, he thought it was fantastic. I thought it sounded bad and tried other ways. I kept going like that during my time at the Royal College of Music. The atmosphere there turned out to be pretty strange. Creatively, older colleagues were hanging over us like ominous clouds of serious electronic music that none of us in the lower grades understood. A kind of snobbery existed around music creation that completely disregarded the receiver. It made it hard for me to find my way. But there were people in my own generation that gave me hope.

Bo Anders Persson:

At the end of World War II, it was like a new era was emerging. The dawn of mass automobile use felt fascinating. It's hard to imagine today, when we see all the downsides. The thought was that cars would become common and publicly owned and that the mechanization of society was underway. It felt unreal but at the same time exciting. There was hope for the future! People were positive, on all levels. Going from that to being called critical of civilization a decade later is a pretty staggering development. I started at Tekniska gymnasiet. Since we were going to gymnasiet [preparatory high school] in different parts of town, we finally disbanded the Dixieland band. I don't really know how I got stuck on becoming an engineer. I knew that culture was difficult to understand, and sexuality, that's deep waters, but machines were something I felt I understood. But I just began feeling unwell after a while. One summer, I had an internship arranged by the school at Imperial Chemical Industries in Runcorn, a small

town outside Liverpool. In Runcorn, I saw the English landscape and its lack of any wild nature. I remember that they said "the forest" and referred to a cluster of trees that I had driven by on my motorcycle. It was the summer of 1959 and it was incredibly hot. But the sun wasn't visible, even though the weather was clear. All summer long, the light was a yellowish-brown, and if somewhere the sky was a little brighter, you understood that was where the sun was. It was pollution from exhaust gases, industrial smoke, smog, and combustion. It affected me physically. There was a club in Liverpool called the Cavern. I met some kids there that were a

few years younger than me. Once, when we were there to see a Dixieland band, a group of youngsters in super skinny pants walked in with guitars. They didn't really play a proper set—their audience just wasn't really there. I noticed that this was something new, and I thought that it must be something from the USA that I hadn't heard of before. I had no idea that I had accidentally witnessed the Liverpool sound. The youngsters were very style-conscious, that's for sure. They had their own thing. It wasn't just the Beatles, there was a breeding ground for that music there. But I wasn't really mature enough to absorb it. Perhaps if I had been more independent, and had other friends, but no, I was going back home to become an engineer.

After a few years, I started having psychological problems. I could no longer attend Tekniska. When I tried going, I caught myself leaning forward. I felt a heavy weight across my stomach and understood that my body was telling me not to go there. After two and a half years, I dropped out. A little lost, I tried music again. I started playing piano. I got into Borgarskolans pianopedagogiska [piano conservatory], where I met the composer Jan Bark. He had been to the US and met Terry Riley and La Monte Young, and he had lots of stories to tell from it. Bark was a very special person. We developed a kind of asymmetrical friendship. He was only a few years older than I was, but he was like a drug. I owe him many thanks. He had an independent approach to the new kind of art music, which had a tendency towards being unavailable and

Above: Postcard of the neighborhood of Weston Point, Runcorn, England. The ICI building, where Bo Anders Persson practiced in 1959, is visible at the top right, along the Mersey River.

ascetic. There was a penchant for being part of an exclusive community, people with a superior, unavailable, incomprehensible air. He had an approach that I could relate to. He demanded something other than just sitting still and being impressed. We also had similar backgrounds. He too had played in a Dixieland band. There were a lot of us who had that journey, like Hoola Bandoola Band, for example. Dixie was the first kind of modern music we all encountered in our teenage years in the 1950s. Modern jazz came around the same time, but it wasn't as accessible and had a different social background. Since I grew up in the free church [born out of the Church of Sweden as part of a nineteenth-century evangelical revival], I carried that tonal language with me, and from there it was just one step over to traditional jazz, they were

so close to each other. Modern art music's roots are from a completely different place, but it also has its magic. I was influenced by all of it. *Ung nordisk music* was a series of concerts with works by young composers, a way to encourage young people to write art music. I created a piece for several tape decks. Ingvar Lidholm thought it had a sound that was needed. I got into the Royal College of Music with it. The others that applied were all too conventional in their compositions. Ingvar Lidholm was a very sympathetic man, but I was probably a bad student in composing class. There was too much going on out in the city.

Dagens Nyheter, September 9, 1965
The following applicants have been accepted as students ... at the Royal College of Music: ... The flute class Students: Arne Persson ... The compositions class Students: Bo Anders Persson.

Margareta Klingberg:

I got to know Bo Anders in the spring of 1967. The first time I saw him, he was engaged. The second time I saw him his fiancée had left him for someone else. I'm grateful for that. He was studying at the Royal College of Music and through that, he had access to Klangverkstaden in Elektronmusikstudion, EMS [national center for electronic music] for his own projects. The kitchen of his studio apartment on Östgötagatan was another important place for him. But he had a strict relationship with consumption. Once a month he went to a large supermarket to do his grocery shopping. Not to look for deals, but to minimize the time spent on purchasing and market forces.

Urban Yman:

That Bo Anders comes from a free church background isn't irrelevant. Out of those accepted to the Royal College of Music, about 50 to 60 percent probably had a free church background. I came from a different social class, but we could meet in the music that transcended all classes. Music and composition made us into a larger unit. We united in the music and

Above: Bo Anders Persson in the kitchen on Östgötagatan in Stockholm, 1968. Photo: Thomas Mera Gartz.

came into existence by creating together. There, my background had no significance whatsoever. The working-class critiques the petite bourgeoisie; I carried that with me. From the beginning, my parents were farmers, crofters, cattle herders, and cleaners. But they climbed the social ladder and became petite bourgeoisie. That was the basis for a lot of youth rebellion in the 1960s: revolt against the fake French petite bourgeoisie. Class-wise, it was a confusing time. Students and the upper classes had the proletariat as their ideal—while the proletariat looked to the bourgeoisie.

Bo Anders Persson:

I was accepted into composition and musical theory education and attended two programs in tandem at the Royal College of Music, I think there was a student shortage. The student rebellion was growing in the composition program. The scene was a mess, including "happenings" at Pistolteatern [an experimental theater space] with Pi Lind and Staffan Olsson. Pistolteatern had its own agenda. I got in on it partly through Jan Bark but without understanding much. Jan and I went to concerts that *Nutida musik* [an art music magazine founded in 1957] hosted at Stockholm Concert Hall with living composers. Contemporary art music was often intellectual and inaccessible. I was utterly unprepared and didn't feel at all qualified. But, I still sat there, and sometimes I liked it. I was fascinated by the French composer Olivier Messiaen. Frank Zappa was also inspired by him. Over the course of these events, I met a youngster who was kind and easygoing. This turned out to be Torbjörn Abelli. Modern art music was cultivated in the scene around Fylkingen [a renowned performance space and label] with that Norwegian guy [Knut Wiggen], who became a kind of dictator. I talked to him as I was starting to try and to play art music, and he cut me down so violently that I started to cry.

Torbjörn Abelli:

Fylkingen was of the Darmstadt School: Stockhausen-style, utterly humorless and emotionless. Incredibly intellectual laboratory-type music, music of the white coats. When Bo Anders wrote a piece for a student concert at the Royal College of Music, he upset the audience. The piece started out very atonal with lots of fragmentary notes but slowly was woven into an incredibly sensual bossa nova. The piece was called "Love Is Here to Stay," which was almost blasphemous. I guess it was his farewell to that kind of music.

Urban Yman:

At the same time as I started at the Royal College of Music, happenings and electronic music were starting to develop in Sweden. Studios like EMS—Elektronmusikstudion—were being built. Fylkingen played a big part in the budding electronic scene in Sweden. That was happening simultaneously with jazz transitioning away from acoustics towards electronics. Bo Anders was inspired by the electric sound. He wanted to investigate what sounds were possible to produce with electronic instruments. I myself was involved with Fylkingen's work. Knut Wiggen, the chairman at Fylkingen, was my piano teacher at the time. I spent a lot of my time in their electronic music studio and met Erik Söderström, who worked there. He made—from what I understood—the world's first electronic violin.

He wanted me to try out its possibilities. In reality, it was a violin-board—a strip of wood with batteries in a box. The new features were that you could adjust the volume as well as the actual timbre. The electric violin could sound like everything from an acoustic violin to an electric guitar. It gave the instrument greater timbre variation and possibilities than any other violin I had played before.

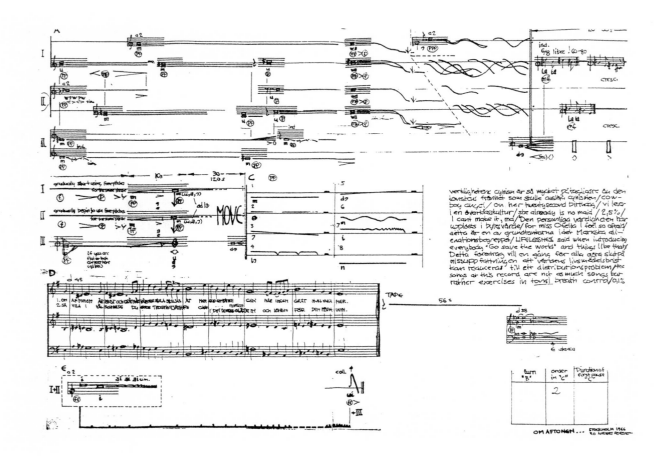

Above: Bo Anders Perssons's sheet music for the composition "Om aftonen," from 1966.

Arne Ericsson:

I got to know Bo Anders around 1965 to '66, at the Royal College of Music when we had music workshops together. It was me and him, Folke Rabe, and a few others. We were in this big hall making sounds. The first one to get sick of it was Bo Anders. That's when he thought of recording audio that he then looped through two reel-to-reel tape players. It felt revolutionary that that was possible.

Urban Yman:

Bo Anders asked me if I wanted to join in on a music experiment that he had been invited to in connection with the *Ung nordisk musik* concerts.

Dagens Nyheter, November 9, 1965

For the concert series Ung nordisk musik, organized by the Nordic music colleges, the following works from Sweden have been selected: ... Arne Ericsson: Partita for piano and En Face ... Bo Anders Persson: "Om sommaren sköna II" and "Love Is Here to Stay" for chamber ensemble.

Urban Yman:

There had to be a band name for those playing. Bo Anders called us Pärson Sound. Aside from Bo Anders and me, the group included Arne Ericsson, who was in the cello program at the Royal College of Music. Björn J:son Lindh was there for both the UNM concert and in other contexts. Maylen

Bergström sang—and I think Torbjörn Abelli was there sometimes, but not as a permanent member of the group yet. That's what the first lineup of Pärson Sound looked like. Those of us who had performed went on together.

Dick Idestam-Almquist
Dagens Nyheter, May 27, 1966
The only captivating piece was performed by the singer Maylen Bergström and some tape players (that the composer Bo Anders Persson sat behind). The tape players recorded her song and sent out distorted fragments of it that created "background noise" to the song that was heard directly without electric amplification. Maylen Bergström is a really talented singer and she creates a strong atmosphere ... Taken as a tendentious collage it was weak. But taken as simple and modest entertainment it was very enjoyable.

Oscar
Dagens Nyheter, November 26, 1966
On Friday night, the Royal College of Music's student body had an evening of happenings. Within the frame-work for camaraderie and guild spirit, the composer named Bo Anders Persson engaged himself in creating a four-hour-long piece.... At 20:00, the composing started. The tape crawled its way through the tape deck and the sound was colossal through Stig Carlsson's speakers, hallowed in these halls. What did it sound like? Sound. Sound from different sources of both electronic and natural origin.... A collage hissed from the Carlsson speakers against the state power's neglect of musical education.... Longing for a more aggressive attitude towards what one is doing. To break away from the worst parts of a tradition that says that students should shut up and that the syllabus is their holy sacrament.

Runar Mangs
Dagens Nyheter, May 23, 1967
Bo Anders Persson ... formulated "Små toner, mer eller mindre" ["Small notes, more or less"]. Here, a measure of talent and an artistic awareness that inspires real respect for the creator is revealed.... The slow, faint movement, the careful, dynamic changes, the relatively long spaces of time with reverberation, and the silence between the contrasting shorter notes against the drawn-out floating ones--all give the impression of a thoughtfulness approaching central reexamination, and not just of music like this, but of serious music in general.

Arne Ericsson:

Bo Anders was talking about forming a band and I was hard to persuade. I still didn't know what I wanted. We called ourselves Pärson Sound and had quite a few gigs. We sounded kind of weird, and Bo Anders tried steering us towards more comprehensible music. We were still into the idea that things could sound any which way. We met in the basement, but also in the living room at Bo Anders's. His poor mom had to lock herself in the bedroom. You can maybe see them as rehearsals— they were some kind of meeting, at least. In that basement, Bo Anders built our first "cello-board." It was a guitar-board with a microphone, but with a cello neck and tuning. We had a bunch of trouble with the mic, because it didn't really pick up what we wanted. We started playing a regular cello with a mic, but after the cello-board was finished, I switched to that instead.

Bo Anders put a lot of work into building amplifiers, speakers, and a guitar there in the basement. He had gone to school at Tekniska and was a pro at electronics. He always did really well with whatever he took on.

Torbjörn Abelli:

We studied music on an academic level, approached it intellectually and analytically, and looked at musical notation and what others had written. But in reality, music is something you do here and now. I wanted to play the electric organ, but it was too expensive, so Bo Anders gave me a bass. I had never played bass or guitar before, and

thought it was kind of fun to handle that bass, because I didn't care about what the notes were called. For me, someone who came from Adolf Fredrik, where notation and pitch and all that was very important, it was a bit rebellious to play by ear. We hung out at the Royal College of Music with a couple of small amps trying to play Rolling Stones songs, but it didn't sound like the record. Anyhow, pretty quickly we figured out that we should approach it from another angle. The band was Bo Anders, Urban, Arne, and myself on some pretty strange instruments. Our first gig was at a large private party at Pistolteatern. Then we played at Moderna Museet where Greta Beling [Lindholm], who was a student at the School of Dance [now Stockholm University of the Arts], was having her graduation show and we were the musical element.

Bo Anders removed the panels from the piano and was crawling around with contact mics and created this big rumbling sound from the piano, then we had an electric bass, upright bass, and cello … pretty bassy. We weren't playing rock or pop, but a kind of large noise. Some sort of rumble.

Anders Lind:

I have a very special memory of when I came up to Bo Anders's apartment on Östgötagatan. He was building a fuzz pedal. I had soldered and done quite a bit of constructing and I was meticulous and thorough, but Bo Anders was not. He built the pedal in a little cardboard box because it was faster that way. He made just a little hole for the potentiometer and then soldered all the resistances in mid-air. Everything was just hanging loosely in this cardboard box and then it was finished. He was always experimenting. I thought it was kind of crazy … but also very fun.

Left: Bo Anders Persson's home, Östgötagatan, Stockholm, 1965. Photo: Thomas Mera Gartz.

Bo Anders Persson

2

På Ung Nordisk Musik 1965 i Stockholm spelades ett stycke som hette **Love is here to stay** av en osedvanligt långhårig komponist vid namn Bo Anders Persson. Stycket gick hem fint: det var musik med ljuvliga flöjt- och sångerskeslingor över en skön bossanovaartad rytm. "Småvacker musik, ett hyfsat stycke. Men nu räcker det inte till för att motivera min existens".

Bo Anders Persson tycks ha behov att motivera sin existens. Han förefaller ha kroniskt dåligt samvete, talar mycket om de svältande miljonerna, det exploaterande västerlandet och "det globala överlevandet", och tycker egentligen att det är en ohållbar situation att han sitter där med en mixed grill och en mellanöl utan att kunna göra något åt eländet.

Föddes 1937. Började med dixieland. "Det gav en gehörsmässig attityd." Man lärde låtarna genom att höra på grammofonskivor, inte genom att läsa noter. Blev emellertid läroverksingenjör, gick ett par år på Teknis. Säger sig ha "plågats" av medvetandet om att allt man sysslade med där "var motiverat av funktionskrav och gick ut på en maximal exploatering." Han slutade. "Egentligen skulle jag ha fortsatt, för då hade jag möjligen haft en chans att bidra till att lindra pressen på naturen." Numera är det här med exploateringen och de svältande miljonerna vad han kallar en "delpryl, men viktig. Ungefär som att vara en ordinärt kristen, som skäms men syndar ändå. Trösten är att det finns så mycket som är helsjukt. Jag känner starkt för provieprylarna. Det är STORT."

På Borgarskolan i Stockholm blev han elev till Jan Bark. "Hade jag inte träffat honom hade jag nog aldrig börjat jobba med musik. Han excellerade i öppna attityder."

1965 började han på Musikhögskolan, i kompositionsklassen och sedan också i teoripedagogiska. Tänker sluta nu i kompositionsklassen. "Min energi är inte obegränsad."

Det hörs nästan. **Små toner mer eller mindre** — en mycket karakteristisk titel på det stycke som framförs i Kammarmusikstudion — är ett rätt stillsamt och statiskt plockande med toner, för det mesta relativt låga och långa. Harpisten har en del att göra, skall stämma ner vissa strängar, slå på strängarna, gnida dem med naglarna, spela med stråke och annat sådant, men annars är stycket minst av allt provokativt. Senare delen är centimeternoterad i stället för taktsrecksnoterad. "För min egen bekvämlighet."

Bo Anders Persson "tror nog att det alltjämt går att skriva för vanliga instrumentalister". Men siktet är inställt på något annat. För något år sedan skrev han **Om sommaren sköna II** för instrument, band och "teaterprylar", och han har länge sysslat med något som heter **Om sommaren sköna III**, där han skall använda bandade intervjuer. Intervjutekniken ger inte bara ord, utan också en massa atmosfär, klang och dramatik på köpet. Intervjuerna ger musiken en yttre anknytning, ger den sociala relationer. Det behöver den, enligt Bo Anders Persson. "Jag tror att lösningen ligger åt teatern till."

Han har ett rätt ljumt intresse för den stora västerländska konsertsals- och operatraditionen. Hans stora upplevelser kommer av pop — The Who's bl.a. Den aktuella "media-mysticismen" — mediet är budskapet — förstår han sig inte på. "Det är för lättvindigt. Dessutom baserar sig det på västerlandets särställning. Plågsamt nog är jag på väg dit själv."

Det finns gott om inkonsekvenser och motsägelser hos Bo Anders Persson. Ännu en: han kan inte inse varför staten och samhället skall försörja honom. "Men jag tar förstås tacksamt emot stipendierna."

GÖRAN BERGENDAL

Above: Article by Göran Bergendal from the magazine *Nutida musik* 8, 1966–67. Photo: Thomas Tidholm. English translation on p. 346.
Top right: Article by Ulla-Britt Edberg from *Svenska Dagbladet*, July 21, 1967. English translation on p. 347.
Bottom right: Sheet music for Terry Riley's composition *In C*.

"Bo Anders Persson Sound"

Det hände något. Det lyfte. Vid onsdagskvällens konsert i "Jazzfestival 1967":s tecken och Sju sekels lokaler fick frenesin, den våldsamma ljudvolymen, den oerhörda satsningen en mening och ett berättigande. Något av det svårdefinierbara i en positiv musikupplevelse infann sig relativt ofta. Det som kanske är identifikation med ögonblicket, med exekutörerna, identifikation med må vara vad det vill. I varje fall är det ganska sällsynt och kunde kanske kallas berikande.

Vid liknande konserter — pop eller utanför pop, jazz eller utanför jazz, nutida seriöst eller avantgardistiskt musikexperimenterande — upplever man alltför ofta den våldsamma attacken som en modemässig knorr, ett ytligt och lättvindigt hanterande med krutdurkar vars innehåll och expansionskraft exekutörerna endast tycks ha en begränsad vetskap om. "Bo Anders Persson Sound" nådde en verklighet man accepterade. Den delgavs dessutom ärligt och utan omsvep.

Aftonen uppdelades i två kompositioner. Bo Anders Persson, flöjt, Arne Eriksson, cello och Thomas Gartz, trummor, spelade. Thomas Tidholm tillkom senare med blockflöjt. Med hjälp av en bandapparat spelade de kanon med sig själva. Ett bandeko förändrade klangen. Överstrykningar, rundsvängningar och överslag tillhörde givetvis de tekniska hjälpmedlen. Ur små motivceller byggdes långa enhetliga rytmiska och melodiska perioder upp. Stegringarna skedde i långa utvecklingskurvor. Intensiteten var total och engagerande.

Senare delen av konserten blev till en början ett medicinskt- mikrofoniskt avlyssnande av slagverket. Man rispar metalliska ytor och avlyssnar med mikrofonen som stetoskop. Sådana studier har bedrivits förut av exempelvis en Stockhausen när han undersöker och framlockar olikartade ljudsensationer ur en gonggong behandlad med alla de slags instrument/verktyg. Men ingenting blir sämre därför att det inte är nytt. I all synnerhet när fortsättningen med tvärflöjt, blockflöjt, trummor och cello blir ett accelerat vibrato. En starkt verkande in- och utlevelse. Den kunde uppfattas rent bildmässigt som ett försök att slå emot sinnevärlden för att om möjligt bryta igenom.

Ett försök till totalteater: en film från svenskt dansbaneliv kördes paralluellt. Att resultatet var mindre stimulerande berodde kanske på filmdukens lilla format? Kanske var filmen mindre luämplig även om den visades både fram och baklänges.

Ingen av musikerna skulle egentligen framhävas på annans bekostnad. Om inte Thomas Gartz nu liksom på måndagskvällens konsert i Kungsträdgården övertygat om sin kraftfulla begåvning för sitt instrument.

ULLA-BRITT EDBERG

Sonja Gransvik:

When I met Bo Anders, he was still studying at the Royal College of Music and had just started making music as Pärson Sound. He subscribed to publications like *Clarté* [a progressive magazine, still in print today] and other left-leaning magazines. I started reading them but barely understood half. It was a lot to take in. Eventually, I gained a broader consciousness of society and saw the world with more perspective. Music became an exciting bridge-builder combining the socio-critical leftist ideology with a newly awakened environmental awareness. Even though there were a lot of leftist views, Marxism and Socialism, it was important to include nature.

Urban Yman:

Bo Anders was the facilitator. He contacted new people, and soon Thomas Tidholm came into the picture. He brought along an alto saxophone that he had just recently learned to play. He was the only one of us that wasn't from the Royal College of Music. The main instruments at this time were Bo Anders's electric guitar, Tidholm's alto sax, my violin, and Arne Ericsson's cello.

Thomas Tidholm:

This was when I was working at Sveriges Radio [Swedish public radio service] with a magazine called *Nutida musik*. *Nutida musik* was about Art Music. Editor Göran Fant asked me if I wanted a job as editorial secretary and photographer. This was fantastic—suddenly I had a salary. For one assignment, I was to photograph a new composer named Bo Anders Persson. He lived in a small apartment on Östgötagatan full of wires. I took photos of him there. Later, he invited me to an event where he was going to conduct some kind of sound experiment. He had hung a microphone from the ceiling and a few people, including myself, were placed under it to sing. A number of reel-to-reel tape decks were dispersed throughout the room, and the tape ran in loops across the floor. The others were Torbjörn Abelli and maybe Arne Ericsson. We sang our notes that looped as overlays to what was simultaneously being recorded. That was the stuff Bo Anders was doing at the time. Later, we would perform some of what we made. It became the concert at Sju sekel in Kungsträdgården [a restaurant and music venue in the city center].

Margareta Klingberg:

Thomas met Bo Anders at his apartment on the top floor of a house on Östgötagatan. Afterward, Thomas told me that he had met such a beautiful person. It sounded like he was in love.

Thomas Tidholm:

Our music didn't have anything to do with the pop music of that time. Still, we had heard what was played out in the city. Anna-Clara and I used to go to Nalen and listen to pop bands. There were Shanes, Tages, and a band we liked called Anna-beeNox. Their sound was something new, but they never became role models for us. Rather, we liked Bob Dylan. But that wasn't the kind of music we played at Sju sekel either. We were playing modern art music. We put the tape ribbons on the stage floor and created a lively drone. A repetitive, variable wall of sound. You could see wonder and delight in the audience.

Thomas Mera Gartz:

After a gig with Mecki Mark Men, Thomas Tidholm and Bo Anders showed up. They asked if I wanted to be in this thing they were doing. It was a gig at Sju sekel in Kungsträdgården. I think we met up at Bo Anders's place once before the show, where I got to know and play together with them a bit. I was supposed to help out with the tape decks—we had two reel-to-reel tape decks

JAZZ
JAZZ

3 LÖRDAGAR PÅ PISTOLTEATERN I
APRIL OCH MAJ
KL.15
22/4 Nisse Sandströms kvartett
29/4 Persson sound
 6/5 Yman & Co.

Above: Advertisement for Pärson Sound's first public gig, at Pistolteatern, April 29, 1967.

that we used to record the music, which was then overlaid in several layers on the tapes. After I had taken care of the tape decks, I was to play the drums, and then Bo Anders would up with a mic pointed at the cymbals. He'd hold it close and record it on the reel-to-reel system. In the recordings, you just hear this big wall of sound, and from that, a rock beat emerges, gliding away into noise.

Bo Anders Persson:

At Sju sekel, the audience was under the impression that there was going to be some kind of cultural performance. They were perplexed: Stig Carlsson was surprised that we were so loud. We were using speakers that he had helped me construct. "If you're going to play this loud, you need to build your speakers in a different way," he said. I met him at a bar and we sat and discussed speakers for hours. I built the band's speakers based on the idea of a round sound instead of a directed sound. I created a

bunch of patents and tried to get the optimal sound. We were in Kungsträdgården as avant-garde decoration. The actual gig was very tense. Catatonic. Chaos. But it was appreciative chaos. We had decided on a few simple things before the gig. Then you always have to answer the crowd's excitement, so there's tension. That tension—the audience's impact on the music—determines a lot of what comes after actually. Afterward, Leif Nylén or Mats G. Bengtsson accidentally pushed over one of the tape recorders and it broke. That was a shame—would have been nice to still have it.

Thomas Mera Gartz:

All sound came through Bo Anders's two eight-inch omnipolar speakers: Arne's cello, Tidholm's flute and his readings, and Bo Anders's guitar and flute. It was an enormous noise, loud as hell compared to standards of the time. The place was full of people and no one had heard anything

Above left: Torbjörn Abelli at Thomas Tidholm's place, Borgmästargatan, Stockholm, 1965.
Above center: 7 sekel, Kungsträdgården, Stockholm, 1969.
Above right: At Thomas Tidholm's, Borgmästargatan, Stockholm. Anna-Clara Tidholm, Thomas Tidholm, Kitte Arvidsson with son Nisse, Mats Arvidsson, and Bo Anders Perssin, 1968. Photo: Thomas Mera Gartz.

like it. The audience at the café tables recoiled. The experience was that powerful. Those who couldn't get in were standing outside with their faces pressed up against the windows. Ulla, my girlfriend, became nauseous. Afterward, the group wanted me to play with them again.

Arne Ericsson:

I wasn't feeling all that well, but I still chose to play my trusted cello. At first, they wouldn't let me in at Sju sekel, but when the others came and said I was with the band, they let me in. We wanted to do a version of "Dies Irae," and Bo Anders later claimed that I was constantly a half-tone below everyone else, but I have no memory of that.

Roland Keijser
Upsala Nya Tidning, July 21, 1967
Restaurant Sju sekel in Kungsträdgården isn't a bad place to present avant-garde music.... The volume constantly turned up to the limit. The feeling of being connected to high-voltage power lines. In direct contact. The body becomes a big trembling elephant's ear. Two options: active listening/leave the premises. These sounds don't work as background

music. They demand total engagement. "You have to be with it." ... electronics as a creative fellow musician: the sounds produced by the quartet were recorded on tape that was connected with other tape recorders which in turn threw the sound back into the space, now partly distorted in various ways and together with new sounds from the quartet; distortions, interferences, reconnections, etc, sometimes the technical machinery seemed to operate independently, emancipated from the musician's control. But, perhaps these ecstatic musicians overestimate the audience's listening capacity. The pieces could probably have been shorter and maybe they should have made it possible for the listeners to move more freely in the space, to move and participate in a purely physical matter.

Thomas Tidholm:

It all started after Sju sekel. We were offered gigs at Klubb Filips and Moderna Museet during the Andy Warhol exhibition. I don't really know how it all happened. We made connections wherever we came and found our place right away! There was a lot of enthusiasm around Pärson Sound and it almost happened on its own.

CHAPTER 2

Protein Imperialism

Protein Imperialism

Jakob Sjöholm:

My first memory of Bo Anders is his first performance at Sveriges Radio with his reel-to-reel tape recorders. I was there with Margareta Klingberg. The first time we talked was when he was the artistic director at Dramaten [the Royal Dramatic Theater], and the Mascots were playing there. I think Bo Anders was hired to be some kind of middleman between the bands and theater and I was there because I knew the Mascots. I remember the dark, grand auditorium and the Mascots' repetition. This was around 1966 or '67.

Margareta Klingberg:

In 1967, references to the theater were often mentioned in connection with Bo Anders's performances. The choreographer Donya Feuer noticed this and got him involved with creating sound for a performance at Dramaten. But that honorable task meant mostly ethical tribulations. He expressed concerns that he couldn't reconcile with her idea of firing a gunshot during the performance. To him, it meant inflicting violence on the audience. The young pop group the Mascots, with students from Stockholm's Musikgymnasium [music education high school], were also involved. After Bo Anders got his paycheck from the director of Dramaten, Erland Josephson, there was nothing more between Persson and the theater.

Previous spread: Pärson Sound with Björn Fredholm as an extra drummer at the opening of Moderna Museet's Andy Warhol exhibition, February 10, 1968. Photo: Jacob Forsell.
Left: In a field in Huddinge, fall of 1968. From left: Bo Anders Persson, Thomas Mera Gartz, Arne Ericsson, Torbjörn Abelli, and Thomas Tidholm. Photo: Anna-Clara Tidholm.

Bo Anders Persson:

The attraction to new pop music was very strong. It started out renunciatory: "Isn't this a little cheap?" But the Beatles' breakthrough was a tipping point; pop music came in through the backdoor into the culture, or maybe jumped in through the window. At least it wasn't a polite entrance. There was a kind of borderland between pop and art music that the improvisation group had our sights set on. But we never really got that far before we became purely a rock band or pop orchestra. In 1967 to '68 there was so much going on that I think it was totally legitimate to lose your footing.

Thomas Mera Gartz:

Mecki Mark Men was the creation of Mecki Bodemark. He started playing songs by Georgie Fame on the Hammond organ— which everything in the band was built on. Mecki Mark Men was a dansband [a Swedish live band genre incorporating blues, rock, and popular dances] that played up to fifty-something songs in one night. Couples dancing to foxtrot, that's how things were at the time. Mecki was the bandmaster and the songs were his. We, the band, played without filling in anything of our own volition. I wasn't really happy with that. Like me, the saxophone player, Hans Nordström, wanted to play longer songs and solos.

I brought Mecki to Moderna Museet so that he could hear new art music— Stockhausen, for example. He was really impressed by that stuff, and I played records for him at my place. When we jammed Mecki started bringing out new kinds of songs, his own songs. We played longer improvised parts, which created a kind of psychedelic tone. Psychedelic music with improvisation and force was

Above: Mecki Mark Men's first single, 1967, Swedish version (left) and Dutch version (right).
Right: Mecki Mark Men. From left: Thomas Rundkvist, Claes Swanberg, Thomas Mera Gartz, and Mecki Bodemark.

something other than foxtrot. We came to these places where girls and boys were standing on opposite sides of the room waiting to dance. But they couldn't do that to our new music—it was too intense. They kept standing to the sides just staring; fascinated but unaware of how to relate to the music. The rituals weren't lining up.

Dagens Nyheter, August, 12, 1967
Mecki Marck Men play a mix of pop and jazz that sometimes has elements of electronic music. When they started playing together they focused on rhythm-blues.... "We want to do something surprising now, something new and above all festive", says Thomas [Gartz]. And then the crowd has been surprised at places such as Jump-in, Gyllene Cirkeln and the dance spot Domino, where Mecki Mark Men have played recently. The seven-man-strong band completely pours sound over the listener.... Mecki Mark Men has two drummers to really get the rhythm out properly. "The audience has to feel the throbbing and the strong pressure. It makes them react. The best thing would be if one could establish a kind of collaboration with the listener, but I don't really know if that's possible", says Thomas.

MOTHERS OF INVENTION
MECKI HANSSON MARK-MEN AND KARLSSON

Konserthuset - Lördagen 30 Sept. 1967

Thomas Mera Gartz:

Jimi Hendrix stumbled onstage when we were playing at Gyllene Cirkeln. He was incredibly drunk. He liked our music and wanted to play with us. The same thing when we played at [Klubb] Filips—he showed up and asked if he could join in. Of course! He borrowed the bass. At that point, his mythological status had grown, so I think I was a bit surprised. When he asked if he could join us I answered wrong, he thought I meant that he couldn't. I vividly remember him backing up, but it was resolved moments later and he started playing bass with us.

Ludvig Rasmusson
Dagens Nyheter, May 12, 1968

Mecki Mark Men brought new ideas to Swedish pop. They were skilled musicians and played fascinatingly. Had they lived in London or San Francisco they would be just as big as Pink Floyd or Grateful Dead. Things didn't go great in Sweden. No one knows why. Some say that what they played was too "difficult." But English and American bands that have play equally "difficult" music have done well in Sweden. Are we too scared to believe in our own pop music? Another explanation is that MMM didn't seem as nice and sweet as other Swedish pop musicians. Maybe people thought that they were hippies. In an interview in Aftonbladet, Mecki Bodemark said that he likes to smoke hash, and that he preferred it over booze. Later that fall the whole band signed a

Left: Flyer for the Mothers of Invention's concert at Stockholm's Konserthuset in 1967.

Above: Jimi Hendrix at Dans In, Gröna Lund, September 11, 1967. Photo: Jakob Sjöholm.

big protest list against the Vietnam war. No other
Swedish pop bands did that. MMM didn't just play
difficult--they acted unusual.

Thomas Mera Gartz:

Mecki Mark Men came from utilitarian
music, music with a specific purpose.
Pärson Sound were interested in art, and
approached music from a different angle
than I was used to. But Bo Anders wanted
to make art music more like utilitarian
music by pulling it into rhythm, moving
it closer to something more functional for
people. He couldn't stand the Royal
College of Music's academic version of music. I had met Bo Anders at Hemstudion
before I started playing in Pärson Sound.
He was processing these tape compositions
with walls of sound, while I made a drone
on a tambura [South Asian string instru-
ment]. I had played it at home on the piano
with the same notes and with the piano
pedal pressed way down. I listened to the
overtones and to how the piano started to
sing. So when Pärson Sound started to play
Terry Riley-sounding drone music, it was
the same kind of music that we had played
at Hemstudion. It was exactly what I was
into, which made it easy for me to slide
right into the band.

Thomas Tidholm:

From the start, it was Bo Anders, me, Torbjörn, and Arne. Mera joined soon after. Both
Arne and Torbjörn understood Bo Anders's
ideas; they were at the Royal College of
Music together. I guess I had some musical
experience, since I had been playing the
clarinet since I was fifteen. I played classical
music in the Huddinge symphony orchestra, and liked to play the recorder by myself.
I didn't find it hard to understand what
Bo Anders wanted to do. When the tapes
started to roll and the music looped, all you
needed to do was fill in with new sounds.
You were involved immediately.

Thomas Mera Gartz:

I went to listen to an art music piece that
Bo Anders had written for a small ensemble. You could hear in his compositions
that he cared about the world. It was a
period of awakening and understanding
that there was something beyond Sweden:
the whole world. But Pärson Sound had a
poet [Tidholm] with ambitions, and others
that had serious musical schooling. Add a
chugging obstinate bass and a heavy beat to
that and the music became unique and very
powerful!

Thomas Tidholm:

I met Terry Riley when I was working with
Nutida musik magazine. He was touring
Sweden, working with long, repetitive
pieces that often consisted of short snip-
pets or riffs. It was called "minimalism."
And we were impressed. In Pärson Sound
we would weave together our own cre-
ations—sometimes it became something
airy and sometimes it was a tight musical
structure. That process determined what
we sounded like. I was in New York in
1967, when the band had been going for
a few months. I looked up Riley. I played
him a tape with our stuff. He mumbled
"Mmm … .ahhh … ", then he said,
"Something can definitely come of this." I
could tell that he didn't really think it was
that great. Honestly—it wasn't. But it got
better.

Bo Anders's piece "Proteinimperialism"
is real art music. It is reminiscent of stuff
that Terry Riley developed. When Riley
visited Stockholm, Bo Anders played the
pieces "Olsson III" and "In C" with him.
Another time I also played on "In C." It
was an enormously important piece to
all of us.

Left: Torbjörn Abelli and Urban Yman, 1969.
Photo: Thomas Mera Gartz.

Bo Anders Persson:

I was creating a piece for an exhibition called Sköna stund [*Nice Moment*], which was very 1968, with [the artist and satirist] Lars Hillersberg and others. Ulf Lauters had made these big sculptures with big fat western capitalists eating while starving people watched. Very severe. My piece was called "Proteinimperialism," a concept I had come across when reading the scientist Georg Borgström. I thought it covered so much. He made a correct assessment that there will be a crisis of protein resources.

Urban Yman:

Terry Riley introduced an entirely new way of thinking musically—a minimal way of composing. This meant repeating short phrases: short sequences that were repeated with minimal changes for a long duration of time. The model was his "In C," a piece that was composed in C-major. We participated in all the concerts in 1967 when the piece was performed. Riley's way of working—especially in "In C"—became our musical idiom, in both Pärson Sound and International Harvester, where we eventually started combining the short repetitive figures with a rock beat.

Bo Anders Persson:

I played the keyboard when Riley was in Stockholm, and started to understand how it all worked. I never thought that you could work so loosely, just decide a few things ahead of time. "In C" consists of fifty-three fragments where all the musicians play through all the fragments without determining the beat. Riley used to say that it was like a field with racehorses that spread out and then come together. A flock of birds would have been a more appealing image. It becomes a progression where you need to connect and not stray too far off on your own. But you never play in unison. If you play the same fragment as someone else you end up in an antiphase movement. "In C" was an instruction book for collective improvisation.

Arne Ericsson:

Terry Riley's music was something completely new, small building blocks that together grew and became this huge carpet of sound. A fantastic show of minimalism. I played the flute. Bo Anders said he felt like his head was buzzing when we played Riley's composition, and I agree. We brought Riley's way of thinking into the band, even though we also had lots of other expressions.

Urban Yman:

We wanted to bring rock and pop music's primitive simplicity into composed music and cross-pollinate these repetitive patterns. Rock had replaced jazz as the musical expression for the youth zeitgeist. Jazz's evocative repetitions predated psychedelic music. That scene was blossoming at this time—from San Francisco to Woodstock. There was an atmosphere of magical seance during the concerts, which concurred with the frequent drug use. People started smoking hash and taking LSD. The drugs pointed in the same direction as the music: magical self-centeredness. But not so much from an aesthetic and musical aspect, more as a kind of spiritual experience, an associative influence directed inward. Actually, it was an anti-intellectual streak that was based on emotion—on the here and now.

Right: Urban Yman in Björkhagen, Stockholm, March 30, 1969. Photo: Håkan Agnsäter.

"Our starting point was to combine a process of minimalist repetition with magical mind expansion to create a shortcut to ecstasy."

Urban Yman

Our starting point was to combine a process of minimalist repetition with magical mind expansion to create a shortcut to ecstasy. You had to let go of the self-discipline that existed at, for example, the Royal College of Music with the memorizing of scales, but it also existed outside in "expert society." From the Royal College of Music's perspective, music was the result of rehearsed intellectual control. Western music composition is based on an advanced compositional and intellectual process with a foundation in counterpoint and Bach. What we did was the exact opposite. No equilibristic instrumental technique was required from us. We could stay on the same musical figure during the entire duration of the piece, which could be very long. Repetition and simplicity were central to us. But that starting point didn't make any intellectual demands. In theory, anyone could play what we played as long as they had the right feeling. Our fascination for minimalism, like Terry Riley's "In C" and psychedelic music's more ecstatic or transcendental centerings—like imploding circles—was a search for a kind of imploding emotional experience with ecstasy as the final goal. A magic, emotional, and complete experience; to allow yourself to lose sanity as an ideal; to try and go outside of yourself. It was a suggestive pull that at the same time was life-affirming—dare to let go!

Bo Anders Persson:

At my place in Tallkrogen, we played acoustically, talked a lot and, to be honest, smoked quite a bit. We rarely had regular rock band rehearsals, although we had those too in the basement. It was just for a short period, a year or so, that we used it as a practice space. We had figured out that we wanted to be a rock band, but me and my feeble imagination thought that we needed to start from the beginning, study rock, and start with a song by the Rolling Stones. Thomas Tidholm didn't share that opinion at all. He had been to San Francisco and seen the bands there. He said you just play. It was a concept that was completely foreign to me. But that is what prevailed. We were influenced by bands with strange names like Country Joe & The Fish and Quicksilver Messenger Service. Music that was a bit strange, but often very well-produced.

Thomas Tidholm:

In 1966 I was at the Avalon Ballroom [in San Francisco] and traveled around the US. There was something very interesting that was brewing, a completely new music scene emerging. There were bridges between the more experimental pop music and folk music. It wasn't rock quite yet. I probably felt that that kind of music was a little too nice, nothing for us to take on. Eventually, we found our own way. Things were going well around 1968 to 1969, and we played everywhere. We made amazing improvised music, and I don't remember any differing views in the band. Just five guys who felt the same way, and who knew a lot about esoteric science. It was a happy, intoxicating time. We just agreed on every damn thing and that's why things were so good! . . . Well, sometimes not great.

We tried building something heavy and unmanageable, a beautiful machine that just stood there chugging along. Sometimes it didn't work. It's like building a house of cards, sometimes it collapses. But when we were there and really hit the spot, there was nothing better. It was close to magic. That's how I felt then, and I can still feel it.

Urban Yman:

> There was a spirit of tacit agreement in the band that made language and discussion irrelevant. There was a stomp-the-beat vibe. One just needed to clear one's throat to get approval. Thomas Tidhold cleared his throat often. He said something weird and everyone nodded—he talked in metaphors a lot—but I wonder how many really understood what he was saying. There was also this feeling that we knew the real secret behind it all, that all the other suckers didn't get. It's a basic sectarian view that gave us a sense of belonging: "We know how things really are."

Urban Yman:

> Our music got a big response right away. We were booked at student unions, theaters, and similar contexts all over the Nordic countries. We played in Helsinki and Oslo, and we noticed that people there were connected to the same patterns of life and musical image that we were. There was a spirit of Flower Power and a hippie lifestyle that welcomed us wherever we came.

Bo Anders Persson & Thomas Tidholm

T'a 6, November 2, 1968

We pretty much use the same instruments as other pop groups, except Arne who plays the electric cello; and then we have some instruments that we use sometimes. When we played at the Diplio festival in Helsinki, Kjartan Slettermark danced with us and that was great.... We started experimenting in the areas between jazz and Terry Riley in the summer of '67, now we start from pop mostly, but try to learn from, for example, Indian and African music. We are attracted to Swedish folk music, Swedish folklore, and Swedish nature, we wonder if we can use that somehow.

Anna-Lisa Bäckman

Dagens Nyheter, October 22, 1967

Black and white light flickers gaspingly in hot cold flashes over young thin people. They swing and twist and move as if by pulling strings. The stroboscope, a lantern in the ceiling, some kind of crazy lighthouse, changes the world. At Filip's patisserie. Outside is only Regeringsgatan, empty and smooth in the evening light. In here: Faces ablaze with sudden explosions, streams of color projected on the walls and running streaks across the bodies.... You sit and move in a tent of sound. A boy with his girl on his lap drums his fingers rhythmically against her belly....

Perssons Sound [*sic*] is playing upstairs right now while people dance to disco on the ground floor. The room they play in is clogged up with tobacco smoke. Red lights shine through the haze like ominous suns. The music roars, screams and cuts through the microphones. They play with faces half turned away, as if searching through what, to a casual listener, first sounds like dissonances. Sometimes a rich cello tone plays.... They play for fifteen, twenty minutes.

Then the playing faded into knocking.... "We use the microphones in a dirty way", says Bo Anders Persson, the leader of Perssons Sound. "Against accepted rules. We want to see where we can go. But still, it is a very small part of the sound that we experiment with, compared to when you utilize the full possibilities of electronics."... He answers the burning question about "psychedelic." What is it? This? "It's a word that feels very distant. Psychedelic elements have always been present in art... But it's clear that the word has its justification now when it comes to certain West Coast jazz and pop."

Torbjörn Abelli:

> Real rock music came in the fall of 1967 when we had gigs at Klubb Filips. It was Stockholm's only real Flower Power club. It was an amazing space—like in San Francisco. On the bottom floor was a big space with lots of strobe lights. [The Pioneering psych bands] **Hansson**

Right: Poster from the opening of the psychedelic club Filips in Stockholm, 1967. Design: Piero Tartagni.

& Karlsson and Baby Grandmothers played there. Upstairs was a smaller space—that could house an audience of a couple hundred—that's where we played. We played a kind of primeval music that I had been longing for: slow variable improvisations. The shows at Klubb Filips were important because we developed a routine, and since the upstairs stage was billed as experimental, we weren't promising too much. There could be a lot of people when we started playing, but after ten minutes, three quarters had disappeared. But the quarter that stayed for the hour or hours that we played almost always seemed just as affected as we were. That's where it started.

Arne Ericsson:

Pärson Sound played in one room and Hansson & Karlsson in another. Sometimes Janne Carlsson would play drums with us so that we had two drumkits going. That was massive.

Thomas Mera Gartz:

Filips was pretty short-lived, but we managed to play there a few times. Filips was the coolest place there was. That was the goal for both audience and musicians. Next to the stage was the door to an old tiled kitchen. In there is where the inner circle of the club used to hang out, those who ran things. Recordings were made from there. To get to what was called the "backroom," you had to walk up some stairs and out

Left: Audience at the opening of Andy Warhol's exhibition at Moderna Museet, 1968.
Above: Pärson Sound at the exhibition opening. Photo: Jacob Forsell.

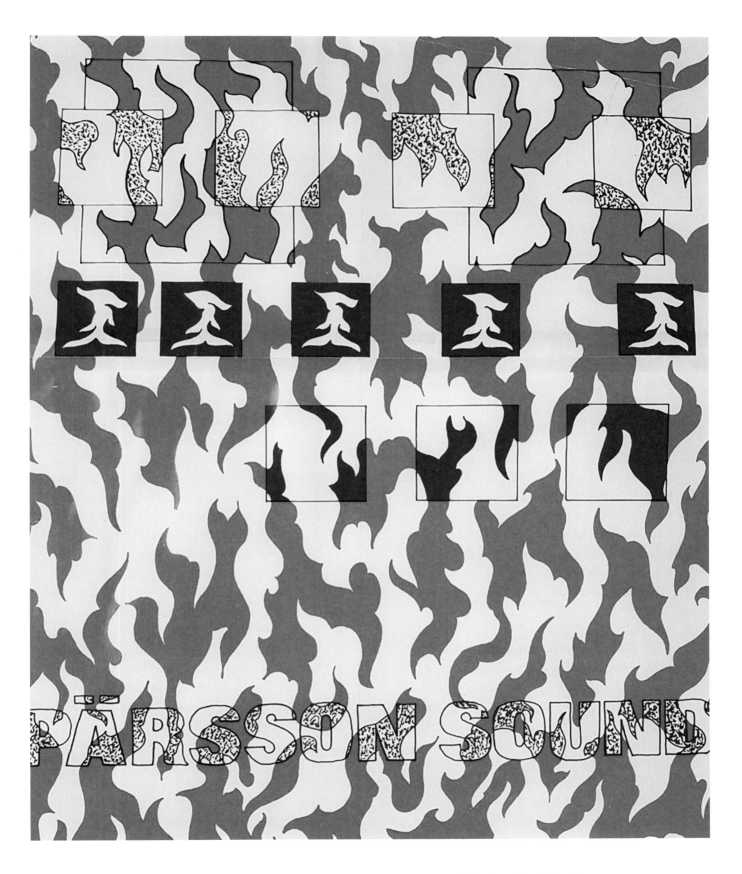

Left: Audience members at the opening of Andy Warhol's exhibition at Moderna Museet, 1968. Photo: Jacob Forsell.
Above: Poster for Pärson Sound, 1968, with the band's name misspelled. Design: Mats Arvidsson.

onto a small courtyard with a roof, that's where we would sit until it was our turn to play. In a room pretty close by, Hansson & Karlsson practiced and kept their things. I got Bo Anders to do this special gig together with Mecki Mark Men. Bo Anders recorded parts of the band's sound with a microphone. He walked up close to the sound sources and played them back on two tape decks and two big speakers. The long loops mixed with the band's music. The method was similar to the one Pärson Sound used at their gigs. The music was incredible.

Tore Berger:

I traveled into Kungsträdgården from my little apartment in Råsunda to go to Filips and cut a rug. It must have been in the fall of '67, the same year that I came home from Formentera with a high-quality chunk of marijuana—something entirely different from the boring hash I had been offered previously. Filips was an avant-garde kind of place with flashing strobe lights, but also an extension of the little discotheque at the beach on Formentera. It was easy to just surrender. I had been to Filips a few times before and experienced Hansson & Karlsson's pulsating, somewhat monotonous,

sessions. This time around, it was Pärson Sound that was playing the dance music. The band played on in excellent style, with a three or four-meter-long audio tape in front of them that delayed and drew out their contemplative yet intense rock music. You could dance slow or fast, completely introverted while simultaneously together with everyone else in the accepting space. Some were really there to be seen—and the constant strobe effects created a graphic collective that everyone was a part of. It was like photographs directly into your memory. I can still evoke them at any time. That gripping, deeply impulsive music. Time had almost stopped. It can't be explained. But the marijuana intoxication was congruent with this. It created wonderful drawn-out moments, but it wasn't liberating. Of course, it didn't last. Where was reality?

Thomas Mera Gartz:

The most important gig we did was at the opening of Andy Warhol's exhibition at Moderna Museet—in February 1968. I think we played two or three times. We had two drummers. I brought Björn Fredholm, whom I played with in Meki Mark Men, and the others in Pärson Sound were into it.

The music we played sounded Indian; one song was forty minutes long with complex drumming that was more free than rhythmical, a mass of sound that flowed out together with the two drummers. We weren't using the reel-to-reel tape decks anymore and Bo Anders had built more speakers. I think we had four speakers and all the instruments—including Thomas Tidholm's vocals, flute, and saxophone—through the same amplifier. It was a fairly small amp that Bo Anders pushed to its very limits so it started sounding distorted. The sound became high and round and filled the entire large space at Moderna Museet.

Then Andy Warhol and his entourage showed up and listened, nodding a little with folded arms. It was exciting that he was there. At those gigs, we created the framework for what the band was going to sound like. After the Warhol gig, I quit Mecki Mark Men, after having played in both bands for a while. Pärson Sound felt a lot more interesting. I preferred drone music, like our piece "Till Indien," where we tried to approach an Indian type of scale that we improvised with.

Ingmar Glanzelius
Göteborgs-Posten, April 21, 1968
Right now there are many who claim that humans are not important. Much more important is the collective, all of society and the interactions between people. These interactions are more important and fruitful than the people acting them out. This opinion can be found in many areas ... We seem to live in a time when a man cannot become a hero. Humanism is a romantic and thus harmful view of humanity.

It makes us self-absorbed and therefore blind. We can discern ourselves only through the collective, our connections with others. And not the other way around: we shouldn't use our friends as a background to make ourselves more beautiful and grand. On Thursday we can hear a group that prescribed to this way of thinking. Thursday at 8 pm at Konsthallen and the following evening at Globe Club. The group is called Pärson Sound. It consists of Bo Anders Persson, guitar, poet Thomas Tidholm, soprano saxophone, Arne Ericsson, cello, Torbjörn Abelli, bass, and Thomas Gartz, drums. It is embarrassing to list the names of the members because they do not play as individuals but as a group.

They think jazz is a nasty form of music because it emphasizes each player as a soloist. Nobody in Pärson Sound wants to sign autographs, if you ask them they will probably write "Pärson Sound."

Above: A child dancing to Pärson Sound at Moderna Museet, 1968. Photo: Jacob Forsell.

International Harvester

International Harvester

Thomas Tidholm
Dagens Nyheter, August 25, 1968
International Harvester, that's a name for all the liberation armies out in the world.... In addition, it is another name for the grim reaper who will kill Western society.... We want people to feel good. We want to help. We hope for a peaceful solution.

Bo Anders Persson
Dagens Nyheter, August 25, 1968
We sound sort of like "All You Need Is Love" by The Beatles.... That part where they aren't singing.

Thomas Tidholm:

Pärson Sound had Bo Anders's last name in it. There was no question about who was the bandleader. That's how it was from the beginning and that was all fine, but changing the name was a good thing. I liked International Harvester more and we changed the name in May 1968. A grand name. It comes from a combine harvester, as well as an entire industrial group. In Stockholm, they had ambulances that were named "International Harvester" [an American automobile and equipment manufacturer]. A patient almost died in one of those due to an incorrectly installed phlegm suction apparatus. The name became a critique of the profit-hungry engineering of the West! Childish but still, we were young. The international harvester—the grim reaper who destroys civilization. It never had to be said, because it was heard anyway.

Torbjörn Abelli:

Thomas Tidholm was very adamant that we should be called International Harvester. I think we had three cars in the band—among others a Volvo PV—painted with drippy letters that read International Harvester on both sides. So the band name was already

Previous spread: International Harvester's outdoor gig at Hötorget, Stockholm, in connection with
Alternativ Jul [Alternative Christmas]'s protest, December 14, 1968.
Left: Thomas Tidholm rests at the exhibition at Galleri Observatorium, 1969. Photo: Thomas Mera Gartz.

established. We got the idea from the Merry Pranksters, a wild group that toured with Ken Kesey in California. They had a multimedia show with film screenings and recordings, live music, theater, circus, etc. The Merry Pranksters traveled in an old school bus, a 1939 model by International Harvester. That was a clue. That story isn't official, but we saw through Thomas after the fact. At first, I felt like it was a little wrong, something about it felt too imitative. But then, when I read Tom Wolfe's book *The Electric Kool-Aid Acid Test* about the Merry Pranksters, I understood that there was a bigger idea behind it all. One thing we hadn't anticipated, however, was that in addition to International Harvester making tractors, combine harvesters, and old schoolbuses, newspaper headlines were made in Sweden when International Harvester's ambulances had such bad brakes that they became completely life-threatening. The janitor who greeted us at a venue said: "So you're International Harvester! Bad brakes . . . heh heh." And when he had heard the music, grinding on and on, his ingenious statement came up again: "Bad brakes . . . heh, heh."

Ludvig Rasmusson

Dagens Nyheter, August 25, 1968

International Harvester is the name of a new Swedish pop band that not many in this country have heard of. So far they have never performed under this name. The group was previously called Pärsson [*sic*] Sound. And before that Persson Sound. The spelling with ä was an attempt to get away from the misconception that Bo Anders Persson was the bandleader. He was, but only for a short while in the beginning. At that time, he used the group to create a sound that he liked. Nowadays, all five are involved. The old name seemed too much like a Persson cult, so they changed it to International Harvester.... From the members' background, one could easily conclude that International Harvester is some kind of intellectual hippie band. Something like the Fugs. And, without a doubt, they play pop music that differs strongly from almost everything else in Sweden. But it's a lot simpler than you might think at first. The music is reminiscent of English bands like the Stones and Eric Burdon and the Animals. The heavy beat is recognizable, as is the lack of refinement and carefree nonchalance.... You will never risk thinking that International Harvester is interested in *Svensktoppen* [Sweden's bestselling-records chart]. The music is big and massive. It is difficult to separate musicians and songs from each other. Everything blends together. One single singer

sounds like hundreds of people talking in one room or like one big choir. There are no limits. Somewhere in the masses of sound and noise, you can make out lyrics. It's not on top and clear as it is in most pop music. Slowly you come in contact with it. Sometimes the Stones also sound like that. This way of sounding is closely connected to the group's ideas. They want to create collective music without any clear-cut border between individual presentations.... International Harvester sees themselves as mainly a political group. The ideas are thoroughly considered. They believe that all western culture is based on preventing people from meeting one another. It's a system for individualists. International Harvester wants people to be together.

Margareta Klingberg:

I got to know Thomas Tidholm at Galleri Observatorium, an art gallery on Observatoriegatan, that was run by art history students from the university, which was located in this neighborhood at the time. Many artists and theorists who would later become significant started their careers here. For a period, Thomas was the curator of the gallery together with the aspiring art critic Mats Arvidsson. At Observatorium everyone helped out, manning the exhibitions and writing invitations to openings. This was done by hand and there was time to talk while you worked. I remember how the talk went when the Beatles had just put out A Hard Day's Night. It was in those exchanges that you made friends. Or enemies. There were several people in the gallery who were interested in pop music.

Thomas Mera Gartz:

There were always friends around International Harvester. We created an exhibition at Galleri Observatorium. A few friends and the band hung up some paintings, drawings, and photos. We had theater performances at Pistolteatern. We held protests. We handed out ballots that were like toys for those who were going to vote. We played on Sergels torg, or rather Plattan [as the square is locally known], with others. Sometimes several hundred people

Above left: Sit-in at Galleri Observatorium, 1969.
Above center: Ulla Berglund, Bo Anders Persson, and other visitors at Galleri Observatorium.
Above right: Bo Anders Persson and Gabi Björnstrand play drums with Jon Klingberg. Photo: Thomas Mera Gart.

Jakob Sjöholm and Gabi Björnstrand (sitting on car)
outside Galleri Observatorium. Photo: Thomas Mera Gartz.

Above: Poster for International Harvester, 1968. Text Reads "Förfäras ej du lilla hop. Synden straffar sig själv." Design: Anna-Clara Tidholm.

"Music, which was the most important thing in the new left movement, was completely dominated by guys. International Harvester was no exception, although girls were sometimes included on stage to ring a bell or play tambourine—contributions that hardly counted. Guys could also build speakers, solder, and fiddle with wires. Us girls often ended up in the periphery. Nor did we participate much in the conversations, but sat and drew or knitted, or held a baby. It was strange, especially since many of the women that belonged to that circle around International Harvester had skills that were overlooked."

Anna-Clara Tidholm

Above: Thomas and Anna-Clara Tidholm at the café by Mälartorget near Pistolteatern in Stockholm, fall of 1968. Photo: Thomas Mera Gartz.

would gather, and the police were provoked because people were spontaneously gathering, playing and having fun. Those types of actions meant that lots of different people were participating. The circle around International Harvester included around fifty people that came and went. People came from other circles too; we became mixed, everything was open and there were no tight-knit groups. This was before people became more decided when it came to political stuff, how you were supposed to be or think. We invited people in and so did everyone else.

Jakob Sjöholm:

Since I knew Anna-Clara and Thomas Tidholm, I became part of the circle around International Harvester. Thomas was teaching at Christer Strömholm's photography school and he bought this darkroom enlarger that we had in this closet in their apartment on Borgmästargatan. We developed photographs in the closet and Thomas demonstrated the magic of an image emerging. My girlfriend Gabi and Anna-Clara did quite a bit of writing. We were a big group around the band. The core was all of us who are in that photograph on the back of their album *Sov gott Rose-Marie*. I was entranced by the organic aspects of International Harvester's music, but sometimes I could get a little impatient. It could be a bit clumsy at times, but that feeling disappeared over time.

Anna-Clara Tidholm:

I came in contact with International Harvester through Thomas Tidholm. We had recently initiated our relationship—we both worked in the culture and media sphere—so music came as a surprise. My book *Tjejdikter* was published in 1966. Thomas had had a collection of poems published a year or so earlier. We belonged to the same circles at the University, worked on the student paper and at an art gallery. Stockholm was small at that time, and it was easy to get ahead—in both media and culture. But Pärson Sound/International Harvester was something new, something a lot more "underground," and a lot more innovative than other contexts I belonged to. The band wasn't just a band but a group of people: more and more people joined, some on the periphery, others more involved. Through music it evolved into other activities—shows at Pistolteatern in Stockholm and exhibitions at the student art gallery Observatorium. Although the "core operation" was the band, there was room for those who weren't musicians. I made posters.

In 1967 and '68, a new generation started to take up space. "Pop music" developed and the leftist movement emerged. There was a lot going on in Stockholm and new movements took off. Institutions like Moderna Museet and Stockholm City Museum, as well as media such as SVT and Sveriges Radio, were open to the new. Everything was moving left. This countermovement had a big need for texts, music and theater; culture was a big part of the independent left movement's early stages, and International Harvester became a resource in different contexts. I worked for [the weekly magazine] *Vi* and [the evening paper] *Expressen*. I wrote reportage and did interviews, reflecting what was happening on what was then still called the "teenage pages." Being both inside and outside the new culture became complicated in the long run, and I ended my budding media career and quit my studies at university, just like many others did. Music, which was the most important thing in the new left movement, was completely dominated by guys. International Harvester was no exception, although girls were sometimes included on stage to ring a bell or play tambourine—contributions that hardly counted. Guys could also build speakers, solder, and fiddle with wires. Us girls often ended up in the periphery. Nor did we participate much in the conversations,

ÖNSKEBRUNNEN

Krister Västlund.................Bo Anders Persson
Birgitta Weisshappel.............Gabi Björnstrand
Max von Sydow...................Jakob Sjöholm
Tuttan, en stackars grevinna.....A-C Tjerneld
Fredag, en vilde.................Thomas Gartz
Thomas Alba Edison..............Thomas Tidholm
Rudyard Kipling.................Sonja Eriksson

Musik: Jan W Morthenson och Magnus Banck

RESUMÉ:

Jorden utsöndras ur solen och börjar liksom cirkulera omkring
denna. Småningom "kalmnar" denna och det uppstår vatten i håligheterna. En del blixtar som slår ner i vattnet orsakar uppkomsten
av ett xxxxxxxx en särskild sorts slem och ur detta slem "utvecklas" en rad djur; ytterst små visserligen men ändå levande. Nu
har det hela kommit igång. Efter bara en miljard år xxxxxx växer,
fullt av örter och ormbunkar i skrevorna och ortoceratiterna kryper på havets botten. Växterna blir större och xxxxx flera skogar
till slut och dom små djuren börjar lägga ägg och föröka sej.
Draködlorna erövrar jorden. Det ser "illa" ut men efter ett tag
dör dom ut och kvar blir bara en liten konstig "hund", det första däggdjuret. xxxxx Det sker en uppdelning i flera arter bl.a.
hästar och apor. xxxxxx En solig och varm junidag i "trakten" av
nuvarande Johannisburg känner sej en ung apa i behov av lite mat
och utan att tänka närmare på saken griper han en sten och slår
o. slår o. slår på en liten hare tills den dör. Efter den dagen, r
är ingenting sej likt längre. Småningom lärde dom sej att använda eld och hjul och att bygga städer och hus och pyramider.
"Många" kulturer och civilisationer såg dagens ljus och många
var mycket vackra. Tillxxxx Men plötsligt började samlades en,
en del folk på en kulle i trakten av xxxxxxxxxxxx Donaus källor. Dom stämde opp en larvig visa och bestämde sej för att xxx
xxxxxxx alltid titta opp i himlen och xxxxx inte äta annat än
xxxxx snask hela livet xxxxxxxxxxxxx. xxxxxxxxxxxxxxxxxxx xxx

---

I ÖSTER STIGER SOLEN UPP
A space Odyssey

Justus Korallus...............Mats Arvidsson
Tekn.dr Uno Lamm..............Bo Anders Persson
(expert på överföring av högspänd likström)
En tjock fjant...............Oscar Hedlund
Stadsråttan/lantråttan och en rabulist....Thomas Tidholm
Pia Jansson..................Christine Arvidsson
En kammarfru.................Sonja Eriksson
Storvesiren av portugal,ett sändebud....Thomas Gartz
m fl
Handlingen tänkes utspela sig med centrum i solistlogen
på Kungliga Operan

Många frågar sig säkert:Men är icke denna ungdomens frigörelse
från det förgångna och förtroende för produkterna av det
egna filosoferandet något gott i och för sig? Till det vill
jag ställa motfrågan:Var i världen finner de det som är bättre
än vår egen kulturtradition – vilka folk har haft större
mänskliga framgång än de västerländska ?

DN's ledarsida den 2o oktober 1968

Pop och dans och saft

Pistolteatern: "International Harvester Good Luck Show". Medverkande International Harvester (f. d. Pärsson Sound) bestående av Bo Anders Persson, Thomas Tidholm, Arne Eriksson, Thomas Gartz, Torbjörn Abelli. Dessutom Gabi Björnstrand, Jacob Sjöholm, Mats och Kitte Arvidsson, Anna-Clara Tjerneld, Ulla Berglund m. fl. Man spelar varje måndag "så länge vi orkar hålla på".

Det är för popare, kvällsdansare och familjen.

Sammanställningen låter kanske ovanlig men täcker begreppen. Någorlunda. På fyra ställen har man ljusprojektioner. När man kommer är det vackert kurbitsliknande bilder, varefter blir det både filmer och stillbilder — de senare mest från underskön natur.

När man går in är det foliepapper mot podiet; fond och lite svag fågellåt i högtalarna. När man går ut är det pop på högsta volym, några dansar på golvet och de andra tittar på.

Under pausen serveras saft. I stor kastrull med slev. Som på landet.

Och det här är egentligen landet, åtminstone ett bortan-land, ett fjärran land där man sitter på stolar eller på golvet och är en enda stor familj i en sorts demokrati där alla verkar liktänkande. Man är omgiven av röda stugor på väggarna, bilder som växlar med sommarlandskap som växlar med vår och höst och vinter.

Det går inte särskilt fort i det här landet. Alla har tid att vänta på de poänger som egentligen inte alls kommer. Men man hinner i alla fall se egengjorda valfilmer där scengruppens medlemmar delar ut valsedlar som är allt utom valslitor och man hinner se radiochefen Rydbeck sitta och säga mot ett annat ljudband att han gillar irländsk tobak. Det gör Wedén också för den delen.

Och så står en flicka upp och dansar. Hon dansar på exakt samma ställe. I en hel halvtimme. Hon har indianband om pannan och jeans.

Bo Anders Persson ritar ett hus. Det är bara ledningar i det. Gas-elvatten — och allt det där. Han gör det väl för att han tycker att vi glömmer bort att vi har ledningar i våra hus — de där stora husen som i förhållande till de små röda ser opersonligt glamoriserade ut.

Fråga mig inte om det är bra eller dåligt. Det är faktiskt ganska skönt. International Harvester sköljer över en med rytm, våg på våg.

När jag går ut är rytmbränningarnas skär jag bara hur alla de dansar medan Sveriges skira och vänliga trädbestånd i form av diapositiv leende kring väggarna och ser på.

ULLA-BRITT EDBERG

Above: Program for the play
Önskebrunnen [The Wishing
Well] at Pistolteatern, 1968.
English translation on p. 348.
Bottom left: Program for the play
I öster stiger solen upp [The Sun
Rises in the East] at Pistolteatern,
1968. English translation on p. 348.
Bottom right: Review by Ulla-Britt
Edberg in *Svenska Dagbladet*,
September 25, 1968. English
translation on p. 349.

but sat and drew or knitted, or held a baby. It was strange, especially since many of the women that belonged to that circle around International Harvester had skills that were overlooked.

Some of us were journalists, one woman was even a music journalist—others attended Konstfack [an art and design university] or had been published. That men made music was a truth that wasn't questioned. Girls were allowed to be creative in the niches that were outside of actual music-making. Artists like Lojsa af Geijerstam and Channa Bankier created album covers for different bands.

Thomas Tidholm:

People around us started to do things, friends and acquaintances. Some of them who came to a lot of shows started hanging with us. Per Gud [Per Odeltorp] often recorded our gigs and bought us beer. He was a grass dealer, so he had money. He had good gear and got these nice sound recordings at lots of gigs. I had read Kerouac's *Dharma Bums*, Gary Snyder, and all the Beat poets. That was at the back of my head: the idea of a good life where you could be an intellectual, Buddhist monk, and lumberjack all at once. When it came to bands and social life there were many role models in the US. I particularly remember one iteration: The Immediate Family. In California, there was a band named that that consisted of many people.

International Harvester
Svenska Dagbladet, September 23, 1968
We are interested in creating some kind of theater but we also believe that there is a need for places where people can meet and be together. "The audience" and those who create the performance should be together. *International Harvester Good Luck Show* will probably be political since we are trying to describe the situation right now, what it looks like, and how it is. It will be about the western world. The show will be improvised in the sense that people can dance, talk to one another, and do whatever they feel like.

Thomas Tidholm:

Together with a bunch of people, we put on a musical show at Pistolteatern—*International Harvester Good Luck Show*— where a pretty modest societal critique developed. It gave the show a slightly ironic nature. Really we mostly just played, but we showed nice pictures of Sweden on the theater's four walls. It was eighty images on a slide projector carousel, one projector for each wall, and we had to switch images manually. We screened our own short films and performed short absurd theater performances—pretty stupid, improvised nonsense. One play was called *Västerlandets historia* [History of the West], which later became a song title. Bo Anders liked using the word *västerlandet*, the west, in different contexts.

Peter Mosskin:

International Harvester Good Luck Show opened in the fall of 1968 at the old Pistolteatern by Mälartorget in Gamla stan. The show was performed on Mondays, since the other theaters were closed that day. The music swelled, and images covered the whole stage, or maybe only half. Pistolteatern, [also known as] Pickan, was all black inside. Black is the color of the theater. When the house lights are off, the auditorium becomes black. All light is on the stage. But the lights were on, perhaps a little dimmed, as you sat on the benches or stood in one of the aisles, talking quietly to someone you knew, that you hadn't seen in a while. Harvester's evenings at "Pickan" assembled people you had known and were happy to see again and attracted new acquaintances.

On stage, behind the band, there was a big screen where images accompanied the music. A green forest, ferns, spruce branches, moss. That's the image I remember best. A calm. A stillness. Eyes resting on the fern's leaves, on the big branches that hung heavy, like huge eyelashes, over the moss. Swaying branches, moss, ferns, seen as if for the first time since childhood, when stones and tree stumps, beard lichens and pine cones spoke their own language. Part of me stepped into the forest, and the music became both weaker and stronger. The city outside of Pistolteatern's doors, with its cars, trains, and airplanes faded away, and the city, with its houses and people marked by the record years [Sweden's postwar economic expansion] disappeared. As if a door had opened up and revealed something else. The images and music and the band highlighted an alternative that I hadn't been aware of. A kind of revolt against the City, against Automobility, again Consumption, against the Record Years. An uprising in the shape of swaying branches, haircap moss, and stillness. A counterpoint to the rushing and hustling, to the traffic. Questioning career, skepticism towards the idea that development meant creating large cities.

International Harvester at Pistolteatern contributed to my moving out to the country. The vibe at Pistolteatern on those Monday nights with International Harvester was immediate, almost mild, and eye-opening. Those evenings were somehow connected to the playground stations that I was involved in that same autumn. "Children are mostly people anyway", as Anna-Clara Tidholm wrote in the program for the playground exhibition *Modellen* at Moderna Museet, where daycare kids jumped around in the rubber foam together with Olof Palme [a Social Democratic politician and future Swedish Prime Minister, assassinated in office in 1986].

If the [Dutch countercultural movement] Provo in Amsterdam was a city phenomenon —with the concept of "the playing man," *homo ludens*, as a symbol—then International Harvester stood for an alternative to the big city. A counterpoint to social-democratic

Sonja Gransvik reading the script before a performance of *The Good Luck Show* at Pistolteatern, 1968. The flower design visible on the wall is the same one Thomas Mera Gartz would later paint on his bass drum head.
Right: Urban Yman concentrating, Pistolteatern, 1968. Photo: Thomas Mera Gartz.

uniformity. A window that was open in the land created by [the Social Democratic leaders] **Tage Erlander and Gunnar Sträng. A window that let air in for young people who dreamed of something else, who were looking for new ideas, for something other than a seven-to-four job or a nine-to-five life in an office. The music opened up an everyday life that wasn't controlled by engineers. The everyday, a reality, a life that wanted something else.**

Ludvig Rasmusson
Dagens Nyheter, September 25, 1968
Things have moved fast for International Harvester. Not long ago they were called Pärson Sound and played advanced modern music with an orientation towards pop. They were good but exclusive. Today, International Harvester is one of Sweden's best popbands. They are part of the Swedish pop map just as much as Hep Start and Tages and they are a good example of how the concept of Swedish pop is growing right now.... On Monday evening International Harvester opened their own show at Pistolteatern, with Urban Yman on violin. It will play again Wednesday and Friday and then on a number of Mondays in October until Christmas. The audience at Pistolteatern was understanding. Friends, and friends of friends, and people that were generally sympathetic to them. The program partly consisted of International Harvester just playing, partly other things.... International Harvester is not content just being a pop band. They want to build in all directions. In principle, it's the same as when the Beatles sell clothes, make films, and meditate. For both the Beatles and International Harvester, the pop group is just a starting point. I think this will become more common in pop over the next few years. Just like the Beatles, International Harvester are the most successful when they keep it in the group. The images projected onto the walls were nice and sometimes corresponded well with the music. But they were only on display on a few square meters throughout the space and people didn't really care to look but looked at the musicians instead.

A color film about the election was shown last Sunday. International Harvester and some of their friends had dressed up as eclectic hippies playing on a schoolyard—a polling place in Stockholm—handing out all sorts of things instead of ballots to the voters. One of the friends was filming and was zooming so enthusiastically that one almost got motion sickness. This film is too obvious and quite banal in its critique of society.... The show was over at around eleven when they moved some seating to make space for people to dance to the music. The poetic, beautiful, Swedish, tender Beatmusic and the audience's quite stereotypical discotheque-shaking, became a grotesque contrast that ruined a lot of the atmosphere. The intention was that the audience would come in contact with International Harvester and their friends. You might have got some contact and lost everything else.

Thomas Mera Gartz:

It was a funny idea, that thing at Pistol-teatern. I think Thomas Tidholm was the driving force behind the show. It was based on us creating these sketches that we played music to. Like, long pieces. On the first night, Bo Anders showed us how everything in society and the world is connected. He made this schematic description on a big piece of paper and illustrated electrical systems and sewage systems. We sit on toilets that are linked to a bunch of other people without even knowing it. That's not private at all. We press the light switch and the electricity is connected to these huge systems. The shows lasted an entire evening. If the weather was nice enough we would continue outside the theater, blowing bubbles, playing, and just hanging out. On the first two nights, we played our weird sketches. The following evenings I remember as just long gigs with accompanying slideshows. It was really fun, but we didn't make any money on it.

Jakob Sjöholm:

I remember the little dark room at Pistol-teatern, and that a lot was going on on the floor. There was no stage, and the audience sat on bleachers while we were on the floor below. It was a happening where pretty much anything could happen. I contributed with pictures and by playing the congas. It was one night a week during the fall, and we made the program the week before, often at Thomas and Anna-Clara's place. We created new material for each show—no shows were alike. When the sources of inspiration ran out, it became difficult to renew ourselves every Monday.

Margareta Klingberg
Aftonbladet, December 1, 1968

International Harvester is the name of a socialist pop group as well as the name of a larger group of people that make film, images, music and simple theater together. One might have noticed them during Aktion Glasburken, the anti-fair against Teenage Fair and at Pistolteatern where they have been performing their "Good Luck-Show" this fall. The show is about what is happening in the world and in Sweden right now. One of the main ideas for the group is that people should have the opportunity to meet—they claim that the environment in Stockholm and Sweden at the moment is developing in the opposite direction. They are also opponents of the western idea of development that contributes to the delay of development in the third world.

Thomas Tidholm:

We also had a protest in 1968 on Sergels torg, because we wanted the empty space under the glass obelisk to become a multi-activity center. But that didn't happen. It was impossible to even try to change the mind of those in power. I debated with [the Social Democratic politician and two-time mayor of Stockholm] Hjalmar Mehr on the radio, but he was too slippery. Mehr was

Right: The poster used to incite a boycott of the Teenage Fair in Stockholm, 1968. Design: Carl Johan De Geer. English translation on p. 350.

STOPPA MÄSSAN !!!!
INTE ETT ÖRE, INTE ETT HAND-TAG TILL LYX-KONSUMTIONEN

a qualified shithead and personified the enemy in Stockholm at that time. But he had to back down when he was trying to take down the elm trees in Kungsan [during the Almstriden, or "Elm Conflict," the May 1971 protest against redevelopment of the entrance of the Kungsträdgården metro].

Ludvig Rasmusson
Dagens Nyheter, November 5, 1968

On this cold and sleety weekend, there were suddenly several places for youngsters in Stockholm to go. Not just T-Centralen. But also the Teenage Fair in Storängsbotten. And the Anti-Fair at Stockholmster-assen, Pistolteatern, Studieteatern and Nyttig. The Anti-Fair was a nice initiative. I was at Stockholms-terassen for two nights. It was packed. I saw an interesting film on the French student riots. It didn't have any subtitles so only those of us who spoke French understood anything. And I listened to the two avante-garde pop groups International Harvester and Sound of Music. Harvester sounded better than any other time I've heard them. "Music" had a bad night.

Vi ska klara av det — med musik Dom gör det med musik — socialistiska popbandet International Harvester gör låtar som heter "Ho Chi minh" och "Ut till vänster". De har många syften, bland annat att påskynda den västerländska kulturens fall. Tycker till exempel att den västerländska kulturen alltid undertryckt människors inneboende drift att vara tillsammans. International Harvester har hela hösten propogerat för gemenskap i sin "Good Luck Show" de kört på Pistolteatern i Stockholm.

Pretty Things played at the Teenage Fair (not very good) and sang Peps [Persson] (very good).

A bunch of teenagers mingled around listening, letting themselves be fooled to drink mellanöl [the 3–5 percent ABV "middle beer" popular with Swedish youth] and buy a car for fifty thousand. At the Anti-Fair, I didn't see any teenagers. Those who actually showed up looked different than those at the Teenage Fair. They weren't wearing any expensive boutique clothes. They were the aware, enlightened, engaged ones. And there were students and people working in the field of culture. People who, thanks to their education or work, have been given the opportunity to see through commercial attempts at indoctrination. They had already been vaccinated. Those people would have been able to go to the Teenage Fair without being fooled into buying expensive boutique garments, drinking mellanöl, chewing gum, wearing leather jackets, going to the movies, driving a car, playing the banjo, riding a snowmobile in the mountains, read [the youth magazine] *Bildjournalen*, playing records, and eating hot dogs. They won't give an öre [the Swedish equivalent of a penny] to luxury consumption!

Per Kågesson/Pär Stolpe
Dagens Nyheter, November 6, 1968

Ludvig Rasmusson--*Dagens Nyheter*'s pop writer--hasn't understood at all what the Teenage Fair was about. He also hasn't understood the meaning behind Aktion STOPPA MÄSSAN [STOP THE FAIR Action]! Nor the "Anti-Fairs" (which, by the way, continue every day!)...Ludvig is of the opinion that the "unaware youth" was forgotten, that the pop music and films were too complex. That is wrong—International Harvester is just as sexy as Tommy Blom [the singer of the band Tages]. The thing is that the band hasn't had the opportunity to show themselves to Ludvig's fifteen-year-old teenage girls during the "Anti-Fairs." And everyone thought that was great.... Most important is, of course, that Aktion STOPPA MÄSSAN! only is an initial focused action. It will be followed by actions against the commercial betrayal that goes under the motto CHRISTMAS and against the entire bourgeoisie-misguided consumer society. One never knows on what day a big department store in the city center will be occupied by determined activists.

Above: *Aftonbladet,* December 1, 1968. English translation on p. 350.
Right: Demonstration in Stockholm against the Olympics in Mexico, 1968. The photograph shows Mats Arvidsson, Thomas Tidholm, and Ulla Berglund, among others. Photo: Thomas Mera Gartz.

Leif Nylén
Paletten, November 4, 1968

"Aktion Stoppa Mässan" was a battle of the youth.
A confrontation between two interpretations of the
youth uprising. The merchants' attempts at exploit-
ing the newly won freedom as a giant vacation par-
adise, characterized by marketable fads and status
values. A new, gigantic freemasonry that without
difficulty lets itself become incorporated into the
already existing societal structure. And the radical
interpretation: that new youth culture sketches an
alternative to bourgeoise individualism, authoritarian view of human beings, property fetishism, and
exploitation. The fair and the "anti-fairs" included
(at least partially) the same kind of things but on
diametrically different grounds.

Thomas Mera Gartz:

For a few years in the 1960s, an awakening
of the context of the world and everyday life
grew among younger people in Stockholm.
The Living Moment was The Apex, everyone who was there was The Intensity. The
books told, the records heated up, newspapers, images, TV and bikers, raggare [Swe-
den's greaser/rockabilly subculture], trips
to other countries, the international travelers
that passed through Kungsträdgården in the
summers, the anti-atom bomb movement,
world citizens, pacifists, poets, "provies" [the
pacifist-anarchist movement formed in answer
to the Netherlands' "Provo" culture] and
radically happy people of all kinds, intense
folklife, and several places to gather popped
up both inside and outside.

FRONT MOT ÖVERKLASSKULTUREN

Från den första till den sista stavelsen har den västerländska kulturen varit en överklasskultur. Nu har det gått så långt att ordet kultur betyder teater eller konserter eller konst. Men vi vill berätta att en gång fanns i detta land precis som i andra länder en folkkultur, alltså en kultur som hängde ihop med människornas liv, alltså en kultur som _fungerade_. På den tiden fick folk leva _ett_ liv men nu tvingas alla att bli schizofrena.

Västerlandets historia har varit tillgjordhetens seger över naturen. I femhundra år har människor i allt större skaror lurats att flytta från sina hem mot löften om pengar och någonting fint. Man har förträngt naturen. Man har också förträngt Afrika, Asien och Sydamerika. Man har kämpat för att uppnå någonting fint, någonting finare..... Det Finaste. Man har flyttat in till städerna och skaffat sej en sportstuga. Och dom människor som vill ha en mening med sitt liv istället för en mening med sin död har man kallat bondlurkar och så har man pressat kläderna en gång till, för skrynklorna vill man också förtränga.

Nu talas om att sprida kulturen till folket. Jaså verkligen. Nu har man alltså tagit ifrån människorna deras liv och istället för deras liv vill man ge dom Teater, Litteratur och Konst. Som ersättning för sitt liv erbjuds man att sitta i en fåtölj och hålla käften medan andra människor apar sej på en scen, tusen mil bort från allt som egentligen var värt någonting. Men inte heller dom lever. Dom är alla döda.

KÄRA VÄNNER

Folk will träffas, men dom som bestämmer vill inte att folk
ska träffas. Utom på vissa villkor: Man får t.ex inte träffas
för länge eller för många och så ska man ha gjort av med mycket
pengar under tiden.

Anledningen till att dom inte tycker att man ska få träffas är
att dom lider av sexualsrkäck.

Pengar och skit är samma sak, det är vetenskapligt bevisat.(Av
bl.a Sigmund Freud.)

Poliserna har dom satt dit för att folk ska köpa ordentligt och
gå hem sen.

Sergels torg ska på så vis bli tummelplats för dom kommersiella
fascisterna (och dom andra.)
"Take a day and walk around
watch the nazis run your town."

Hjalmar Mehr,PO Hansson och Nils Hallerby kan sticka och beckna
sig. Dom ska i vilket fall inte få vara med i några diskussioner.
Stadsfullmäktige är fullständigt genomkorrumperat.

Åhléns berömda potatissallad har en ohygglig bismak.

Vattnet i fontänen är dyrare än köttsoppa.

Konserthuset ska byggas om för 17 milj. Vore det inte billigare
att skicka symfonibögarna direkt till Wien med Club 33.

Vi är snällare än dom nånsin har v arit.

Gå till torget på torsdag och titta på när Hantverket inviger
sin lilla utställning av överklassprylar i vårt kafé. Ni får
inte komma in så klart men tryck näsan mot glaset ordentligt så
kanske ni får se en skymt av prinsessan Sibylla.

Bu för den västerländska utvecklingstanken. Håll öppet åt Vänster.

GOOD LUCK

                    INTERNATIONAL HARVESTER

Above: "Dear Friends." Announcement by International Harvester, 1968. English translation on p. 351.

The threat from the left, the Security services'
surveillance of communists, anarchists, etc. 1965-2002
(SOU [Swedish Government Official Report] 2002:12)
[During] the mid and late 1960s, a younger generation
of anarchists began to make themselves heard. In the
shadow of the Maoist movement, groups with a more
libertarian socialist orientation began to emerge.
Alternativt Samhälle, Arkiv samtal, and International
Harvester, which later developed into Träd, Gräs
och Stenar, were perceived by the security police as
interesting or even as part of subversive Sweden.

Bildjournalen, November 14, 1969
International Harvester have been called Sweden's only
political pop group.... International Harvester's politics aren't the same as the government's, parliament's,
or the municipality's politics, but a way of living
in a constant struggle against capitalist interests,
standing outside the society of luxury consumption. "In
the beginning all pop music was political," says Tomas
[*sic*] Gartz, drummer. "And it became a dangerous threat
to passive couch society. So society had to render pop
harmless by diluting it, commercializing it and ranking
it into the system.... Beatniks became an industry in
jeans, hippies necklaces and jackets with fringe, the
NLFers [united antiwar protest groups] have meant a boom for
Vietnam patches. International Harvester have nothing
to sell. Our politics aren't a gimmick. The industry
people—managers, producers—will never be interested in
us."

Margareta Klingberg:

In May of 1968, the students occupied the
student union house on Holländargatan in
Stockholm. As a new mother, I was satisfied
following the developments at a distance.
One evening, as the occupation was nearing
its end, we—the band and close supporters
and girlfriends—had gathered in an apartment on Borgmästargatan on Södermalm.
Thomas had left his family and moved in
with Anna-Clara Tjerneld, who was studying History of Literature and had made
her debut as a poet at Bonniers [a Swedish
publisher] the same year as Thomas, 1966.

We had understood that the occupiers were
going to go out on the streets and continue
to protest that night. There were rumors
of plans to storm the opera. That lit the
rebellious fire in our more anarchist friends.
Everyone left the apartment. But there were
several children to take into consideration.
My role as the babysitter was chosen. I
stayed at home with my sleeping son and
Tove Tidholm, who was a few years older.
The rebels returned after midnight and I
received reports from the political battle-
field. No storming had taken place.

Thomas Mera Gartz:

We opposed cultural imperialism (on the
part of the Europeans and Americans) that
wanted to pull in all people and cultures,
all ways of living and thinking, and gods in
their commodity sphere and confiscate their
natural resources, put a price tag on them
and their lives and their picturesque dress to
be seen by rich tourists. We saw ourselves on
the side of the Vietnamese, on the side of the
Paris revolutionaries, the Prague youth, the
hippies, the Black Panthers, the American
Indians, and the Samis.

But we were also on our own side, on
the workers' side, kids' side, because we
saw that we were also occupied and partly
shaped by commodity imperialism's industrial production and point of view, that our
culture had once had had a different content, not too long ago, that showed its face
inside of us—perhaps deformed, but still.

Jakob Sjöholm:

Mera was the great anarchist in the band.
But the rest of us were sure of ourselves.
We worked with a conscious expression.
We were of the idea that political people
were way too square, that reality is usually
way more complicated and layered. We felt
political anyway, just not tied to a party.

Torbjörn Abelli:

Joining any particular faction was out of the question—partly because unity and not division was strongest within the left, partly because there was an inherent block in the group's ideology. The anarchists were the group that was closest to us, but there was never an ambition to cement an official group ideology.

Arne Ericsson:

I was probably more political in the beginning if we're talking Marx, slogans, and NLF demonstrations. But that rigidness disappeared pretty quickly, and as a band, we never wanted to create political propaganda. We weren't preaching. We wanted to make good, nice, and true music. But that meant that we were quite obnoxious towards society, while at the same time sympathizing with left-wing ideas.

Thomas Tidholm:

In 1967, when Anna-Clara and I were in the USA, the atmosphere had already changed. The previously positive and open culture that we saw in California in 1966 no longer existed. Not in New York either. The climate had become a lot tougher, with more police on the streets. The police cracked down on hippies and almost everything new that emerged. A radical political movement arose. During the 1968 election year, a lot came to a head: both Robert Kennedy and Martin Luther King were assassinated. The American military staged the Chicago riots during the Democratic convention. At the same time, people began to move out of the cities. The same thing happened in Sweden, with a little delay.

Above: Torbjörn Abelli being chased by mounted police in Stockholm at a demonstration against the shutdown of the multi-activity center Gamla Bro. *Expressen*, November 5, 1970. Photo: Kenneth Jonasson.

International Harvester with friends out in the water by Albysjön, late summer of 1968.
From left: Jakob Sjöholm, Gabi Björnstrand, Kitte Arvidsson, Mats Arvidsson with son Nisse,
Rathje Vierth, Arne Ericsson, Margareta Klingberg with son Jon, Urban Yman, Erik Tidholm,
unknown, Ulla Berglund, Torbjörn Abelli, Thomas Mera Gartz, Anna-Clara Tidholm,
Thomas Tidholm, Stefan Teleman, Bo Anders Persson, Sonja Gransvik, and Sofia Teleman.
Photo: Thomas Tidholm (with tripod).

CHAPTER 4

Sov gott Rose-Marie

Sov gott Rose-Marie

Torbjörn Abelli:

> **The commercial companies were sincerely uninterested. Signing us was out of the question. And the small labels hadn't really gotten started yet.**

Peter Mosskin
Expressen, January 7, 1969

In November, a short program in color was broadcast late one evening about International Harvester. Some Indians were shown, to orientally-saturated pop, an impression of dusty India that moved in time with the music. The images matched the music. Then the image changed to Swedish haymaking, slouch hats, and the turn of the century--or maybe later. Same beat, same music. The wonderful thing: film and music were still synced. Suddenly, a connection between the developing country India and Sweden had been established which said more about humanity, and solidarity, than several lectures and jarring testimonies combined. Several examples of International Harvester's ability to combine and connect can be found on the group's first and newly released LP, *Sov gott Rose-Marie*. The record begins somewhere in the Swedish Middle Ages, Catholic mass, blackbird song. Vilhelm Moberg's "Rid i natt" is on a tree stump. The air is thick with inland forest, tall trees, and moss. Some distant voice, far away from our memories, sings "I villande skogen." The trees split. At the lake in the forest, two electric guitars strum through the clearing, and long-haired people gather around "The Runcorn Report on Western Progress." The Prime Minister is sitting a little further away.

He can read, write, and count, but can he really understand the second industrial revolution (electronics, cybernetics), is he the right man to lead the post-war generation against Looting, Starvation, and Poisoning? One by one the young people get up.

Previous spread: International Harvester rehearsing before recording for the TV program *Number 9* at the Narrenteatern at Gröna Lund, February 14, 1969. The performance was broadcast three days later on Sveriges Television as a test program for color TV. Photo: Jakob Sjöholm. Left: International Harvester with families and friends on Kungsholmen in Stockholm, 1968. Photo: Jakob Sjöholm.

The Second World War generation looks out from their windows in the high-rises on the other side of the lake, and sees the young people walking by chanting "Ho Ho Ho Chi Minh" and "It's Only Love." They carry a Georg Borgström quote, "It's very late now," on a large hand-woven sheet from Mockfjärd. Forest, moss, 1968. Again forest and it's summer, the hay is raked. Despite war and demonstrations, we can meet, and we meet in common history, recognizing familiarity and summer, to start with hands and hearts and continue the walk toward the future. We have to. And we can. "Sommarlåten" helps us on our way.

Arne Ericsson:

When we recorded the first LP, *Sov gott Rose-Marie*, we started to create an outline and knew what we wanted. There was a hidden poetic social critique in a lot of the lyrics; they became melodies and it felt well thought out, even though nobody was controlling it. However, we weren't exactly instrumental acrobats, which meant that we had to work quite a bit to get where we wanted to be.

Jan Nordlander & Urban von Rosen
Svenska Dagbladet, December, 29, 1968

The most striking LP this Christmas comes from International Harvester. Just like the group, the LP can be characterized as the first "underground production" in the country. The record includes several numbers that makes one think of American predecessors of the genre. The LP has two main themes in its textual and musical content. One clearly marked political stance—they make fun of the Prime Minister and celebrate Ho Chi Minh.... Further, the music has a strong closeness to nature--which is probably to be interpreted as a protest against unrestrained environmental destruction. It is both welcome and promising that a record company dares to invest in such a controversial group, and it is even more gratifying that the result has been well beyond expectations.

Ludvig Rasmusson
DN, February 12, 1969

In the last six months there have been quite a few attempts with Swedish pop. A few were acceptable. Most of it has been garbage.... No one has come up with a really effective Swedish pop style. In any case, a very interesting attempt has been made. It is International Harvester's LP, recorded and produced in Finland ... *Sov gott Rose-Marie*. That's also the

INTERNATIONAL HARVESTER
SOV GOTT ROSE-MARIE

L♡VE RECORDS

LRLP 1005 A

SIDA 1
DIES IRAE (trad) 2.29
I VILLANDE SKOGEN (trad) 3.12
THERE IS NO OTHER PLACE (Tidholm, Abelli) 2.39
THE RUNCORN REPORT ON WESTERN PROGRESS (Persson) 3.25
STATSMINISTERN (International Harvester) 0.18
HO CHI MINH (trad)
IT'S ONLY LOVE (Jagger) 1.29
KLOCKAN ÄR MYCKET NU (G. Borgström) 3.23
UT TILL VÄNSTER (Tidholm) 0.46
SOMMARLÅTEN (Abelli, Persson) 2.45
SOV GOTT ROSE-MARIE (Tidholm) 3.36

INTERNATIONAL HARVESTER
SOV GOTT ROSE-MARIE

L♡VE RECORDS

LRLP 1005 B

SIDA 2
I MOURN YOU (Tidholm, Persson) 12.45
HOW TO SURVIVE (Gartz, Eriksson) 11.53

name of one of the album's songs.... It is a completely "Swedish" song.... It is clear and clearly pop, just like Bob Dylan or the Rolling Stones. It's not Swedish in the way that it has a bunch of violins from Dalarna or other shortcuts. It's straightforward, natural and unsentimental.... The atmosphere is Swedish--just as Swedish as a Pressbyrån stand [chain of convenience stores] in the country, or rental apartments on Söder or, a breakfast of oatmeal with coffee and a hardboiled egg in a café.

Anders Lind:

The Finnish record label Love Records wanted to make an album with International Harvester, and Bo Anders got in contact with AB Ljudåtergivning, where I was working at the time. AB Ljudåtergivning archived all of the philharmonic rehearsals in the Royal Concert Hall and I was there to record it. I learned a lot about big, uniform sound there. International Harvester didn't want their album to be a traditional pop album but to have a whole sound, a sound where things weren't able to be distinguished individually. It was really a thorough idea they had, that the speakers would direct the sound in all directions. Actually, it was intended that the B side on the record would consist of the song "Skördetider." Our demands regarding how things should sound musically were quite high, and we didn't think the song was good enough. So, right before the album was to be released, the B side was changed to "I Mourn You" and "How to Survive." There were things I didn't really understand, like when

they chanted "Riksdagsman, åh Riksdagsman, vad åt du väl idag" ["Parliamentarian, oh parliamentarian, what did you eat

Left: Front and back cover of *Sov gott Rose-Marie*. Love Records, 1968 (LRLP 1005). Cover design: Mats Arvidsson.
Above: Center labels for *Sov gott Rose-Marie*.
Bottom right: The Finnish Love Records logo.

International Harvester and friends in Vårby, 1968. From left: Erik Tidholm, Jakob Sjöholm, Margareta Klingberg, Gabi Björnstrand with Jon Klingberg, Mats Arvidsson with son Nisse, Kitte Arvidsson, Sofia Teleman, Sonja Gransvik, Bo Anders Persson, Ulla Berglund, Thomas Mera Gartz, Rathje Vierth, Urban Yman, Anna-Clara Tidholm, Thomas Tidholm, unknown, Torbjörn Abelli, and Arne Ericsson. Photo: Thomas Tidholm (with tripod).

today?"] on Sergels torg. When I heard it, I thought it didn't fit on the record. I didn't think it was music, I just thought of it as a statement. I later understood that it did fit in the context. I think that Bo Anders has broadened my view of why you make music, how you can express yourself and what kind of music you can release. It has brought me a lot of pleasure.

Tidningen Vi, November 8, 1969
International Harvester's latest record *Sov Gott Rose-Marie*, ... a cruel little lullaby that deals with both darkness, starlight, birdsong and politics: "The Prime Minister can read / The Prime Minister can write / The Prime Minister can count / but he can't dance, rocka/bugga, rocka/bugga dong-dongdong"--Does a prime minister have to know that? How to dance? In other words, how to be mobile? Yes: because "THE CLOCK CLOCK CLOCK IS LATE NOW, YES MY FRIENDS THE CLOCK IS PROBABLY RIGHT," i.e. according to G Borgström, the time is nigh. In "Dies Irae," which means "Day of Wrath," the approach is more of a rhythmic chorale, it fades away and instead, you hear the birds chirping. Someone picks up the melody from *Värmlänningarna* [a nineteenth-century Swedish folk play]: "In the wandering forest, I herd my flock." Soon after, the prime minister comes followed by an impatiently increased dramatic stomp HO HO HO CHI MINH HO HO HO CHI MINH! Bo Anders Persson (formerly Persson Sound [*sic*]), who made the music together with Thomas Tidholm and others, said a few years ago in an interview in *Nutida Musik*: I want to make music in the kitchen. Now one understands what he meant: music with steaming everyday ingredients. Some have been listed above. The kitchen window is wide open.

What must be added is that this music is fresh and angry like a dragonfly. She can, as you know, lift twice her body weight. It is a musical contribution to the nature conservation debate, which simultane-ously applies to both Sweden and the world. The range of tempos is astonishing: from mumbling, and humming folk tunes, to spoken word chorus plus liberally used material from the Stones.

Lester Bangs
Rolling Stone, November 67, 1970
Of all the Finnish [*sic*] groups, undoubtedly the strangest is International Harvester. One hesitates to call them a group at all--on the back cover stands a congregation of 20 or 30 people, and the album itself is more a series of sounds than an arranged mu-sical production. The first side lists eleven "songs," but many of them are largely silent.... But right in the middle of these soporific meanderings lies the thundering "Ho Chi Minh," a fierce chant for martial drum and massed female voices which simply repeat the North Vietnamese leader's name over and over again in a wildly insistent rhythm and reminds me of nothing so much as the haunting chants of the choirs on Elektra's classic *Music of Bulgaria* album. Side two features two long jams for string instruments somewhat reminiscent of early Velvet Underground pieces such as "Black Angel's Death Song".... A thick multi-textured modal drone which could make a very effective statement if harnessed properly.

Urban Yman:

The strength of youth music lay in its progressive questioning tone. It was an attempt to find alternative ways out of society's closed norms. At the same time, there was an awakening against the US's war in Vietnam. Music and the youth movement took off from that awakening. When the Vietnam War entered people's living rooms, we were more affected by the image of the horrors of the war—and what it did to people—than the war itself. From that came an idealization—which perhaps in some way can be found in the song "Ho Chi Minh." Even though we are really just repeating the words Ho Chi Minh — the words say so much. And by repeating the words, the stance becomes central and suggestive.

Thomas Tidholm:

"Ho Chi Minh" came about by pure chance when we were going to play at Kåren in Lund. Someone who liked us had pushed

Above: "Ho Chi Minh." Design: Håkan Nyberg, 1970. English translation on p. 351.

Members of International Harvester in Vitabergsparken's pavilion. Here International Harvester recorded "How to Survive" (September 1968) and "När Lingonen Mognar" ["When the Lingonberry Ripens"] (June 1969). Photo: Thomas Mera Gartz.

for us to play there. When we got there, we noticed that the student union organizing the concert thought we were unhinged hippies and that the audience was mostly conservative students. It felt as if the student union was going to "exhibit" us in some way, that we were there to make fools of ourselves. So we started singing "Ho-Ho-Ho-Chi-Minh" over a rhythm that we played. They couldn't take that. Things became pretty tense! People tried to pull our instrument cables out. We've only felt such a menacing atmosphere a few times. A soup of conservative values was cooking there.

We toured in an old VW bus, and after a long journey from Stockholm, we had arrived in Lund early in the morning. The police had surrounded the entire festival area; they thought there was a risk of student rebellion in Lund, as well. I took a picture of the university building in the morning sun with an endless number of Amazon Volvo police cars lined up in front of the fort-like university.

Margareta Klingberg:

The recording of the folk song "I villande skogen," which is heard in the introduction to *Sov gott Rose-Marie*, was made during the late summer. Early in the morning we, the band and a group of close friends, went to the forest on Korpberget in Huddinge, a dramatic place at Vårbyfjärden [a strait in Lake Mälaren, southeast of Stockholm]. We sang a beautiful stanza placed in different places in the terrain. The idea with the essentially different short pieces on one side of the LP was to create a sound collage beginning with the medieval hymn "Dies Irae." Inspiration came in part from the American band Vanilla Fudge, who earlier in the year released the album *The Beat Goes On*, where sound fragments and documentary recordings alternated with the group's instrumental parts.

97

After our morning liturgy up on Korpberget [a rocky promontory in the Vårby area], a group photo was taken. Jon is the youngest both in the recording and in the photo. It became one of the covers for *Sov gott Rose-Marie*. Thomas's friend Mats Arvidsson drew the picture on the cover.

Thomas Tidholm:

I thought songs and song titles together became like poetry or secret messages. There is music on *Sov Gott Rose-Marie* that we played at gigs, but most of it is songs that we rarely or never played at our shows. They are only on the record. I don't remember why it was like that. We agreed on what we wanted to put out. That's how I understood it.

There are recordings of long repetitive songs from the same occasion that never made it onto the album, but which are now available as bonus tracks. But there is a nice recording from the music pavilion in Vita Bergen [a park in central Stockholm] where we managed to take up the surrounding sounds, with dogs and children.

I had another idea, that we should play on a truck bed while the car was driving. Then we would rig microphones along the street as the car slowly drove by. Then the sound would go from vague, at a distance, to very close, and then disappear again into noise. But it never happened. When it came to lyrics, I had ambitions, but they somehow didn't fit.

When I sang into the mic, it became just one voice. The words disappeared in the strong common soundscape. Therefore, I usually didn't even sing any words; the singing was mostly a kind of sound or abracadabra. Some songs just didn't work, I used them on my album *Varma Smörgåsar* instead.

Bo Anders Persson:

Thomas Tidholm had an entire concept for *Sov gott Rose-Marie*. He had thought out exactly what was going to be on it. Admittedly, there were some songs that we had already played. But others couldn't be played at all, as in the opening song "Dies Irae." It was a brilliant idea, but it wasn't followed up by any magic in the music. I tried to make songs, but felt like I was completely disconnected. It was hard. But it was a decent record anyway.

Thomas Mera Gartz:

When we improvised or played live, it was Bo Anders or Thomas who came up with an idea, and we said we'd try to record this. It was usually just one take. We never made any other recordings over it afterward. The first record was recorded with only two mics in Nacka Aula [auditorium].

Urban Yman:

Often it was Tidholm who came up with the text-based material and—I think—Bo Anders who came up with the music. But both had strong opinions about how things should be. It was a contradiction that neither of them really wanted to resolve. I myself was never drawn into those discussions. Essentially, their thoughts were compatible. But I felt strongly that the situation didn't need much more disagreement before it would become senseless.

Låt Harvester spela i skolan!

Ett par hundra människor hade stämt träff med International Harvester på Arkivmuseet i Lund i går kväll. Någon imponerande publiksiffra var det väl knappast, men ändå ungefär vad man hade anledning att vänta sig. International Harvester är en udda popgrupp och dess berömmelse har inte nått särdeles långt utanför huvudstadens gränser.

Då jag recenserade bandets första LP-skiva för en månad sedan, skrev jag någonting om International Harvester i en svensk sommarhage. Det finns ingen anledning att ändra på den karakteristiken. Sextetten inbjuder i stället till associationer av denna sort genom att illustrera sin musik med landskapsbilder.

I annonsen kallades detta sistnämnda Ljusshow — några flackande spotlights med blinkande färgfilter inrymdes emellertid inte under den måhända publikdragande rubriken. I stället gick det hela mera i stil med de gamla stumfilmsbiograferna med pianospelande äldre damer längst fram i salongen. I går var det naturligtvis det omvända förhållandet — musiken illustrerades med fotografier och teckningar, men dessa kunde man nästan varit utan.

International Harvester kan svårligen förväxlas med någon annan popgrupp av svenskt ursprung. Sättningen är ovanlig såtillvida att den inrymmer två stråkinstrument med ovanlig klang och utformning. Det ena ger från sig ett svårdefinierbart knarrande ljud som ibland för tankarna till amerikansk jag band music. Ovanpå det välfyllda kompet figurerar en gitarr som väl går in i ljudmöstret.

Raka motsatsen till Tio i Topp — hur låter den? International Harvester kan vara ett av svaren. Man kan inte dansa till deras musik, nynnande och fotstampning möter också många hinder. Gruppen börjar på låg nivå, ett efter ett faller instrumenten in och tempo och volym stegras tills en kompakt ljudvägg fabricerats. Kring denna vävs sedan klanger från koskällor, bjällror och flöjter, alltmedan bilden av ett svenskt sommarlandskap framträder på näthinnan.

Så upplevde jag International Harvesters musicerande den här gången. Det var fascinerande i all sin påfrestande monotoni och dess närmande till den svenska folkmusiktraditionen är intressant. För ett år sedan skulle jag säkerligen haft betydligt svårare för den här sortens musik; trots att den inte är speciellt rolig att lyssna på har den nu en ganska svårförklarlig attraktionskraft som möjligen bottnar i svärmeri för det svenska landskapet.

International Harvester skall absolut inte höjas till skyarna — det är gruppen inte värd. Men varför inte låta bandet spela på skolorna? Då och då turnerar svenska musiker ur klassiska, modernistiska och jazziga och spelar för skolungdom. Musikerna går ut till publiken. Varför inte låta popmusiken göra detsamma? Skolornas musikundervisning trampar på i gamla nötta fotspår och måste förnyas.

OTIS

Left: The pavilion in Vitabergsparken, Stockholm, 1968. Photo: Thomas Mera Gartz.

Above: Text by the pseudonymous Otis, published in *Sydsvenska Dagbladet*, February 25, 1969. English translation on p. 352.

CHAPTER 5

Playing Together

Playing Together

Thomas Mera Gartz:

Our audience was the big city audience that was used to going out to some cool place like Filips or Gyllene Cirkeln, where the music was what was important and not the boy-girl ritual. Out in more rural areas, it was more difficult and incredibly ritualized with places where girls and boys stood on different sides of the venue. They didn't know what was going on: "Are they playing to dance or what are they doing?" I think International Harvester played at a discotheque once and it was not good.

Ludvig Rasmusson

Dagens Nyheter, September 21, 1968

[The Doors] performed at Stockholm Concert Hall on Friday night. It was two performances in a row, both sold out with a violently applauding audience. One understood that it's wrong to talk about the Doors as psychedelic or underground or experimental or revolutionary. They are simply entertainment artists.... During the first half of the show the Swedish band International Harvester played. Many people in the audience were enthusiastic, but most of them seemed puzzled. International Harvester is one of very few Swedish bands that can surprise and bring something new to the table. They played and sang some of their own Swedish-folksong-inspired songs that clearly showed how independently they relate to American and English pop. I believe that if Swedish pop is ever going to be something other than a good copy, musicians need to try the same paths as International Harvester. Even if it sounds unusual at first. The contrast between their friendly, soft and unassuming music and the Doors' showy, sexy and somewhat square style could hardly be bigger.

Kjell Genberg

Nöjes-Aktuellt, October 1968

A writer in our largest daily morning paper sharpened his pencil to write something about International Harvester (previously Pärsson [sic] Sound) in connection with their performance at Stockholm Concert Hall on September 20. The writer emphasizes the group as groundbreaking Swedish pop music

Previous spread: International Harvester soundchecking at Stockholm Concert Hall. Photo: Jakob Sjöholm.
Left: International Harvester during their Norrland tour, 1969.

and representing a revolutionary style. I can agree with him on this if the criteria for that would be:

1. It's groundbreaking to not be able to tune your instruments.
2. It's groundbreaking to have the sound be so unbalanced that one often can't hear anything but random tones from a plastic saxophone.
3. It's groundbreaking to have practiced so little that you can't play in unison.
4. It's groundbreaking to sing out of tune so much that it sounds like a parody.
5. It's groundbreaking to use extra instruments (recorder) that you can't play.
6. It's groundbreaking to perform sloppily on stage.

... It sounded, apologies in advance, like a drunk elementary school orchestra on their first rehearsal. The ambitions might have been great, but still.

Ludvig Rasmusson
Dagens Nyheter, October 6, 1968
Kjell Grenberg has protested my review, in the magazine *Nöjes-Aktuellt*. His point is that a group that is so unrehearsed, has such bad balance and where the singer

and saxophone player sing and play so badly--can't be groundbreaking? But I stand by my opinion.... International Harvester doesn't put on a shiny, well-rehearsed show. They are journeying forward, tentatively and carefully. By removing the use of external effects and techniques as much as possible, the musicians are trying to get people to listen and interest themselves in the music's content. The fact that International Harvester sings out of tune and plays the wrong notes is something that I find incredibly striking.... The more pop music is built on sounds, noise, words, show and contact with the audience, the less conventional musical rules will mean. International Harvester isn't alone in playing in this new way. Mick Jagger in the Rolling Stones is a great example. He sings out of tune on many of the Stones' best albums. At first, when you hear it you become horrified, but then you start liking it more. American bands such as the Fugs and Velvet Underground also deliberately work with sounds and songs that aren't perfect.

Bo Anders Persson:

I borrowed a guitar that had problems with the tuning pegs, so it was constantly out of tune. I had also pulled together singing

Above: Flyer for the show with the Doors and International Harvester.
Right: Ray Manzarek and Jim Morrison from the Doors, Stockholm Concert Hall, September 20, 1968. Photo: Jakob Sjöholm.
Following spread: Backstage at the performance at Stockholm Concert Hall. Arne Ericsson, Torbjörn Abelli, Jakob Sjöholm, and Erik Lidström, September 20, 1968. Photo: Thomas Mera Gartz.

gear because we weren't allowed to use the Doors' stuff. I wasn't very harmonious, I was overworked. The Doors weren't interested in us. They cruised by our space outside their dressing room with their noses in the air; anything else would have been impossible. We would never get to play with a band of their stature today. It was all a bit confused. That we were there was a mistake, but at the same time, it was right, because afterward, I heard that we opened a lot of people's eyes.

Jan Nordlander & Urban von Rosen
Svenska Dagbladet, September 21, 1968
It was both a difficult and thankless task to play in front of a band whose promotion had been so intense. But our personal view is that International Harvester proved to be ripe for the task. They performed a form of monotonous, slightly nonsensical crescen-do-music with influences from Swedish folk music, Mothers of Invention, the group's own personality, and oriental musical forms. The group's closing number ... "Sov gott Rose-Marie" ... was performed in Swedish and was effectively illustrated by Tidholm putting some little cute dolls to bed on stage, which he stomped down as a finale. That's how much he has left over for the sleeping Western world.

Thomas Mera Gartz:

The Doors weren't like Jimi Hendrix or Frank Zappa, who said hi. They were too preoccupied with their drugs or whatever. They slithered in, and played, and Jim Morrison was there in his leather pants doing his thing. It was out of the ordinary, since they were a band from another country and they were famous. But when you're contemporary with something that hasn't reached mythic proportions, it's much easier. I never worried that I would play worse or that our music was insignificant compared to theirs. It wasn't like that. We just played and hoped for the best.

Torbjörn Abelli:

On one of the first tours [to Lund in Skåne], we stopped for a cup of coffee on our way home. A few young boys asked us for our autographs and we signed, a little surprised. Later we understood why. The trailer we had rented had previously been used by the Kinks, and their name was still on it. The boys thought we were the Kinks.

Thomas Mera Gartz:

When we went on tour with International Harvester, we often played at museums, libraries, and stuff like that; totally different spaces. If we played at a library in Gävle [two hours north of Stockholm], we were part of a cultural segment, since we were at a library and not a music venue. The right kind of people came, and they received us in a completely different way. We played two songs that were forty minutes each, with a break in between. They were very taken because it was so powerful, rhythmic, and manic. And since it was a different environment than the rock venues—where things were supposed to be a certain way—there was room for that to happen. It was noticeable in the audience that they felt it was something new: "What is this? Now things are happening!"

Iwan Erichsson
Gefle Dagblad, February 6, 1969
International Harvester, a so-called pop group, visited the public library on Wednesday evening. About 400 mainly young people had come to see and listen to the much-talked-about unconventional group. It's a relatively new group so many were probably eager to hear what they were going to sound like.... The performance at the library was both good and bad. First off, you don't have to have the volume turned all the way up for the music to be enjoyable and "hit home." They seemed ill-prepared, which might be part of their style. After some tuning--because they were tuning their instruments, right?--the group started playing a number that lasted over half and hour. They improvised endlessly on a given theme. One got a headache from their music, even though they say that it's supposed to make the audience feel good.

"After some tuning—because they were tuning their instruments, right?—the group started playing a number that lasted over half and hour."

Iwan Erichson on International Harvester, *Gefle Dagblad*, February 6, 1969

Leif J Andersson:
Arbetarbladet, February 6, 1969

What one must not forget when discussing International Harvester is that the pop group (if they can be called that) is just one part of a larger tribe of people. A tribe that lives with a strong social commitment, reacting to unnecessary technology of war, destruction of the environment, and working to create a bigger understanding between humans. This background can be found, for example, in Thomas Tidholm's stories about the images that are part of International Harvester's performances. Strong political commitment that attracted the audience's applause, little thoughts about beautiful patterns in peasant textiles. For those not used to the expressions of youth music this realization must come as a shock....Unfortunately, it's not easy to decide how one feels about it. In any case, your ears will hurt.

Torbjörn Abelli:

Pärson Sound and International Harvester tours were like a continuous ongoing seminar, because in the tour vehicles, there was constant discussions going on, about popular versus societal governance, about upper class and lower class, and there was a huge interest in old Swedish peasant culture, which of course often was idealized. Things maybe weren't equal or beautifully and stylishly done, but there was a certain measure of realism.

Margareta Klingberg:

In March of 1968, Bo Anders and I had a son. The day that Jon was born Bo Anders was preoccupied with concerts during the *Kulttuuripäivet* ["culture days" festival] in Helsinki, Finland, where the band's first LP was being put out by the record company Love Records. There were gigs where

Left: International Harvester at a pit stop during the Norrland tour, February 1969. From left: Thomas Tidholm, Anna-Clara Tidholm, Gabi Björnstrand, Arne Ericsson, Torbjörn Abelli, Bo Anders Persson, Urban Yman, Ulla Berglund, and Thomas Mera Gartz. Photo: Jakob Sjöholm.

neither Thomas Gartz or Thomas Tidholm participated, and so they were carried out with a stand-in Finnish drummer. But Jon and Bo Anders met for the first time a day later. A little over a year after that, Jon played the harmonica on the LP *Spela själv* that Bo Anders produced and released with Rikskonserter [the Swedish state foundation and label/publisher]. I started bringing Jon to musical, cultural, and political events during the spring and summer of 1968. Tucked in with blankets in a basket, I brought him along to a show one Walpurgis Fair Eve with International Harvester in a practice space in an industrial building on Åsögatan. I was attacked by other adults in the audience for doing so. I should have understood how anxiety-inducing the music was for a small child. But I myself felt like the situation was reassuring: both the child's parents were there and participated throughout the evening.

Charlie

Norra Västerbotten, February 8, 1969

The international pop and jazz group International Harvester was supposed to have performed at Expolaris in Skellefteå on Friday evening, but after a visit during the day, the seven group members decided to refuse to play in the venue. Their reason was that the space was too materialistic and too commercially-oriented. The music school and Kanalskolan's student council, which were organizers of the concert, had to move it to the Folkets hus [community arts and culture center] instead.... "Those who built Expolaris probably think it is a very beautiful building, but it is ugly, terribly ugly, there is nothing uglier in the whole of Skellefteå," said the guys in front of the 300 people who had turned up. "We want to preserve the beautiful and natural!" And it might be so, but International Harvester did not lead with any particularly good example. The seven group members seemed unkempt more than anything else, and suitcases and other things were piled into one big mess on the stage. The group is fully aware

Left: Ulla Berglund, Thomas Mera Gartz, Sonja Gransvik, and Thomas Tidholm study a review of the previous day's performance, 1969. Photo: Unknown (taken with Thomas Mera Gartz's camera).
Above: International Harvester outside Expolaris Convention Center in Skellefteå, February 7, 1969. Photo: Thomas Mera Gartz.
Following spread: Concert in the Pit, Leksand, July 7, 1969. Photo: Mats Erikson.

of this. "It's no coincidence that we look the way we do," said one of the musicians. "We look different and that's because we think differently and want society to change. We want to protest, for example, the way that Western industry buys cheap raw materials from poor countries. They pay nothing of what the item is worth, but then it is used to raise our own standard of living, while other people starve and suffer.

Västerbottens-Kuriren, February 10, 1969

Pop group International Harvester from Stockholm gave a well-attended free concert in Umeå city library on Saturday evening. The venue was filled to the brim with an audience of youngsters ....After a few introductory songs, Thomas Tidholm, one of the musicians, asked if Umeå didn't have a bigger space. "Are there any officials here?" he wondered. "In that case, I would like to speak to them." It was eerily quiet. Everyone looked around. Finally, the head of culture in Umeå, Bengt Skog, stepped up to the microphone. "It's not our fault it turned out this way," he said.... Then someone said: "We could at least move the chairs." And that's what happened.

In a flash, all the chairs were taken away and the audience sat down on the floor around the band ... As a complement to the music, color images were projected onto a white screen. The pictures represented untouched nature, fields and meadows, mountain ranges, and red cottages. And as contrast, sterile urban environments and artificial suburban areas. Thomas Tidholm, who had taken most of the photos, spoke and described the images. The projector was manned by Anna-Clara Tjerneld, pop writer and author. "These pictures show how we would like society to be," said Tidholm. "We want to preserve the beautiful and natural. This is a warp flower pattern from Värmland, something that they are trying to hide away in the museums. There is no reason why such a pattern should not be used anymore, so we intend to paint it on the drums." "When one, like us, comes out to the countryside from Stockholm, you discover how big everything is," said another of the musicians. "Never travel to Stockholm!" Then they showed a film depicting the entrance to the Riksdag [Sweden's legislature]. "Nothing is happening", someone shouted in the audience. "Well, exactly," said Thomas Tidholm. "Nothing happens in the Riksdag. There are those who say there is nothing at all behind that big door."

Peter Mosskin
Expressen, September 17, 1969

On a rainy July evening last summer, cars stopped for long stretches of time at the edge of the large maypole pit in Leksand. From down in the middle of the pit, on Rune Lindström's Himlaspel stage, a strange, slightly monotonous music was playing--as if it came from far away. But it was also familiar--as if it came from the forest, from the shacks on a high summer's evening. On stage, in front of a beautiful painting in Dalecarlian-style with kurbits [a traditional folk painting style from the Dalarna region], a lot of people were playing, sitting or moving about.

Beneath a large, heavy, kurbits flower, a blonde-haired, meditating San Francisco boy sat on two guitar amplifiers. There was a large platter of fruit on two other amplifiers, and in the midst of this beautiful image, the music swayed and flowed from Harvester's instruments.

Thomas Tidholm:

> Our sound was mixed directly on stage and everything went into the same speakers. It was pure chance and unmanageable on stage. You never knew what was heard or not heard. You could stand up there and make far too much noise—without even knowing it—or nothing was heard. Overall, it was difficult to bring out the wind instruments in the soundscape and the intonation was adjusted accordingly. It's strange that it turned out so good after all, judging by the audience. If we had today's equipment, with someone mixing the sound and with a sound check—that wouldn't have been half bad! Now I listen retrospectively and hear great things, but I also want to shout: "Turn it up!"
>
> At times, Arne Ericsson's cello is next to nothing, and at other times he completely dominates the soundscape. Sometimes Bo Anders had decided that he would reverse the beat and cranked up his guitar to the max—and that then took over the entire sound.
>
> We had to rely on the sound that bounced off the walls where we played. But our speakers were very beautiful. They were small works of art in themselves.

Bildjournalen, November 14, 1969

[International Harvester's] music is not difficult to approach. It allows the audience's imagination to work. It searches for ways of expression that anyone can understand. It wants quick contact with people. That's why International Harvester plays at Sergels torg in Stockholm. Or even better, for small groups of people out in the countryside. You can do that when you don't care about the money.

Folke Rabe
Dagens Nyheter, May 14, 1969

In recent years in Sweden, we have been able to meet musical forms with the obvious intention of giving a strong experience of a way of working together on equal terms. One example is Terry Riley, ... another is International Harvester, plus some more anonymous organizers of collective "audio games" for children, housewives and old men, etc.

Thomas Tidholm:

We participated in part of Thomas Wieslander's Aktion Samtal project [a Stockholm activist group dedicated to interventions in children's pedagogy and urban design]. **Around 1968, there was this large construction-themed playground in Vasaparken, where people could build and hammer. A lot of kids came there, and that was the idea. It was actually a bit dangerous; kids could hurt themselves. "They could step on a nail," someone said. That would never have been allowed today. It went on for about a week and we played there. We handed out instruments so the children could join in and play. It was really fun. At that time, I was teaching at Christer Strömholm's photography school. All my students wanted to go out on the town and take pictures of what was going on. They were always curious. They held exhibitions and formed their own photographic group, Sepå. Some of them—everything was overlapping—were part of Aktion Samtal's group, including Roger Gustafsson, who became an expert in making instruments from plastic pipes. He created different flutes, which the children then used.**

Ⓒ SEPÅ

Previous spread: Poster, Sepå 1971.
Below: First release in Rikskonserter's LP series
"reportage," 1970. The record cost SEK 10.
Right: Catalog from the exhibition "Folkets musik,"
which was created by Bo Anders Persson
and Leif Ljungberg under the auspices of
Riksutställningar, 1969.

Thomas Mera Gartz:

"The people" were all the rage in many ways. It was like simultaneously being in and creating a situation together. We talked about it a lot in the band. Because the situations were usually controlled by the organizers. There was a boundary consisting of a cover charge and rules and a set system where musicians had to perform something. For us, it was a matter of opening up. But what was being opened? Maybe anyone should be let in; there should be no cover; maybe [we're] at another location in a completely different space where the audience is playing with us. Then it became clear that the audience is the music, and the band is just the band. A lot of American hippies did that kind of thing. We started including the audience when we played in the Stockholm City Museum's courtyard [in May 1969]. There was a group of people who came to

"spela själv" ["play it yourself"] which was a totally new idea. We got roped into that with them. They had made six and eight-sided wooden drums. We asked people to bring their own instruments and we played together in the courtyard. That's where the idea of "spela själv" was clearly formed.

Bildjournalen, November 17, 1969

Some time ago, nearly 1000 people gathered at Stockholm City Museum for a huge jam session, equipped with anything that can make sound, from trumpets to pot lids. The initiative came from International Harvester, a politically radical pop group. And just as International Harvester had intended, the music became an expression of the individual's situation in society--a common rhythm, that some are trying to break. For over six hours they jammed at the museum —they continued long after International Harvester had taken down the instruments.

Hans-Jörgen Nielsen
Dagens Nyheter, May 2, 1969

International Harvester's ... drum party at Stockholm City Museum ... is one of the most convincing forms of a socialist art activity that I have experienced in Sweden. Here, the entire old concept of art was eliminated. There were no "artists" here. No rare animals, whose actions had a false added value. No false notions of quality. The quality here was the human presence itself. A lot of people who were just together as equals and drummed and played and smiled and were happy in a big collective presence.... It was not about politics. It was politics.

Arne Ericsson:

It was super fun to hang out and for the kids to participate. It wasn't just kids; different kinds of people came and wanted to play. We opened up for participation around us. People got on board, and at the Stockholm City Museum, they were there and played. It was so fantastic!

Urban von Rosen
Svenska Dagbladet, 19 jun 1969

International Harvester played at Ceders Café in Vitabergsparken on Wednesday evening.... There are few groups that want to gain new members while playing, but International Harvester gained exactly as many new members as there were listeners.... The ones who did it immediately were the children. Perhaps International Harvester has created a new concept in the multifaceted world of music: pop or music for all people or children's pop—because the children apparently enjoy experiencing International Harvester.... Bring yourself or your children and come along and participate with International Harvester. You are always welcome, they say so.

Thomas Mera Gartz:

We played for a long time in Vitabergsparken and Kjartan Slettemark [a pioneering artist-activist] **was doing his thing.**

It was a nice evening in June 1969, and lots of people came, and it was a success. Kjartan was a well-known figure in the counterculture. He had been my painting teacher at Grundskolan för konstnärlig utbildning [preparatory art school]. He did a lot of actions on his own with his art and about his life. This was part of that, and was about how you are treated when you are seen as mentally ill. About the pills they give you, downers that take you down chemically. Kjartan was his art, and completed it by taking a stand for himself and his own life.

Kjartan Slettemark
Dagens Nyheter, December 21, 1969

I was raised on goat's milk, I come from the forests of Norway.... But I have ended up here in civilization and have to eat Hibernal [an antipsychotic of the era, also marketed as Thorazine] instead of food and come to Långbro [a Stockholm-area psychiatric hospital] instead of getting a place to live.... People have said that I'm imagining that society is conspiring against me. But these are not hallucinations, they are realities. I do not think that homeless and unemployed people should be called mentally ill. I don't think you should treat housing shortages with Hibernal.

Above: Kjartan Slettemark and fellow artist Hans Esselius, 1970. Photo: Jakob Sjöholm.

OÄNDLIGT TACK

till dem som anordnade International Harvesters framträdande i Bollnäs 10 febr.

Ett speciellt tack, för att ni vågade bryta de stela konventionerna och släppa fram denna fantastiska samling musiker i full frihet.

International Harvester är en av en knapp handfull svenska grupper (även Sound of Music, Mecki Mark Men, Hansson & Karlsson), som har lyckats kasta av sig kommersialismens tunga ok.

De har något väsentligt att säga, till skillnad från den stora mängden.

Det avstånd, som åhöraren vanligen känner mellan sig och de uppträdande, är i International Harvesters fall helt utplånat. Publiken är ett med dem genom deras musik, som kommunicerar med samtliga närvarande på ett utomordentligt sätt.

De är en samling individualister, och sådana är alltför sällsynta, inte bara inom musiken, utan på alla områden. Ganska signifikativt var emellertid, att publiken till 99 % bestod av s. k. "konstiga typer". Man beklagar verkligen, att inga representanter för "vanligt folk" behagade infinna sig. De kanske skulle ha fått sig en tankeställare.

Till alla, som av en eller annan anledning missade evenemanget, och för övrigt även till den skara som slöt upp, vill jag säga:

Kök International Harvesters LP "Sov gott, Rose-Marie". Ett belopp på 25:— är sannerligen inte för mycket för en stunds upplevande av suggestiv och medveten musik.

"Idioten".

International Harvester i full aktion i festsalen på Bollnäs Folkets Hus. Medlemmarna heter Bo Anders Perssen, Thomas Gartz, Arne Ericsson, Torbjörn Abelli och Thomas Tidholm.

Above: "Endless Thanks." Letter to the editor, 1969. English translation on p. 353.
Right: Poster for International Harvester's show at Ceders Café, Vitabergsparken, Stockholm, June 1969.
Design: Mats Arvidsson. Photo: Svenskt Rockarkiv. English translation on p. 353.

CEDERS KAFÉ
VITABERGSPARKEN
HARVESTER
SPELAR OCH NI MED
KJARTAN
GÅR PÅ LINA
17 JUNI ½ 8

International Harvester playing at Ceders Café.
Kjartan Slettemark walked a tightrope during the evening.
Shortly after the show, Ceders Café burned down and
their operations ceased. Photo: Jakob Sjöholm.

CHAPTER 6

Hemåt

Hemåt

Jakob Sjöholm:

The band rehearsed and recorded the album *Hemåt* at Kafé Marx. I took pictures and just hung out. It was like an open house; they had set up all the gear and played, and people came and listened when they were playing

Anders Lind:

Kafé Marx was located in a big industrial space. I think it was Urban—he was a Marxist—that thought of the idea of recording at Marx. We just went with it. For the rest of us, it wasn't about taking a political stand. We were there for several days rehearsing and recording. Recording was hell, because you could hear the music in the control room, which made listening difficult. Recording there was more limiting than recording in Nacka aula, with its huge space.

Bo Anders Persson:

On *Hemåt,* we did the opposite of what we did on *Sov gott Rose-Marie.* We just played. But we all agreed on the cover. Mera had made one and Anna-Clara Tidholm another; hers was actually very good. Anna-Clara had drawn these two mice that were carrying a passed-out person on a gurney. But Mera had put a lot of work into his picture, drawing it for the cover. I couldn't say no.

The thing was that Thomas and I were the oldest in the band, which was a factor in this context. Mera had probably been able to argue his point of view, but it was all so difficult. I just wanted to remove myself from the situation, but I didn't have the energy and things weren't getting done. Recording wasn't that fun—things were pretty tense. But there was undeniably an intensity around the recording.

Previous spread: Arne Ericsson with his electric cello, next to Bo Anders Persson's hand-built speakers.
The speaker on the right has a declaration of love to the Rolling Stones. Kafé Marx, 1969. Photo: Thomas Mera Gartz.
Left: International Harvester photographed for the cover of their LP *Hemåt*, on Nytorget in Stockholm, 1969. Photo: Bertil Bylin.

Ludvig Rasmusson:
Dagens Nyheter, June 19, 1969

I listened to a tape of International Harvester's upcoming LP. It will be in stores in a month or so. The music is very reminiscent of their previous album. It's heavy, powerful, romantic modern pop music. One of the songs is "Kristallen den fina." Sometimes the music gets a little too grand. But it is very evocative and something completely unique in Swedish pop. International Harvester has never been as good as when they made this LP.

Thomas Mera Gartz:

Anders Lind came to Kafé Marx with his tape decks. Like with the first album, we only had a few microphones. We were using Carlsson speakers with a round, radiating sound, built by experimental sound techs, who had the same idea that Bo Anders had had when he built ours. It was an ideological as well as a technical thing that the sound shouldn't have a central point. It was all about the entire surroundings. The sound bounces in all directions, and it's impossible to know where the center is. It's just as true that the world is big and we are in there somewhere. This Carlsson concept meant that we recorded with two stereo microphones placed at a distance, so that it was possible to record the big hall at Kafé Marx or the big stage at Nacka aula. Bo Anders had more microphones for *Hemåt*, but there were still only two tracks. Everything was recorded at once. Anders built this recording device in one room, where he could close the door and listen to it on headphones.

Sometimes, Bo Anders, Thomas, Tobjörn, or Urban had gotten into something and would be playing that. Then we jammed and used parts of it or Thomas showed up and said, "Let's play 'Ack Värmeland du sköna' [a traditional song known in English as "Dear Old Stockholm"]," or Bo Anders wanted to play "Kuk-Polska."

Above: Front and back cover of *Hemåt*, Decibel Records, 1969 (DSR 3701).
Right: International Harvester during the recording of *Hemåt* at Kafé Marx in Stockholm, May 6–11, 1969.
Photo: Unknown (taken with Thomas Mera Gartz's camera).

But the recordings were stagnant compared to the real musical act. It was as if we were leaving a trace, frozen in a moment. Of course, it felt special to get to make records, and it was fine if someone listened to it. But it was nothing compared to when we played for real, live. The living situation with the audience was what was important. That's when everything was alive and moving. That was unbeatable and not something that could be caught on vinyl. We didn't think the recordings were as important. It was something frozen, what we sounded like at that moment, a memory. A recording is just a pale image of a certain situation. It's almost nothing, just something you hear in your ears.

Anders Lind:

Sound installations and tech were created at AB Ljudåtergivning, but since we bought mixers we sometimes got requests for recordings. So I formed the company Studio Decibel together with Ljudåtergivning. My initial funding came from a recording I did with Hansson & Karlsson, which was pressed in an edition of 100,000 cardboard singles titled *P som i Pop*. It accompanied an article in *Dagens Nyheter*'s Sunday edition that had a feature on new music and flower power. I think I got 2,500 kronor for the recording. It was a lot of money at the time. The reason we were the ones who put out *Hemåt* was that contact with Love Records was lacking. There were no actual settlements from them. So we formed Decibel Records, to be able to put out their next album.

Above: Plastic-covered cardboard single by Hansson & Karlsson, titled *P Som i Pop*, included with an article in *Dagens Nyheter*, 1968. The record was recorded by Anders Lind at Klubb Filips in Stockholm, December 1967. Right: Anders Lind during the recording of *Hemåt*, May 1969. Photo: Thomas Mera Gartz.

Releasing records was fun. But getting distribution for Decibel Records was backbreaking work. It wasn't possible at the time. If you went up to GDC [Grammofonbolagens distributions-central, a Swedish record distributor], they didn't want to deal with it. A record was a hassle, there were settlements, and a bunch of papers; they said it didn't sell. No one was interested in the record company. However, after a lot of ifs and buts, we found a Swedish record company called Cupol and we were able to distribute Decibel's records under their wings. Everything was fine initially, but then we had this record with a song called "Kuk-Polska" [literally "Dick-Polska"] that they weren't too happy about. But they swallowed it, and we felt that times were changing.

Aftonbladet, February 23, 1969

Harvester has for some time been trying to interest various record companies to distribute an anti-single "Jag vill ligga med dig" and "Kristallen den fina." Despite our willing help, they have failed. Maybe it's because they chose the wrong songs. The only natural single the group has recorded is "Ho Chi Minh." Through both the song's simplicity and the suddenness with which the meaning of the words turns to the listener, it should capture the actively primary-school-educated Tio-i-Topp [public radio record chart] jury of today.

Arne Ericsson:

I felt that the time with International Harvester and Harvester was the most fantastic. There was a creative pioneering spirit. It brought people together around us, physically, who in some way were part of the band, even though they weren't playing. But then Urban Yman and Thomas Tidholm disappeared, and suddenly there were just the four of us. It goes without saying that that affected us as a band.

Friends of the band hanging out and
listening during the recording of *Hemåt*,
Kafé Marx, May 1969. Photo: Jakob Sjöholm.

How to Survive

How to Survive

Torbjörn Abelli:

The collective shouldn't be overvalued—the collective activity in International Harvester was more about ideas than practice . . . . Working in a group is simultaneously stimulating and demanding; democracy wasn't formalized and not always carried out, so there were times when members would feel overpowered. At the same time, the music was dependent on all members taking responsibility for their "piece" of the whole. But of course, there were conflicts and, unfortunately, the preparedness to deal with them was quite poor—it was not in line with the spirit of the times.

Thomas Tidholm:

Eventually it became clear that some of us couldn't talk to each other like we used to. People are different, very different in fact. I have a maladjusted middle-class background, which never worked very well for me. Bo Anders was the son of a preacher, from a free-religious Christian background. They were two completely different worlds that didn't really have the slightest thing in common.

Still, it had been a real friendship in the beginning, not to mention attraction. We could talk then.

Previous spread: Dancing to Träd, Gräs och Stenar on Stockholmsterassen, July 7, 1970. Photo: Kostas Kakoseos.
Left: International Harvester with friends on a walk in the forest, fall of 1968. Photo: Thomas Mera Gartz.

Bo Anders Persson:

Thomas Tidholm was very philosophical; he was educated and had breadth. I admired him a lot. We talked about Western culture—it was very interesting, and I was very influenced by him. In every field in which I have been active, he has been better. But he was difficult to work with. When Thomas joined the band, he started to call the shots and boss us around. My energy went into sorting out our dealings, and everyone else ended up a bit on the periphery. I couldn't stand him in the end, or it was him who couldn't stand me. He was very good at coming up with suggestions for songs and melodies, and he really surprised me with his sense of harmony. The sense of improvisation was very rustic. His songs were good, but they stood on their own. They didn't evolve organically, so I finally had enough. I had a hard time working with him in the end, and I felt like I was missing something when we played.

Thomas Tidholm:

A sad schism had developed in the band. I still don't know what the conflict was about, really. Bo Anders is and was a depressive person. After gigs, he could say: "Oh, guys, we blew it. We were so bad, everything went wrong…" but actually people had been fired up during the show. He was like an alcoholic who had had a great high but was struck with regret and remorse afterward. It was like we had been sinning, I just really don't know how. Hard to take. There were power plays that also ate away at us. An air of competition had developed in the band. But Bo Anders was the only one that was ever considered for the leader's jersey, simple as that. If he ever thought I wanted to take over, he was kidding himself.

Right: Bo Anders Persson and Thomas Tidholm during the recording of *Hemåt*, May 1969. Photo: Thomas Mera Gartz.

Thomas Mera Gartz and Bo Anders Persson at
Thomas Tidholm's home, 1969. Photo: Anders Lind

I was just so naively enthusiastic, which was surely annoying. Torbjörn didn't have an opinion. He never said anything. He was a rock on the bass and a purely kind person. Same with Arne—he never had an opinion, he just played, very beautifully. Bo Anders, Mera, and myself were the ones that had the opinions. But Bo Anders and Mera weren't really on the same page, either.

Urban Yman:

Bo Anders and Thomas Tidholm dominated International Harvester. I don't have any memories of deeper discussions—maybe they were had with others, but I was never invited. Bo Anders was very goal-oriented

in his silence. He was always consistent in everything that he did. The silence had meaning, and that was probably where he and Tidholm clashed. Since we were all musically oriented, we could see possibilities in places other than in intellectual thinking. The spatial also has sound. Silence becomes creative and has meaning. We approached a kind of meaning of life, at least a meaning we found in the void of silence, from stillness until the music slowly moves forward again. We came closer to something common in creation. Partly, I think it was because we were so connected, and partly because we felt the same thing—we came out of the same point in the void. There was a search for emotional explanations in the creation itself—in the experiences we had while performing the music ourselves. It almost created itself out of nothing. Our feeling was our guide into that landscape. That was the main idea behind International Harvester. In contrast, intellectual thought was considered short-lived and fickle. I wonder if Bo Anders was actually quite isolated in his thoughts. He once said: "Urban, you have so much I need to learn. You have so much inside you that I don't know." Now, if he wasn't pretending or wanting to flatter me, I think he had respect for what I mastered in my musicality. He never forced a particular musical expression or style of playing; I was never questioned musically. I would have remembered that—because that's what you remember most clearly.

Arne Ericsson:

Things were periodically pretty difficult. Bo Anders could quite demonstratively interrupt a rehearsal and go and lie down in a corner with his back to us. It wasn't fun. We had a crisis meeting about whether to disband or continue. Neither I nor the others took part in the actual exchange, it was between Bo Anders and Thomas Tidholm. Thomas could be a delightful person, who pushed us in a positive way. He had the ability to see others.

Jakob Sjöholm:

They reacted so differently. Bo Anders reacted quietly and went inward; Thomas was the opposite. I don't remember any confrontations. They weren't easy to deal with, those two. But things were really uncomfortable when Bo Anders issued an ultimatum that forced everyone else in the band to choose between him and Thomas, and Thomas quit. I don't think he said it right away, it just happened that way. Bo Anders had a hard time accepting that Thomas easily expressed himself in speech and writing, and that he generally was more forceful than Bo Anders himself was. Then, they probably had different ideas about how the music should sound.

Thomas Tidholm:

I know now that Bo Anders had decided that it was his band, and that I was just too much. And Mera … that I was skeptical to his attempts at establishing himself as a shaman made him keep a distance. Not always though—we could have fun too. But he wanted people to look up to him. If he was more of an occult seeker, I definitely took a skeptical stance. But Mera was a phenomenal drummer. Actually, there were a lot of things he didn't know, but he had tremendous precision. We could not have become what we became without him. When Mera had to choose sides, there was obviously only one he could choose if he wanted to continue playing. Then it was over. We had a meeting upstairs in a former dairy in Alfta, Hälsingland, where we were

Left: Thomas Tidholm and Bo Anders Persson with unknown passenger.
Above: Thomas Tidholm, Bo Anders Persson, Jakob Sjöholm, and Gabi Björnstrand during the 1969 winter tour. Photo: Thomas Mera Gartz.

143

to address the bad vibe in the band. "What is it really about?" I tried. I really wanted to know. "Do you have something against me? Did I say anything that bothered you?" But they said absolutely nothing, just glared at each other. The worst part was that they couldn't say what it was about. They couldn't fucking express themselves! In the end, it just wasn't working anymore. I was forced to say, "Bye, I'm quitting now." It felt incredibly sad.

Anna-Clara Tidholm:
When Thomas's involvement in International Harvester ended, we were already heading away from Stockholm. Simultaneous with the urban actions, there was a movement away from the cities and into the countryside. The first major international environmental conference in 1972 was held in Stockholm [the United Nations Conference on the Human Environment], and in the Skarpnäck camp-ground you could meet real hippies from the USA: Hog Farm, a famous rural commune. In Sweden, the hippie movement never became as big as in the USA, which, by 1968, probably had already had its heyday.

But communes were also formed in the Swedish countryside. The previously open and free alternative movement gradually became a rather rigid left-wing movement organized into different factions, which over time started fighting each other. Progressive urban projects in Stockholm failed, mostly due to drugs and social tensions. We left most things behind. It was fun to have been a part of the International Harvester project, and that music is forever in my heart. But life in the countryside was interesting in a much more concrete and tangible way. I still feel that way. Later, we resumed our careers again—I as an illustrator and creator of children's books—but this time, outside Stockholm's cultural scene, and without belonging to a group. It has continued to work.

Bo Anders Persson:
I feel bad that things never clicked between Mera and myself as one would have wanted them to. I had backed out of the Baptist church and was skeptical toward spirituality. He was a devout Buddhist. I miss having a belief system and knowing my place in the universe. But I've seen too many deviant forms. If you have left the Free Church, you are not inclined to jump on something else that aspires to that dimension. We didn't understand each other on that point. I'm really sorry that Mera and I ended up in a deadlock. It was impossible to talk about it at all. He could not respect that I could not accept his view of how indisputable Buddhism was to him, as an identity.

Urban Yman:
International Harvester—and the more romantic side of the music movement—believed that the main conflict was between capital and nature. It could take the form of purely conspiratorial thinking: if the company directors paved nature, it was because they hated nature. They believed that there was an emotional conflict between making money and liking animals and nature. In International Harvester, there was a natural philosophical orientation. At that time, I also played with Gunder Hägg [later Blå Tåget] and in a way, the two bands were diametrically different from each other.

The artistic form of music was a natural part for everyone [in International Harvester], as we'd studied at the Academy of Music. The Gunder Hägg members, on the other hand, had their roots in concrete poetry—with people like [interdisciplinary poets] Bengt Emil Johnson and Åke Hodell. Bob Dylan showed that it was possible to combine poetic works with fairly simply structured music, and it absolutely became the most important source of inspiration when Gunder Hägg started. The boys thought, "I guess no one buys our poetry collections

anymore, so why not take the opportunity to buy musical instruments and start performing our poems?" There was no major musical thinking with Gunder Hägg, not in the earliest edition of the group; instead, it was a general playfulness and an open way of working.

With Gunder Hägg, the music started with a mass of words and the rhythm in their poetry—where there was also a clear political purpose and content. With Harvester, the musical expression was absolutely most important. Thought and feeling! There you have the difference between Gunder Hägg and International Harvester. International Harvester started from the inner world of feelings and experiences, while Gunder Hägg strove for a material understanding and logical conclusions. If International Harvester—and later Träd, Gräs och Stenar ["Trees, Grass and Stones"]—believed that the main opposition was between capital and nature, Gunder Hägg focused on the class and economic opposition in the world. In Gunder Hägg's early repertoire, there is a song called "Uppå landet" ["Up in the Country"]. It is an ironic presentation of the idealistic and romantic views of nature. The song goes something like this: "How wonderful it is in the country, you avoid all awkward class-related questions, there you can weave your own clothes and love each other," haha.

Above: Träd, Gräs och Stenar playing at Moderna Museet, June 6, 1970.

During the opening of Andy Warhol's exhibition at the Modern museum, Pärson Sound played before Tjalles Horisont (as Gunder Hägg was then called). I was in Tjalles Horisont at that time.

When Pärson Sound played, they turned off the lights and had incense in the room. When Tjalles Horisont was about to go on, Tore Berger turned on all the lights and said: "There's not going to be any fucking magic seances here!" Then International Harvester responded by pulling out our power supply. They confronted me. Bo Anders, Torbjörn, and a few others came up to my apartment and demanded that I choose a side. I would have liked to continue playing in both groups, but they didn't accept that. The ideological contradictions were far too fierce.

STÖD VÄNSKAPEN MELLAN DE SVENSKA OCH KINESISKA FOLKEN!

SVENSK-KINESISKA
VÄNSKAPSFÖRBUNDET

Bo Anders Persson:

When the band became Träd, Gräs och Stenar, I simply asked Urban to quit. I felt him drift off in a direction that I couldn't stick to. I feel like shit about that. I was ashamed and felt like a traitor because I had brought him into the improv group. There wasn't really anything between Gunder Hägg and us, but he was undeniably a better fit there. It was around that time that I began to fantasize about rural life. I wanted music and life to be one. Those kinds of total ideas are a bit difficult to handle.

Thomas Tidholm:

Suddenly, Urban wasn't there anymore. I know that Bo Anders thought he played too nicely, too beautifully. Bo Anders used to call Urban when it was time to play, but in the end, he was apparently asked to leave. There was no decision-making system in the band, so I don't really know how it happened. After all, Urban had been both in and not in International Harvester.

He didn't show up every time.

He thought we were bad Marxists, and he was right about that. The rest of us were quite apolitical. Urban had to take care of the Marxist ideas. And the boys in Blå Tåget [formerly Gunder Hägg] were much more orthodox than we were. Personally, I always liked Urban. He was a nice person and a real musician. He was certainly right in his reasoning. I think he thought we were poorly organized, and that could absolutely be true. We could certainly have been better by speaking more clearly and structuring ourselves more, even when we played.

Bo Anders Persson:

Urban Yman had been one of the leaders of the Rebellrörelsen ["Rebel Movement," a Maoist offshoot group], and was constantly trying to convert us to Marxism and Leninism. They had meetings where they could sit and look at each other—so they would develop as revolutionaries—and

Above: Poster from Swedish-Chinese friendship association, 1970s. English translation on p. 353.
Right: Urban Yman, 1969. Photo: Thomas Mera Gartz.

could say: "I see in your eyes that you do not believe in this." Rebellerna also exchanged apartments and identities with each other in order to create new revolutionary identities for themselves. Urban was the backup bass player for a while, so when we had a gig one Saturday, and Torbjörn was going out for a walk with his little daughter—Torbjörn always claimed that this was completely wrong, and now he unfortunately can't object anymore—I had to call Urban. It was someone else who answered: "No, Urban doesn't live here." I thought we had to cancel the gig, but two days later Urban called: "Were you trying to get hold of me?" He came to the gig and played, and then crawled back under that umbrella.

Urban Yman:

I was faithful to the band to the fullest, at least as long as I was allowed to be in it. I think I was there every time we played out. I don't think my participation in Rebellerna contributed to my having to leave the band. Both Channa Bankier, who was with Mera Gartz, and Gittan Jönsson, my girlfriend at the time, were in the Rebellrörelsen. Mera was on the fringes, but never fully in.

Torbjörn Abelli:

Rebellrörelsen was mostly young people from the upper middle class who had become very, very, very socialist. Double Maoists. They were taking instructions from Mao's little red book, and they were going to do away with their bourgeois past. Urban once showed up with a crooked smile and told of how they had smashed a grand piano, since the grand piano was the ultimate representative of bourgeois music. I could understand the argument, that it is a bourgeois instrument—but to break such a magnificent instrument . . .

Urban Yman:

Rebellrörelsen was a short-lived story. It lasted at most a couple of months during the summer of 1968. It had absolutely nothing to do with my musical work. Every now and then someone brings up the Rebellrörelsen based on some theory they want to prove. Firstly, "the Rebels" were never a unified group. Everyone who was involved was part of the movement, but it was by no means a homogenous grouping. There were groups within the movement that did not form cells, or that were particularly ascetic, that continued to live ordinary lives. For me, it was partly the love for Gittan that kept me going, and she was much more determined than I was. I also found our literature circles interesting. Otherwise, I continued to live a fairly bourgeois life during this short time. Others within the Rebels, unfortunately, had more negative experiences.

I belonged to a group of writers who had published books and who were prominent in the theoretical structure of the movement, and therefore commanded respect. Maybe that's why we were left alone? They probably didn't know what to do with us. We were in an almost protected bubble compared to many others in the larger group. The ideological basis was quite clear. We had the Chinese Cultural Revolution as our model for how a future revolution would take place. Now, we never went that far, but we did a lot of reading and discussed what it would look like. We studied Marx, Hegel, and other important thinkers. At the same time, it was a reflection of what was around us. It was a very emotional time that made me more radical—I think because the Vietnam War was so palpably present. The Vietnam movement attracted broad groups of young people who aligned themselves with the NLF [National Liberation Front] movement. By getting involved politically, they saw themselves and the demonstrations as an opportunity to make the world better.

Left: "Vietnam." Printed poster of an ink drawing. Design: Carl Johan De Geer, 1968. English translation on p. 353.

Dagens Nyheter, August 13, 1969
Around Sergels torg, on Tuesday evening, scattered
tones were heard, which assumed a somewhat
more definite organization up in a corner of the
Stockholmsterassen. Four musicians played music
from the recently reduced International Harvester,
newly titled "F d Person Sound" ["formerly known
as Person Sound"]. Audiences standing, sitting,
lying down and balancing on the railings as well as
children and pets made up the physical framework.

Anita Livstrand:

> I remember a gig on the Stockholmsterassen
> [terrace on the roof of Sergels torg's
> Kulturhuset]. I sat right in front of Thomas
> Mera Gartz's drums and I enjoyed myself
> with all my body and mind. Oh! What power!
> The whole music took a new hold on my
> perception of time, I think, because it led me
> into something that didn't have to end at all.

Channa Bankier:

> On one occasion, for example, the police
> were forced to intervene at a party on
> Stockholmterrassen at Sergels torg, where
> Träd, Gräs och Stenar held a seance. The
> people were dancing and the music was
> flowing, and it kept going and wouldn't
> stop, and the proper bourgeois citizens just
> couldn't stand having this African tribe
> jumping and screaming in the middle of
> their own living room, so there was a regular
> colonial police intervention. The officer in
> charge pushed his way through the dancers
> to what seemed to be the center of the ritual,
> namely the drummer, and fixing his eyes
> on him, as best he could under the existing
> rhythmic circumstances, asked: "Who is
> in charge here, really?" The drummer:
> "It must be God!"

Right: Dancing to Träd, Gräs och Stenar on Stockholmsterassen,
July 7, 1970. Photo: Kostas Kokoseos.

Träd, Gräs och Stenar

Träd, Gräs och Stenar

Jakob Sjöholm:

Mera and I lived close to each other, so he started coming over. He had begun making some songs and probably felt that it was too difficult to present them to Bo Anders and Thomas. We sat at my place and played them, around the time that Träd, Gräs och Stenar was formed. Pretty soon after, Mera suggested I join the band. Not everyone thought it was a good idea, and some conflicts of loyalty arose, but I said that I have to do what I feel like. I told them about what Mera and I had created when we'd played together. Things were very sensitive when I joined, and stayed sensitive for many years.

Thomas Tidholm:

International Harvester stole some riffs and used them however we chose in the big spinning wheel of music. Träd, Gräs och Stenar quit doing that. Unexpectedly, they decided to play just regular rock, sometimes with original song structures. I thought they lost what had been so interesting about International Harvester. Instead, it was just more rock. At the same time, they sounded—in my opinion—blander, and they had also added all that silly stuff about friendly cultivation. It became boring and apolitical. There were no programs for action or ideas on how society should change, except for the stuff about cultiva-

Previous spread: Träd, Gräs och Stenar rehearsing in the closed Grönås school in Järvsö, August 1970. Sonja Gransvik is dancing, and Arne Ericsson's shadow can be seen on the floor.
Left: Thomas Mera Gartz, Bo Anders Persson, Arne Ericsson, Torbjörn Abelli, and Jakob Sjöholm by Klarälven in Likenäs, 1971. Photo: Jonas Wikander.

tion and crops. Actually, I was also interested in nature and had moved away from the city and did a bit of farming myself. But they became idealists, and I have never been that. It might have been a good thing that I quit, so that they could develop more in that direction on their own.

Nowadays, it sounds like Bo Anders thinks that what we did in International Harvester was just something I made up. That is pure falsification of history. He was undisputed as the musical leader, which you can also hear on the recordings. He could have taken it wherever he wanted. You can hear how he dominates with the guitar, and it was fine that he did that. Considering his background and education, I feel like he could have directed the

music more, and given some instructions to people. That would have been interesting, but for some reason, he didn't want to.

Dagens Nyheter, October 7, 1969
International Harvester--one of Sweden's few remaining pop bands--has now changed their name and will henceforth call themselves--in the most Swedish manner--Träd, Gräs och Stenar, a name that corresponds with the group's ambitions to perform music with Swedish lyrics and a Swedish connection.

Th. Edman
Bohuslänningen, April 1, 1972
TGS is something of a cultural movement in pocket format. It goes against the grain in many respects. That's the best thing about them. A thoroughly sympathetic group.

Bo Anders Persson:

[The name] **Träd, Gräs och Stenar** was no accident; we meant to highlight the plant life that we depend on. There are a lot of things in nature that work, and that have nothing to do with human life, except that they are destroyed by human life. Ideologies and religions are a consequence of having language. Language forces us to highlight ourselves as the only thinkers—despite the fact that animals can think and even understand symbolism in certain situations, they just don't express themselves in the same way as we do. I absolutely puke on this alleged human sovereignty. If there is a core in our music, it is to imagine the music of a modern natural religion, a religion that does not exist but should exist. That is my attitude. I don't know if my free-church childhood contributes to the fact that it is natural for me to connect music and cult. [In the natural religion], our spiritual dimension would be dedicated to the totality of life and creation. With that perspective, you can play music and rise above the human. Not to rise to a deity—there is none—but to expand towards the vegetative environment around us.

Otis
Sydsvenska Dagbladet, December 15, 1969
Träd, Gräs och Stenar, do you play pop music?
- "That's the best description of our music we've heard so far." Bo Anders Persson scratches his left sideburn and brings the teacup to his lips.
- "We are a band, a real band, I think. We are working towards unity. We do our best if we can establish emotional unity. It is a service to other people." ...

Eva af Geijerstam
Dagens Nyheter, February 21, 1971
Träd, Gräs och Stenar say they know that they are dependent on the economic system and its consequences for the people. "We are forced to accept it in some cases," says Bo Anders Persson, who plays violin and guitar in the group. But the group wants to counter that. They want to tear down the professional role of the musician, and his position as an expert.... "Neither the musicians nor the listeners have asked to participate in that authoritarian situation," says Bo Anders. "The musicians appear to be special, both in their knowledge and in their way of life, and when they stand there on stage and play for an audience that has paid thirty kronor for their ticket and is not allowed to move freely ... The musicians must be given a chance to play, but what they do is influenced by what the audience likes." For more and more people who play, it is no longer important to have a career as a pop musician, to live off of music, but to be just a Musician. "That's a good thing", says Träd, Gräs och Stenar. "The experts, those who think in right and wrong, are not the important ones right now."

Jakob Sjöholm:

Financial insecurity is always onerous, but performing also gave you a lot that you didn't want to live without. We could have had jobs, of course, but then we wouldn't have been able to go around performing. We managed, in some peculiar way, to live off of it. I was even taxed more because they didn't think you could live on as little money as I had stated in my tax return. I was even sentenced in court to pay taxes on money I had not earned.

Alserud
Oskarshamns-Nyheterna, March 20, 1972
Träd, Gräs och Stenar's modest wage claim--seven men shared 400 kronor--means that the band will certainly have the opportunity to return to Oskarshamn.

Left: Träd, Gräs och Stenar playing at Konstfack's kite festival on Gärdet in Stockholm, May 16, 1979. Photo: Låke Stomfelt.
Following spread: Träd, Gräs och Stenar trudging in the snow at Hertsjö during the Norrlands tour, 1970. Photo: Jonas Wikander.

Thomas Mera Gartz:

There was no gig money, except for the tours we did with International Harvester, which Bo Anders and Thomas arranged. At library gigs, we could sleep in these really swanky hotels. With Träd, Gräs och Stenar, it was as poor as it gets. There was no compensation at all. It was basically just enough for gas and food. We were extreme when we were out playing—we used to say to the audience, "Fix us a gig, and we'll come." Then gigs were arranged, and we passed the hat around to raise money for gas. Once in a while, we could get paid if there was an organizer behind it. We lived off of that money. When I was completely destitute, I had to take a job. I packed boxes in a basement for a couple of weeks at Konsum [a grocery store chain] and worked at a youth center where Bo Anders's girlfriend worked. The Swedish Tax Agency considered it impossible to live the way we did. They calculated a minimum cost of living and you had to get it somehow. They came up with a cost that they thought made sense, and all of us in the band lived well below it. We lived on brown rice and vegetables. I wrote them a letter, several pages long, detailing exactly what I had bought, which wasn't much. I described how old my shoes were and explained why one lives without money, without any surplus and without saving anything. A life where you give away things and give away music almost for free; you know, one or three kroner for admission, as it said on the handmade posters. I also wrote about staying at people's houses and so on. I never had to pay anything or was ever convicted of tax evasion. But Jakob did not have the ability to explain it in the same way, or at least not as extensively, and appeal to the heart of someone at the Tax Agency who could see how it actually was. So Jakob had to pay ten thousand kronor or something like that, which they claimed he had not paid in taxes. It was a hell of a lot of money back then.

159

JOEL JANSSON OCH DEN MÖJLIGA SVENSK-ROCKEN

ett öppet brev

Nu ska jag försöka berätta för dig, Joel Jansson, hur det var när jag hörde ditt spel första gången. Jag hade hittat en platta i en bok, (Jan Ling: *Nyckelharpan*)det var en liten 45-varvs som satt inkilad längst bak. Dom första låtarna på den lät alldeles riktigt just som illustrationer till en bok.

Sen när dina låtar kom, så råkade jag faktiskt ut för en riktig tvättäkta upplevelse, en känsla jag sällan haft i samband med svensk folkmusik. Först var det förstås takten eller beatet som man brukar säga ibland. Och dom äppelkäcka raka svenska melodierna, inget att vara rädd för, vem man än råkar vara.

Ungefär samma gods som den här gammeldansmusiken som man **alltid** har hört och liksom gillat, fast på avstånd. Glädje och kraft, levererat med nyckelharpans rika ljud. Det var första gången jag hörde det gammalmodiga spelsättet som är anpassat till instrumentet med basen och kvinten med i mest svartenda stråk, så att dom liksom matar in ljud i resonanssträngarna. Ett ljud som ligger och pumpar och förser den enklaste melodi med en gloria av läten.

Det enda jag kan jämföra med är trummor, gitarr och bas när dom ibland går ihop till ett enda ljud. Och just som det hela började verka hemtamt och självklart, började jag märka att du hörde ännu mycket finare på den tiden.

Jag menar hålen mellan stråktagen, det stora lugn som gör att också dom snabba och lite obehärskade rörelserna får gott om utrymme mitt i all upphetsning. Precis det som jag trodde att jag lärt mig av Rolling Stones och alla andra svarta och vita storstadsmusiker som gett sig in på att tränga ner genom alla lager av idéer och abstraktioner för att komma fram till kroppen, det raka och fysiska. Glädjen att finnas till manifesterad i ljud.

Det var som att komma hem och upptäcka att man inte behöver glömma eller släta över sin historia, att man har en rätt till den, att den duger som redskap för framtiden. Även om man alltså vill spela rock.

Jag undrar lite hur det kommer sig att jag hör såna ovanliga kvaliteter just i ditt spel, när det finns så mycket bra svensk folkmusik.

Men jag gissar att det beror på att du har spelat till dans, så länge som man över huvud taget ville dansa till nyckelharpan, tills man började tycka att dess läten blev för nyckfulla och o-moderna. Och kanske var du inte tekniskt slipad nog för att bli uppskattad på spelmansstämmorna när konstnärer och folkskollärare och hembygdsvårdens övriga märkesmän sökte efter något nationellt att luta öronen mot, något som var slickat nog för att passera som folkets kultur i deras öron.

Jag har faktiskt stor vördnad för spelmännens krokiga takt, den som hela tiden liksom stannar upp och tar fart igen, och deras egenartade melodier.

Det känns som om musiken vittnar om en vilja till hög kultur mitt i skogen, en kamp mot naturen men på justa villkor. Det skulle varit intressant att veta vart den musiken, det sättet att leva på, hade kunnat ta vägen om det hade fått möjlighet att utvecklas några århundraden till, i stället för att brytas upp av teknologerna och den kapitalistiska ekonomins krafter.

Jag känner mig släkt med den musiken också. Men inte har den talat till mig som ditt spel med dess regelbundna raka takt, en direkt och trygg inverkan på kropp och sinnen.

Jag hade väl kommit hit när du bjöd mig det sista och avgörande beviset på att jag hade hört rätt. För du gjorde vad jag alltid har tyckt varit det högsta hos en del former av rock.

Jag menar, att mitt i den enklaste musik bjuda på universum gratis. Jag vill inte vara religiös eller galen, men jag har inga andra ord för att beskriva känslan, när man hör hur musiken mitt i allt rytmiskt och kroppsligt plötsligt stannar till. Ja, beatet rullar vidare, men du har hittat ett ljud på harpan och du håller ut det en halv takt eller

i varje fall lite för länge, så att man kan höra din önskan att lämna melodin med dess enfaldiga trevligheter bakom dig och dyka direkt in i materien.

Du skiter för bråkdelen av en sekund i vad som är upp eller ner och låter ljudet spricka upp i alla sina små beståndsdelar. Och du bjuder på den sensationen gratis, utan åhävor. Jag menar, Flamingokvintetten är kanske populära för att dom låter snällt och Hoola Bandoola för att dom bjuder på en begreppsmässig trygghet på ett medryckande sätt.

Och så finns det ju Kebnekajse som försöker lyfta fram det storslagna i dalamelodierna i rampljuset. Men vill vi över huvud taget ta steget fullt ut till nån sorts svensk folkrock behöver vi inte stanna vid det medelmåttiga, högdragna eller lite ytliga. Det finns att ösa av, även om källorna är få.

Det var ett par år sen jag träffade dig. Jag hoppas att du mår bra, du var väl 71 år då och man kan ju aldrig veta.

Hälsningar
BOANDERS

Jan Andersson
Aftonbladet, July 4, 1971
Träd, Gräs och Stenar are professional musicians. But don't make a lot of money--about 8,000 kronor per man per year [around 72,000 kr/$7,000 USD as of 2023].

Eva af Geijerstam
Dagens Nyheter, February 21, 1971
"We have to listen to the old guys instead." One of Träd, Gräs och Stenar's old guys is Joel Jansson, nyckelharpa [or "keyed harp," Sweden's national instrument] player from Uppland. On their records and at their concerts, there are songs from Joel Jansson, freely interpreted for electric guitar, violin and drums. Reckless? Disrespectful? Folk music experts frown and say that it's just for fun. "No," says Bo Anders Persson. "The best thing we can do for Swedish folk music," he says, "is to play the melodies we like, as well as we can. It doesn't matter if you play electric. We use it because it has to do with us.... Joel Jansson's music swings in a way that pop swings. There is such a rich world in his music--it is not refined like so much other folk music, but it's pure Raggar-music. If we take an interest in folk music as a function and manage to make our music work the way folk music did, then we have done something radical."

Torbjörn Abelli:

Swedish folk music was already of great importance to International Harvester—the cultural heritage was rediscovered and reinterpreted: the same ear and the same attitude you used to listen to the Rolling Stones could be suitable for Swedish folk music. Turns out that this historic musical treasure was also often much more multi-faceted, rawer, rockier than the polished

façade—the rather orderly, "official" version of folk music. [There was] a book about the nyckelharpa published at the end of the sixties, that included a vinyl record. Among other things, there were songs by an Uppland player, Joel Jansson. His technique and "sound" were pure rock! We picked up some of his songs, including "Tegenborgvalsen" ["The Tegenborg Waltz"].

Bo Anders Persson:

Joel Jansson's music had many appealing features. He certainly had a fairly modern repertoire with exclusively steady beat (we didn't understand the uneven Polska [dance form], so it was just as well) but he harmonized these fairly familiar songs completely recklessly, through irrationally resonant loose strings; the instrument was in control. And he had an unbeatable rhythmic drive. Apparently, he wasn't overly fond of chord changes. Neither were we. He really played the nyckelharpa; he didn't play the nyckelharpa as if it was a fiddle. [I wanted] to find a role model that clearly differed from both old-time dance orchestras and spelmanslag [amateur folk ensembles comprising mostly fiddle players]. This is probably because I heard Leksand's spelmanslag every summer growing up. I had a hard time understanding how some other bands could take, for example, "Rättvikslåten" ["Rättvik Song"] and just play it as is. I felt that this idiom was used up, yet I had a hard

Left: Arne Ericsson in Hersjö, Hälsingland, March 1970. Photo: Thomas Mera Gartz.
Above: Träd, Gräs och Stenar in the forest near Grönås, summer of 1970. Photo: Unknown (taken with Thomas Mera Gartz's camera).

Bo Anders Persson, Folkets park, Rättvik, July 7, 1970. Photo: Mats Erikson.
Right: Tour poster from 1969. Design: Bo Anders Persson.

time explaining *why* I didn't think it was a good idea. Joel Jansson's sound was exotic enough to stand out from these categories, and his somewhat primitive playing style lent itself well to the unsophisticated playing style we wanted to have in Träd, Gräs och Stenar, a playing style that would appeal to close friends but still be absolutely incompatible with the wishes of the record industry (one can probably say that we succeeded with the latter).

Björn Håkansson
Svenska Dagbladet, November 16, 1969
International Harvester is now called Träd, Gräs och Stenar.... The group cannot play their instruments.... As everyone knows, it is permissible for anyone to try their hand at an entertainment profession. Likewise, it is perfectly permissible to take yourself seriously, even if you lack the prerequisites for the profession. This is something that Träd, Gräs och Stenar are not alone in. The question is whether the audience can take these kinds of entertainers seriously.

Jakob Sjöholm:

Instrumentally, we weren't that skilled, that wasn't what we were after. Instead, we tried to build a whole. Of course, one did feel inadequate as a musician at times.

Bengt Eriksson
Aftonbladet, July 4, 1970
Träd, Gräs & Stenar and Gunder Hägg have set Swedish pop free. They have given people confidence --you don't have to be that skilled to be able to play music and all people can express themselves through music. This is the closest to the "People's Music" that we have ever been in Sweden in modern times. The future will prove uncertain and dangerous for the big commercial record companies, for pop managers and for pop bands striving for success and money. The future will probably also show small record companies that can successfully compete with the big, established underground magazines which have music as a strong feature, and a Musikcentrum [nonprofit that supports freelance

165

musicians] that stands against the creation of elite musicians. The last part is already underway as a protest against the Musikcentrum that already exists. We are facing the revolt of Swedish pop music.

Mats Olsson
Arbetet [*The Work*], August 13, 1971
Political pop is awkward. You can do it badly--like Träd, Gräs och Stenar--or good--like Contact [a commercially successful progg group].

Dagens Nyheter, December 28, 1969
This week's TV family lives on Lidingö [an island suburb of Stockholm] and consists of Ulla ..., vocal pedagogue, Rolf, 20 years old, who is in his last year of high school, and Mårten, 15, who is in grade 9.... "The young people were not satisfied with the pop programs. Personally, I only saw Träd, Gräs och Stenar on *LIV* [TV show]. Rolf and I agreed that that group can be an example of the famous left turn in TV--the fact that they are invited to participate must be more due to their politics rather than their musical qualifications. Heavy monotonous music to mushy double-exposed images."

Träd, Gräs och Stenar:

> We encouraged people to play at Gamla Bro, Hagahuset, and in Christiania. We built speakers and soldered cables, we pasted posters from Kiruna in the north to Rudkøbing in the south, we drove and drove, we fixed cars from Drammen in the west to Helsinki in the east—everything based on the understanding of what is necessary in "All power to the people."

Bo Anders Persson:

> It was believed that the alternative to a left-wing regime was a kind of fascism. That was not the case. There was no need to implement a right-wing dictatorship; today's economic system was much better at that, and certainly gentler. In our ideological reasoning at the beginning of the 1970s, I had begun to lean more and more

towards the fact that we must get the relationship between man and nature in order. That was my number one priority. Mera was more into Situationist-influenced actions. I think they always tend to get annoying.

Jakob Sjöholm:

With International Harvester, creating music had always been a kind of collective process, but when Thomas Tidholm left, Mera and Bo Anders probably became dominant. Mera could lose his temper sometimes, not verbally but more in the way that he played, the way that he fumed, there behind the drums. Then there could be confrontations, but they were usually passive, below the surface. Bo Anders is very self-critical, but he is also very critical of everything else. If someone had an idea, he rarely said anything encouraging. Presenting something to him was always tough. I never heard him say, "Oh, that was good." Mera was much more direct. We got along, and found it easy to communicate through music. I was very cautious when I first joined the band, and took no clear role. I was on stage trying to learn the songs, because there was no time to rehearse; I just had to jump in and try to play along as best I could. It became an organic process, and since there were very few chords and notations, I had to start with my ears. We were good at listening to each other or rather to the whole of the music.

I have a different musical background than Bo Anders and Mera. I was born in 1950 and grew up in Vasastan in Stockholm. After school, I would run down to the park and play soccer until it got dark. The neighborhood kids met out on the street and hung out. In the summers, I was with my grandmother and grandfather outside Svenljunga in Västergötland [a province in the country's southwest]. They had a small cottage with a couple of cows, chickens, and pigs, and they had an organ that my grandfather bought when he was eighteen. When my uncle came there in the summers, he played the organ. For me, it was the highlight of the year. The way he could make the organ sound and sing was magic, and my first strong memory of music. My mother put me in piano school. But I only went there a few times; then I skipped school and played soccer instead. At first, I didn't say anything, but mom found out and, wise as she was, she said, "If you'd rather play soccer, of course, you should." The first record I bought was Elvis Presley's *King Creole*, which must have been in 1958. I went to a small record shop at Sankt Eriksplan in Stockholm and had to listen with two handsets, like old telephone handsets, one in each hand. Something happened there that never let go. In my early teens, I went to Nalen [a historic Stockholm concert hall] a lot. They had something called the Sunday Matinee: every Sunday at 1:30 pm, different bands played. It was sold out almost every time. There could be queues all the way down to Kungsgatan. It was packed, sweaty and hot. All the Swedish bands played there: Shanes, Mascots, Tages, Friends, and Hep Stars. The musical development happened incredibly quickly. It didn't take very long until what hit in England reached us in Sweden. Jimi Hendrix's first gig at Gröna Lund was a great experience. I had the privilege of standing at the front of the press area,

"Träd, gräs och Stenar" i Skärholmen

"Träd, Gräs och Stenar" får hjälp av publiken med låtarna.

"Träd, Gräs och Stenar", en massa barn och ett härligt oväsen samlades i helgen på biblioteket i Skärholmen.

Det var den första i en serie familjesöndagar som ska hållas på biblioteket. Meningen är att alla åldrar aktivt ska delta och tillsammans göra något.

I söndags var det under mottot "hör och gör musik". Det var inget vanligt uppträdande av en popgrupp. Programmet började långt innan killarna i bandet hade fått i ordning sina instrument och elektriska apparatur. Redan när den första trumman packades upp var barnen tätt samlade omkring den och slog.

De som inte hjälpte killarna i "Träd, Gräs och Stenar" att skapa musik på deras instrument, hade med sig enklare instrument. För dem som inte hade något att blåsa i eller slå på ordnades plastmuggar innehållande risgryn. Det gick utomordentligt bra att hålla takten med ris, även om golvet på vissa ställen började likna ett risfält.

Alla hade roligt, alla var med och skapade, och det var ju huvudsaken. MARGARETA BOGSTRÖM

Previous spread: Träd, Gräs och Stenar with Bengt Berger and Urban Yman on the right, 1969–1970.
Left: Jakob Sjöholm at Channa Bankier's place on Döbelnsgatan in Stockholm, 1974.
Above: Article by Margareta Bogström, published in *Söderposten*, October 28, 1970. English translation on p. 355.

169

Träd, Gräs och Stenar at the Konstfackskolan's kite festival
at Gärdet, Stockholm, May 16, 1970. Photo: Låke Stomfelt.

right by the stage. The music washed over me and went straight into the inner recesses of my mind and stayed there forever. That's as close to salvation as I've come in my life.

Arne Ericsson:

I was tired of grinding on the cello. One fine day I brought a clavinet, which I found in an ad. Bo Anders had said before: "A little plinking would be fun." I was quite happy with that electric piano, and the others also thought it was fun to have a new instrument. It's clear that we changed the soundscape a bit, but the music kept its soul. The cello was about long notes and walls of sound, sometimes following the melody and sometimes following the bass. The piano was more about shifting the rhythms and amplifying what the guitar did. I was able to adjust the sound of the clavinet in four different modes with a filter function. Then I used different pedals, including a handy little reverb box that Bo Anders had built. We liked to distort the sound in different ways: a less recommended approach was to turn the volume up to the max, but it still happened quite often. Other than that, we used wah wah and fuzz pedals, plus the reverb box, etc . . .

Dan Backman:

Arne Ericsson was an important, but perhaps slightly overlooked, cog in this collective. His function in the group has always been supportive and complementary rather than stepping forward and being seen. With Pärson, International Harvester, and Harvester, his cello formed a dark, enveloping and at the same time driving foundation. A drone. When the music broke away from the slow kraut beat and the cathedral-sized soundscapes, and became more dry rock and rhythmic, he switched to electric piano. The Hohner piano has a tone that differs from the soft tone of the Fender Rhodes and Wurtlitzer—rather it is closer to the clavinet. It's a sound that blends so much with the guitars that you easily forget it's there. Nevertheless, the distorted electric piano fulfills an indispensable driving force function. In the organic process, you can easily hear how the guitars step forward with melodic loops and solos, while the electric piano consistently stays in the background. It is also an art, to not step forward.

Arne Ericsson:

The second time Bo Anders said it would be fun with a little more plinking, Jakob was there. I don't really remember how it happened, but Jakob joining created this spark. After all, he was a little younger than the rest of us, and contributed the wisdom of youth. There was something special about his chord playing; he had a singing guitar. We hadn't split things up with a lead guitar and an accompaniment guitar, but it often worked out that way.

Jakob Sjöholm:

When I joined, we were more drawn to my roots with rock. The band was probably already on its way there, but it became more accentuated. At the time, rock wasn't mainstream. The Stones, for example, were associated with youth rebellion.

Björner Torsson:

I remember how Mera was attentive to the universal power of music. Music is in everything if you listen carefully and draw it out. He showed that you can play on anything. People have suggested the idea that Stonehenge was actually a musical instrument. Mera played on fences, rocks, and empty barrels. Ingmar Glanzelius wrote that the fabulously powerful rumble from Mera's drums rolled out a soft carpet on which the music wandered. It was an invitation to eternity, beyond all sensible daily current affairs, with the same sound as the sound of the sea or when the wind wanders through the treetops. Mera kept bobbing his head as he played. It added extra love to his playing. You can still feel it when you go inside and walk among the "träden-gräset-stenarna" [the trees, the grass, the stones].

Thomas Mera Gartz:

There is not much that can compare to the creation when you play together. There are no other situations where you don't speak, but just make sounds. It is communication in a different state. When it's at its best, you're just present in what you're playing and that's when something can happen that no one has control over. Something common is created whose form is free. We created by jamming. It is a basic form that pulls something out, something that rolls and moves forward without the need to do anything spectacular with it. You slide, move, push it, and create some polyrhythmic figure so it swings a little. This time is short, but it is long between each hit. An infinity divided into small pieces. It shortens and lengthens, hits hard, *swoosh!* and see what happens.

Torbjörn Abelli:

I have always built basslines to be supportive and clear. I haven't learned those fast runs. Instead, I've made it a virtue to keep my playing down to a foundation that goes around, around, and supports and lays a base. Sure, I can be fascinated by bass players doing virtuosic solos, but I've never wanted to do it myself. When I hear old recordings, I am quite satisfied. Persistence can be a virtue.

Peter Mosskin:

Repetition was the opposite of Volvo's time studies, where the North American MTM [methods-time measurement] system broke the worker's grip down to tenths of a second. What could be more provocative than playing the same tune over and over again?

Not working overtime? Live in a commune? Move to the countryside? It didn't take many years before the Stalinist KFML(r) [Swedish Communist Party] called Träd, Gräs och Stenar, Kebnekajse, and Samla Mammas Manna [fellow progg bands] too far out.

Thomas Mera Gartz:

The band changed around 1969 when Thomas and Urban left and we became Träd, Gräs och Stenar. We embarked on long tours in the Nordic countries, which were mostly carried out without established organization. We left cultural life and became "lawless"; we found our audience by sympathizers arranging gigs in their hometowns. We lived as we and our audience wanted, creating a free and co-creative situation with the help of music, dance, a light show with slides and 8mm films, serving food, and letting people play the instruments that we had brought. We wanted to get started, engage and get the audience to play themselves: "You are the music, we are just the band!" The people's music. Organize yourselves— people power. We urged people to start their own meetings, find their own spaces where they could develop their own culture, their "counter-culture", which is there for our collective imaginative life creation, our way of living in solidarity with each other and together with nature.

Jakob Sjöholm:

Often, we played in places where they had no experience of participatory culture. They might have just started a local music club. We made sure that people came and that things could then continue, perhaps through Musikforum and Kontaktnät [national organizations for nonprofit cultural associations]. We were a piece of the puzzle. We had that feeling with us all the time. It wasn't just that we were Träd, Gräs och Stenar; we were part of a new, larger movement.

Thomas Mera Gartz:

I remember that Thomas Tidholm once said: "We play music where everyone is included." That was right, because the door was open and the room was so big that everyone could fit. People could hear and see what was happening. The music went on for so long that eventually it became boring for the audience to stay out. Either they left or they joined in, started swaying together, and joined the big sound that just kept going without saying anything in particular.

Jakob Sjöholm:

We often played on the floor to show that we were one with the audience. People sang and danced. We gained power and energy from the audience's participation in the music. Seeing someone move to music creates positive energy—it's the funnest thing there is. There was no room in our music to do your own thing and just holler out something, because then whole thing dies. If people did something, they made the music better, and if they didn't, it died. If that happened, we kept going a little longer because we were the ones with the electrically amplified instruments.

Above: Träd, Gräs och Stenar on Sergels torg, in front of what was to become Kulturhuset (at the time of the photo it housed Riksdagen), Stockholm, February 1971. They are holding a photo of a clear-cut area in northern Värmland. Photo: Roland Janson.

Torbjörn Abelli:

We coined the expression "play yourself," and spread the gospel of music as an unpretentious way of getting together, where everyone could participate. Some interpreted the ideological stance "everyone can play, everyone should join" literally, and stepped onto the stage with their instruments. It didn't always work with what we were doing. They failed to realize that our interaction was something that we had actually worked a lot on—targeted communication.

Roland Keijser
Upsala Nya Tidning, September 29, 1969
Träd, Gräs och Stenar played at the all-arts evening at V-Dala nation [one of thirteen regionally derived student organizations at Uppsala University].... There were many people who had brought instruments. But most people just listened. The music was nice. But one could perhaps notice that everyone (including the musicians) really wanted to do something else. It was only when the music had stopped and the organizers started threatening to turn the place into a discotheque that something happened. Suddenly everyone started banging on the tables and playing the instruments they had brought. At first a bit desperate and aggressive but then more nuanced, relaxed and responsive. A nice and steady rhythm that everyone had a place in developed quite quickly. But after a while V-Dala's disk jockey came and announced that it was all over. The musicians didn't want to play anymore and since nobody wanted to play the old worn-out discotheque game, it was just as well everyone went home. But no one understood what the disk jockey said. It wasn't that late, and everyone had started to enjoy themselves. You can't just go home all of a sudden. So they continued to make music as best they could. And it went very well. Eventually Träd, Gräs och Stenar came back, and everyone could make great music together. Then everyone started dancing. You could see that they were all happy. I think it's called "creative joy." And it was a collective one.

Landskapsposten, October 1969
We were not at all negative to the idea. However, we do not approve of any disorder.... If people have paid for discos, then this must be implemented. We regard the fact that they started "making music together" partly as mass psychosis.

Gunnar
Sundsvalls Tidning, November 26, 1969
International Harvester was the name of a pop band that for a long time belonged among the better bands in the country. But their big breakthrough was long overdue, so the boys completely changed their style. The Sundsvall audience got to know the new version, which is now called Träd, Gräs och Stenar, at Wiwex on Monday evening. Social criticism is what they have invested in.... In this way, the music has to take a backseat to features such as long monologues about how bad society is and look at pictures of how good it could be.... The music is probably the most essential thing in a context like this, and they seem to have stagnated there.... Social criticism simmers inside all of them, it was quite clear, and they would very much like to voice it. To a large extent, it fell flat, as destructively and incoherent as it was now performed.

Östersunds Posten, November 29, 1969
This week, the protest group Träd, Gräs och Stenar (formerly International Harvester) spread their cultural message in the county. The youth cheer and the elderly put cotton in their ears.... In Hoting, a couple of hundred mostly children and young people, eight- or nine-year-olds and up, enjoyed the deafening entertainment. Sitting, standing, while some preferred to listen lying on the floor. They also got to refresh themselves with juice and make music with the instruments provided, and the evening ended with everyone dancing to the shake. Among the few older people in the audience, some thought that the pictures shown with the music had the most depth. The actual music almost made some of them keel over.

Gärdesfesten
1970

·FESTEN·

Skeppsholmen

STOCKHOLM
12-14 juni
gratis

Gärdesfesten 1970

Eva af Geijerstam
Dagens Nyheter, June 10, 1970

On Monday evening Träd, Gräs och Stenar played at Pistolteatern to collect money for the festival that was supposed to take place at Skeppsholmen [a small island in the middle of the city] on Friday-Saturday-Sunday, but which now has to be moved to Gärdet [a huge field northwest of the city center].... The reason why Träd, Gräs och Stenar played at Pistolteatern was that the organizers of the Skeppsholm festival, who are largely the same as those who are participating in it, suddenly received a demand from the city of Stockholm's Housing Commitee for 50,000 kronor for any damaged lawns. The organizers then had two options: either cancel the festival or try to move it to Gärdet. To be able to publish a special festival magazine, prepare macrobiotic food, and obtain materials for musical instruments and children's activities, the organizers had already received 21,000 kronor from the City of Stockholm, Rikskonserter, and Modern Museet. This money came with the condition that the festival would take place on Skeppsholmen. Everyone who has worked for the festival has done so at cost price. The thirty or so bands that are to perform will do so for free. Those coming from out of town will only receive travel compensation. For a long time, it, therefore, looked as if the event would be canceled. Planning since January would have gone to waste. Permission from the police and health authorities is now required to be at Gärdet. The new permit requires that another approx 14,000 kronor must be given by the institutions that previously allocated 21,000 kronor. In any case, there will be a festival this weekend, a free party for everyone, with jazz, pop, and folk music, with theater and the opportunity for all kinds of activities--if permission from the police arrives on time. The demand for the 50,000 would otherwise prove to be the same as a "No" from the authorities.

Previous spread: Sunset behind the stage, Gärdesfesten, June 1970. Photo: Jakob Sjöholm.
Left: Poster for the first Gärdesfesten, 1970. Photo collage by Thomas Mera Gartz. Peter Zanders finished the poster.

Audience in front of the stage, Gärdesfesten, June 1970. Thomas Mera Gartz can be seen in the middle of the picture, and Joakim Skogsberg is behind him. Skogsberg recorded several concerts with his Nagra tape recorder, and his recording of Träd, Gräs och Stenar from the festival was released in 1996 under the title *Gärdet 12.06.70*. Photo: Jakob Sjöholm.

FÅREN FÅR BÅDE VARA OCH SKITA PÅ GÄRDET. DET ÄR BRA.
VI FÅR VARKEN DET ENA ELLER DET ANDRA. DET ÄR INTE BRA.

TROTS DET BLIR FESTEN PÅ GÄRDET AV PÅ FREDAG (FRÅN KLOCKAN 15:00),
LÖRDAG OCH SÖNDAG (FRÅN KLOCKAN 12:00). KOM SÅ TIDIGT DU KAN. OM
TILLRÄCKLIGT MÅNGAKOMMER SÅ KAN FESTEN INTE STOPPAS.

Ta med käk och instrument så skall vi visa myndigheterna vad gräset är till
för. Med dom har vi käbblat om tillstånd sen februari. Det har gällt toaletter
hit, parkeringsplatser dit och oro för att texterna innehåller politiska(!)
texter. Myndigheterna har systematiskt motarbetat oss. Om man inte har privata
kontakter och expertkunskaper om byråkratin kan man inte få alla de egendomliga
tillstånd, som minst femton egendomliga myndighetertrakasserar oss med. I syfte
att sabotera vår Fest.

Alla är välkomna.

Först tänkte vi vara i Hagaparken. Det fick vi inte.
Då flyttade vi till Skeppsholmen.
För en vecka sedanlämnade Byggnadsstyrelsen (som äger gräset där) ett plötsligt besked om att vi i förväg måste betala minst 50.000 kronorför förstörda
gräsmattor.
Vi har inte 50.000 kronor.
Operan får varje år 30 miljoner kronor i anslag av skattepengarna. På operan
går bara en liten elitpublik. De flesta av operabesökarna tillhör socialgrupp
1. Det är deras nöjesbiljetter alla skattebetalare får subventionera.
På Festen på Gärdet blir det popmusik, folkmusik, jazz, gammaldans, lekar för
alla, film, teater, dans för alla. Och musik av alla. Ta med enkla saker, som
du kan spela på där. Festen är till för människor. Därför har myndigheterna
försökt stoppa oss. De kommer inte att lyckas.
Vi har bestämt oss för att Festen skall hållas på Gärdet vid Borgen. Sextio
olika musikgrupper, teatergrupper, och sångare tänker delta. Dom kommer från
alla delar av Sverige, fast mest från Stockholm. Det kommer också mängder av
andra människorhitresande från andra orter.

Vi kan nu inte avlysa denna Fest. Vilket myndigheterna föröker tvinga oss
till. Det vore att svika en mycket stor publik. Vårt mesta arbete har gått
åt på denna byråkrati. Vi har inte kunnat syssla så mycket med musiken, teat-
rarna och dom andra praktiska arrangemangen, som vi velat. Eftersom byråkraterna hela tidenhar uppehållit oss. Dom myndigheter, som borde ha hjälpt oss
har istället efter bästa förmåga saboterat oss.
Nu har vi inte tid med byråkraterna längre.
Vi tänker ordna vår Fest - Festen om Gärdet - utan tillstånd. Och vi hoppas
att så många, som möjligt kommer till Gärdet. Det är viktigt.

TA MED EGNA AKUSTISKA INSTRUMENT ELLER SÅNT DU KAN GÖRA TILL INSTRUMENT,
UNDER ALLA OMSTÄNDIGHETER MÅSTE VI KUNNA SPELA, DANSA OCH GÖRA TEATER.
TA OCKSÅ MED MAT OCH POTTA.

Dom här grupperna och artisterna spelar på festen på Gärdet:

fredag mellan 15 och 17:
Maria Jerena, Guineas, Roland von Malmborg, Sweet bunch of roses, en orientalisk sång och dansgrupp, Gläns över sjö och strand, Freedom Singers, Diddlers, Skäggmanslaget

fredag mellan 17 och 23:
Dra till och lägg ifrån med Peps, Snabb lindring, Figaro, Hackat o malet, Guineas, Diddlers, Skäggmanslaget, en blåsorkester, Solen skiner, Maces Spering, Music Is Happening, Träd gräs och stenar, Bernt Rosengrens grupp, Stepmother's Blessing.

lördag mellan 12 och 18:
Welcome, Charlie's Electric Band, Old Timey String Band, Det europeiska missnöjets grunder, Stepmother's Blessing, Freedom Singers, Fire, Bonnie o Blues, November, Gläns över sjö och strand, Slim Notini Blues Band, Opus 3, Terrible Ones, Herbert.

lördag mellan 18 och 24:
Roland von Malmborg, Guineas, Skäggmanslaget, Diddlers, Gudibrallan, Snabb lindring, Träd gräs och stenar, Dra till o lägg ifrån med Peps, Nisse Sandströms grupp, orientalisk sång och dansgrupp, Love Explosion

söndag mellan 12 och 18:
Roll's Express, Hackat o malet, Peter Unge, Michelles, Bernt Staaf, Red White and Blues, Atlas, Ljudbolaget, Arbete och Fritid, Gunder Hägg, orientalisk sång och dansgrupp, John Zetterberg, Högdalen, Fire, Träd gräs och stenar,

söndag mellan 18 och 22:
Herbert, Gläns över sjö och strand, Det europeiska missnöjets grunder, Blue October, Music is happening, Solen skiner, Turid Lundkvist, Jan Hammarlund, Atlantic Ocean, Telefon Paisa, Vetlanda Landsortsband, Blues Quality

    Vi kommer att göra mer detaljerade program som kommer att finnas på Gärdet.
    Naturligtvis kommer det att bli en hel del ändringar. Det finns ännu möjlighet för nya grupper och artister att anmäla sig. Eller kom bara och ta med instrument!

Left and above: Flyer for the first Gärdesfesten, June 12, 1970, in Stockholm (front and back). English translation on pp. 356–357.

Margareta Klingberg:

Planning for the first Gärdesfesten started in the fall of 1969 in Aktion samtal's basement space by Odenplan [a plaza in central Stockholm]. Aktion samtal, later Arkiv samtal, was formed by a group of activists that, since the summer of 1968, had been trying to involve citizens in the city as their local environment and worked to build creative playgrounds and foster closeness between generations. Together with Jon, I participated in every preparatory evening meeting until it was time to start cranking the stencil press and handing out flyers on the street before the first party on Gärdet in June 1970. There was no permit from the authorities, but the concerts were still carried out. Bo Anders's negotiations with the authorities are well documented by the filmmakers Olle Eriksson and Rainer Hartleb. In the end, it was still overwhelming to see the very improvised and simple stage rise up and become covered with tarps, and to hear the mobile gas-powered generator that made the amplified music possible—not least, the beautiful fusion between the rock band Contact and the young violinists of Skäggmanslaget. The list of bands eager to play, whose names you had previously neither heard nor known about, gradually became longer. After three days of free concerts under the open sky, the Swedish music movement was underway.

Bo Anders Persson:

Stockholm, Gärdet, 1970. The stage floor had been driven there the night before; it lay stacked outside Konstfack, covered by a tarp. It was Friday, June 12—the morning was overcast and the clouds would eventually turn out to contain rain. But the weather didn't stop us, we just had to keep going. Because we had worked for a long time to realize the *Party*. The organizing group contained a relatively fixed core, consisting of around thirty people who had met regularly for six months. We had had discussions with the city's authorities for just as long: first of all, the Parks Department and especially their park theater section, represented by a woman whose name I have forgotten. She probably did her job extremely well and became our very special anathema. Now, twenty years later [*sic*] . . . it is easy to smile at the questions we received and also at the answers we delivered. In summary, it sounded like this, freely from my memory:

— What is the name of your association?
— It's not an association, we have formed a group for this occasion.
— Who are the leaders?
— We don't have a board. Everyone participates on their own terms. Power corrupts.
— These music groups you speak of, what are they called?
— Oh, there are many, Handgjort, Gläns över sjö & strand, Telefon Paisa, Smutsiga Hundarna, a band from Skåne that call themselves "Hoola Bandoola" or something like that, and then Gudibrallan, Träd, Gräs och Stenar, and Gunder Hägg of course.
— Are these groups of any quality? I certainly haven't heard of them!
— Oh, but we are going to have children's games, folk music, and immigrant groups as well! And a dance hall with old-time music.
— If there is to be dancing, you must have a special permit with hired security guards.
— We can't guarantee that people won't dance!
— How are we supposed to give a permit to an event which can't be defined?
— Exactly, we want a new kind of party, parties of a kind that doesn't exist these days!

184

Neither side was interested in communication flowing too easily across the lines of interest. So we didn't have a permit. There were no police in sight, but we took for granted that a truck out on Gärdet's grass would be a sure way to get them to come. So we carried the stage floor out in sections, about three hundred meters to the east, and started screwing the pieces together. A small crowd formed around the stage. A couple of police officers arrived and warned us against trying to carry out the event, albeit in rather general terms. After an hour or so of arguing, the police withdrew, the excitement died down, and the sky was even grayer. Towards the afternoon we had managed to rig up a simple roof over the stage; it looked like it was going to be needed. I yanked the string to the dirty gasoline-powered generator we'd rented. It started sputtering, but after a while, got its twelve hundred watts in order. The party could begin.

Above: The Uppsala band Gudibrallan, with singer Örjan Terje, at the first Gärdesfesten. Sten Wallin and Thomas Tidholm can be seen to the right of the stage. Photo: Jakob Sjöholm.

Peter Mosskin:

The band had this good-naturedness about them, an open attitude, regardless of whether you liked their long swaying songs or not. That Träd, Gräs och Stenar played an active role in making the first Gärdesfesten happen is no coincidence. When I casually mentioned that I had started playing with some guys in Gagnef [a small city in central Sweden], where I had moved, Bo Anders Persson or Thomas Gartz put us on the list of groups that were to play on Gärdet. Then they called and reminded us that we needed a name for the band. Thoughtful to say the least. OK, "Gläns över sjö & strand" [the opening line of a poem by Viktor Rydberg,

the basis for the famous Swedish Christmas song "Bethlehems stjärna"], a friend in the kitchen in Gagnef suggested, and so it was. Mera played drums when Gläns över sjö & strand played on Gärdet. Everyone was so close together on the little stage. As I remember it, Träd, Gräs och Stenar were there like some kind of mentors to us

Bo Anders Persson
Dagens Nyheter, May 22, 1970
This is a different way of experiencing music, a way that we feel is very important.... A festival that, for example, Gröna Lund [a Stockholm amusement park] will organize is too narrowly commercial. It's just a way to attract people to the slot machines.

Aftonbladet, June 11, 1970

The whole week has been hectic and all around. Ever since the Swedish Building Agency rejected the permit for Festen På Skeppsholmen.... The party has of course been moved from Skeppsholmen to Gärdet because it is the only place the police cannot cordon off if one is forced to keep going without a permit. The dates are unchanged. Friday, Saturday, Sunday, June 12-14 you will help get this amazing thing inside your ears, eyes, and skin, as planned. Let's stomp down Gärdet's grass together!

Dagens Nyheter, June 13, 1970

Twelve colorful chamber pots framed the inauguration of Festen om Gärdet. Hampered even by the weather, it set off on Friday afternoon. A cold north wind and a lot of rain forced music and theater into a makeshift tent. The weather improved slightly during the evening, and the several hundred who braved the cold came and went, sat, danced, and drank chamomile tea. On Saturday, when the party continues, another stage will be added. The electricity comes from a cheerfully puttering generator. When it started up together with Träd, Gräs och Stenar, the heat rose significantly.

Thomas Mera Gartz:

Not many came to the shows we hosted in the beginning, but they got bigger and bigger. There were more of us who were moving towards openness. In the end, there were tons of people. Just like with the Gärdesfesterna. The first one was small; the third one had twenty-five thousand visitors. Everything was not-for-profit, with volunteers and no money. How do you serve food for twenty-five thousand people? It wasn't possible, it was too big.

Arne Ericsson:

I'll never forget Gärdesfesten. The thing of being outside, music from morning to evening, and we got to play. Even if it was an attempt at mimicking Woodstock, there were lots of people and a positive atmosphere, except when the police tried to make us leave. I think we played more than once a day if I remember correctly. But you were there the entire time, and if you want to be a bit idealistic, you can say that it didn't matter if we played or were in the audience.

Left: Träd, Gräs och Stenar on the little stage wrapped in tarps at the first Gärdesfesten. Photo: Björn Nyman.
Above: Audience members basking in the sun at the first Gärdesfesten. Photo: Thomas Mera Gartz.

Eva af Geijerstam

Dagens Nyheter, August 24, 1970

"Träd, Gräs och Stenar" didn't have one of their
better nights--but despite that, it's quite clear
that Thomas Gartz is a very good drummer, that Bo
Anders Persson is an excellent guitarist--and not
least that their music leads directly to the audience. All of Gärdet's kids--who have had the most
fun during these four days--danced.

Lars Åberg

Aftonbladet, June 11, 1971

The new pop quickly became an established concept
after the music parties at Gärdet last summer. All
the labels were immediately put on it--Swedish pop,
community-oriented, rural romantic, amateurish.
But behind the clichés, a broader debate was finally
started about the authoritarian concert situation,
about music versus capital and authorities and about
the role of folk music in plastic society....
The festivals on Gärdet became anchor points, two
beams of light to look for in the darkness. New Pop
has become a strong alternative to Commercial Pop.
The English language was replaced with Swedish,
polished sound was exchanged for an amateur musical
group feeling, and the love lyrics had to compete
with clear political positions.

ÅTAL MOT
GÄRDET'S FESTEN
25 DAGSBÖTER (JUNI 1970)

Sten Bergman var i Stockholmb Rådhuset 7/3 1972
och dömdes för anordnande av illegal tillställning.
Anledning till åtalet var att för alla tillstånd som
ges måste en person stå ansvarig enligt deras
principer. En grupp människor har i vårt sam-
-hälle ingen möjlighet att tillsammans ansvara
för sina handlingar. DOMEN SKALL ÖVER-
KLAGAS TILL HOVRÄTTEN.................

Above: From the paper *Huvudbladet*, 3, 1972.
English translation on p. 358.
Right: Bo Anders conversing with two police officers
that are informing him that there will be no festival
since there is no permit or toilets. They then left in
a big black American car and the event organizers
started rigging the stage, people gathered, and the music
started to flow. Photo: Carl Johan De Geer.

188

2:A FESTEN PÅ GÄRDET
AV OSS SJÄLVA FÖR OSS SJÄLVA

20, 21, 22, 23 AUG.
FRÅN TORSD. KL 18.

FOLK FEST POP ALL MUSIK

i GRÄSET

GRATIS

TA MED MAT, FILTAR, M.M.

Above: Poster for the second Gärdesfest, Stockholm, August 1970. The festival had been moved to an area close to Borgen, on Gärdet, from its previous location in the middle of a field two months earlier. English translation on p. 358.

Above: Poster for the third Gärdesfest, Stockholm, June 11–13, 1971. One of many Gärdesfests designated "the last." Design: Peter Zander. English translation on p. 358.

Sanningens silverflod

Sanningens silverflod

Anders Lind:

Träd, Gräs och Stenar had been commissioned to create the music for Öyvind Fahlström's film *Du gamla, du fria* [recorded 1969, premiered 1972]. I think Thomas Tidholm was commissioned by Öyvind Fahlström. Thomas was not on the green [self-titled] album, but he still deserves credit. I don't really know how things were regarding the schisms; maybe things were difficult around the time when Thomas quit. Maybe Thomas participated in *Du gamla, du fria* and then went home. The soundtrack and the album were recorded in the same week in Nacka aula, in March 1970. We used the venue to record the album at the same time. There was always a lot of thinking, twisting, and turning everything over in the band. It was probably about waiting for inspiration, because either it turned out well, or it didn't turn out at all. Maybe they held themselves to a higher standard, since they were entering into a genre where people would have opinions. It had not been easy to have opinions about International Harvester. What could you say? No one had heard anything like it before. Träd, Gräs och Stenar became more rock 'n' roll.

Musically, there was a difference between their first two records and those that followed. The first three were recorded live, mixed directly from the same mixer. I think we did some overlay on "All Along the Watchtower" in Talstudion, and added singing. Then we made a master copy of the entire recording while they were singing so that the master copy had the added song. It was a common way to go about it when there weren't that many channels. I think the record barely came together financially. Having an album cover with matte lamination was the most expensive thing you could do at the time. It's a very nice record and we had fun making it.

Previous spread: Träd, Gräs och Stenar with friends, Grönås, summer of 1970. Photo: Torbjörn Abelli.
Left: International Harvester during the filming of *Du gamla, du fria*. Öyvind Fahlström can be seen in a light blue shirt with his back to the camera. Photo: Jakob Sjöholm.

Left and right: Front and back cover of *Träd, Gräs och Stenar*, Decibell Records, 1970 (DRS 3702).

Torbjörn Abelli:

Bo Anders had always been bothered by "Sanningens silverflod" ["The Silver River of Truth"]. He wrote the song in January 1970, when we were traveling by boat from Amsterdam to Gothenburg, and then by train to Stockholm. When we recorded it, he had to add a verse because the song was way too cute at first. It sounded hippie-romantic. All accusations that we are romantic hippies oblivious of the world around us and only singing about nature and that we "ser ut över landen när månen stiger upp" ["look out over the land when the moon rises"], all that comes from that song. So, Bo Anders had to add a verse that's on the album.

After the song has faded out with its sentimental flute, and everything is so beautiful, we stood on Sergels torg outside the Riksdag, clapping and singing,

"Oh Riksdagsman, oh Riksdagsman, what did you eat today? Was the broiler chicken watery and smelled fishy, was the ham tasteless? We know you don't have it easy, your position is pretty weak, what needs to be done is already done, at the Bank of America... they send their fishmeal here from Japan and Peru, and all you can do is eat up and think that everything is normal, everything is normal, everything is normal." And then we faded out, like a comment.

Bo Anders was always extra careful with our form of political correctness. But if you can't agitate credibly, then it's completely meaningless.

Dan Backman:

The lyrics make up another chapter of Träd, Gräs och Stenar's story, just like the record covers, posters, and Bo Anders's

196

homemade constructions. The texts aren't that many—the group is mainly an instrumental band—but they are significant and, as with everything else about Träden, deeply original. Take "Sanningens silverflod," for example, an important and in every way mystical and poetic song. When Bo Anders Bo Anders sings "allt genom lunden gröna rinner det en flod / vi vilar vid dess stränder och vattnet är så gott" ["all through the green grove there flows a river / we rest on its banks and the water is so good"], **it is as if a door opens up towards an ancient and unknown folk culture. The same archaically natural lyrics and poetically solemn approach mark almost all of their texts. Often paired with a utopian and escapist appropriation.**

Håkan Sandblad
Göteborgs Handels- & Sjöfartstidning,
September 21, 1970

Is crummy music especially close to the people? A new musical philosophy has emerged in Sweden; it was strongly represented among those behind the festivals at Gärdet in Stockholm. Somewhat exaggerated, it goes on to say that the worse you play, the closer your music is to the people. It is thus anti-professionalism and anti-elite thinking pushed to its peak. In and of itself this is a sympathetic thought. Everyone should be able to join in and play, no one should feel hampered by a lack of technical knowledge. Everyone is their own musician. Definitely tear down the barriers between practitioners and listeners.... If you push this idea to its extreme ... it does have, however, some unpleasant and peculiar consequences. It entails, among other things, a rather strong contempt for the People: only shit is simple enough for the People

197

to follow. There are a few too many thoughts like
that in, for example, Träd, Gräs och Stenar's musical
perception for me to want to join in. But thankfully,
when it comes down to it, they're not consistent.
Because how could they then go about releasing a
new, completely commercial LP (Decibel Records). To
do that is, if anything, reserved for a small elite
group. Now, it's admittedly not a very ordinary
record. Judged by strictly technical criteria, it's
pretty bad. Still, at least for me, most of the songs
work--"Sanningens Silverflod" and "Tegenborgvalsen,"
to name two.

Bengt Berg:

> Without the lingering, swaying beat,
> isolated lyrics appear like desolate,
> withered remains of trees in a clearing in
> northern Värmland, but within the body
> of the music, the words form a kind of idea
> and backbone of thought, which points
> out the direction of the will that drives
> the group forward. When Träd, Gräs
> och Stenar play Dylan's "All Along the
> Watchtower" or the classic Stones hit
> "I Can't Get No Satisfaction" (on the LP
> *Träd, Gräs och Stenar*), they do it in a way
> that creates landscapes, new images and
> contexts around the old lyrics. They
> transform a kind of musical energy into
> another cultural climate; they turn the
> sidewalk into a forest trail.

Svenska Dagbladet, March 8, 1971
Träd, Gräs och Stenar find their way on their own paths
and are never tempted by shortcuts to commercial
success. The group's steady circle of admirers will
surely grow with the newly released album, even though
it probably won't make it onto the radio charts.

Previous spread: Collage album gatefold from *Träd, Gräs och Stenar*.
Left: Träd, Gräd och Stenar sunbathing with friends, Grönås,
summer of 1970. Photo: Thomas Mera Gartz.

MERA MUSIK

TRÄD, GRÄS OCH STENAR

Nu har det av Sveriges "internationella" popband kommit ut med sin tredje L.P. Det är Träd, Gräs & Stenar, och dom är "internationella" bara för att jenkarna börjat intressera sej för dom och för att Country Joe-i "Country Joe & the Fish"-en gäng satt i en studio och lyssnade på dom glatt, förvånat, gillande och instämmande.

Men i Nya Guineas djungler har man förstås inte hört något från dom, där har man väl varken radio eller grammofon och allra minst "studios". På sin höjd har man en flöjt, en trumma och sin egen röst att komma med. Det är sådan enslig och enkelt tillkommen musik som kallas folkmusik. Och om inte folkmusikerna lyssnar på popbandet så lyssnar popbandet desto mera på folkmusiken. Sen kommer den nya musiken till, och är "internationell"-inte för att den spelas på amerikanska radiostationer-utan för att den har sina rötter i hela världens folkmusik.

Man kan höra afrikas trummor, indiens flöjter och hälsinglands felor i deras musik. Man kan höra hummandet och lallandet från klippiga bergen, men dom spelar också Stones och Dylan, för Stones och Dylan är vår generations folkmusik, framfödda ur en ofantlig hop bluesgitarister och skifleband.

Träd, Gräs & Stenar berättar om hur det är, hur vårat liv ser ut just nu. Musiken visar när den är som hetast-när den är "live", förstås-att människorna flyter in i varandra för instumenten går att skilja åt lika lite som människorna och deras handlingar & vibrationer. Alltihop blir en visa, alla mänskorna blir en stam och så börjar det nya samhället, med det som stammen har gemensamt. Dom sjunger Stones-låten "I can´t get no satisfaction". Jag känner mej otillfredsställd för allt är så "plastic", så mekaniskt, dom som har makten är på väg att förstöra vår jord. Men det är inte helt hopplöst för det är vän som sitter på vår rygg och om vi reser oss så faller han; hjälp honom att falla. (Svarta pärla"). Den svarta pärlan är nära fast den ligger på botten av havet. Den är vårt eget liv när det får blomma i frihet. Som i mitten av L.Pins utvikningsbild, där fyra sittande buddhor och två stående gatsopare delar en stunds fullkomlig soluppgång. Eller som glada, befriade ansikten på unga kinesiska kvinnor eller när en naken flicka stiger upp ur det klara vattnet, långt borta från stadens förgiftade nyttighet. På utvikingsbilden som hör till den här L.P.n och i musiken finns många mänskors drömmar, det är "folkliga"önskningar om egen musik (där man ger "musikern"hans brödbit i handen i stället för att hålla enorma grammofonbolag under armarna), om rent vatten, meningsfyllt arbete ren luft, oförgiftad natur och ett liv nära jorden i stället för i skuggan av maskinerna.

Vad inte alla människor vill instämma i är att drömmarna bara kan förverkligas till priset av sänkt produktion och konsumtion, till priset av decentralisering och lägre standard. Och vad som är ännu svårare att förstå är det pris som den väpnade Svarta Pantern är beredd att betala för att få bestämma över sitt eget liv.

Men Träd, Gräs & Stenar solidariserar sej med honom också, liksom med alla andra förtryckta mänskor, som med eller utan vapen vill störta monstret med grävskopehänderna, och bygga det nya samhället.

Och vad har allt det här med musik att göra undrar någon?Nöjen och politik hör väl inte ihop?Om dom vill förändra samhället ska dom väl inte ägna en massa tid åt onyttig musik?

Och det är just dom som frågar så, som verkligen borde lyssna på Träd, Gräs & Stenar. Dom säger det finns bara en mänska, och var och en kan fråga sitt hjärta efter hennes behov. Sjukdomen är just splittringen, att inte leva ett helt liv. Att dela upp verkligheten i arbete & fritid, allvar & nöjen, plikt & lust, när alltihop egentligen borde hänga samman, som det gjorde en gäng när skörden varr allvar och fest på samma gäng. Då kunde man inte köpa glädje för surt förvärvade pengar.

Och samhället är ju allting-det är hur man gör musik, hur man älskar, hur man pratar, hur man arbetar, hur man bor. Om man tycker samhället är fel, kan man börja precis som man helst och ändra det, ändra sej själv. Man behöver inte börja med politik i snävaste bemärkelse. Man kan börja som Träd, Gräs & Stenar, med musik. Det är möjligt att man hammar i häktet ändå nån gäng, som en av dom gjorde häromdan för att ha demonstrerat för ren luft, rent vatten, ren mat & fler bostäder. Det var en demonstration mot allting som förstör oss precis som Träd, Gräs & Stenars musik i sina skönaste omständigheter (som på Gärdet i somras) är en-demonstration av allt som är gott för människan och som allt för många saknar. Allt som är bra börjar med gemenskap, men det behövs en annan gemenskap än pratets. Någon trummar, någon spelar gitarr, en som aldrig vägat förr, sjunger: "All along the watchtower", som om det var han själv som hade skrivit alltihopa, som om det var han själv som hade känt alltihop, som om det var han själv som hade drömt alltihop

Hej min vän
så glad att vi träffas igen
Jag är så ensam
Alldeles ensam
Jag kunde bara inte klara av det.

Har du hört Baby
vad vinden för med sig
Har du hört Baby
många människor på väg ner
kommunikation mindre vrångt
spelar ingen roll Baby
om håret är kort eller långt

Jag sa klättra ur din grav
alla dansar på gatan
gör vad du vet var inte slö
du måste leva som du lär
för de dags för dig och mig
att inse verkligheten

Glöm det som varit Baby
det e inte som för
fortsätt bara rätt på
vi måste stå sida vid sida
Dom säger makt åt folket
de e de dom skriker
frihet åt själen
skicka t vidare
skicka t vidare till unga o gamla

du måste säga barnen sanningen
dom behöver inte en massa lögn
för en dag nån gäng Baby
kommer dom att ha hand om prylar

att när du ger dem kärlek
ge det på rätt sätt
kvinna-barn-man och hustru
den bästa kärleken är att älska livet

Hej min vän
så glad att vi träffas igen
varit alldeles ensam
jag tror jag klarar det ensam
fortsätt att kämpa.

Jimi Hendrix
Augusti 1970

Unga i gammal skola
gör pop av folkmusik

I en gammal, och sen flera år nedlagd, folkskola i Grönås, Järvsö har det i sommar bedrivits ett intensivt musikaliskt experimenterande. Den ytterst jordnära och helt försvenskade popgruppen Träd, gräs och stenar har insett det oskattbara värdet i gammal svensk folkmusik och vill nu göra allt för att föra den vidare på det sätt de spelar den. Två av gruppens medlemmar avbröt sina studier vid Kungl. Musikaliska Akademien i Stockholm för att kunna ägna sig åt den musik de tycker är mer betydelsefull. I dag är Träd, gräs och stenar den i särklass mest intressanta gruppen i nysvensk pop.

SIDAN 12

Left: Article from *Huvudbladet* 1, June 1971. English translation on pp. 358–360.
Above: Piece from *Söderhamn-Hälsninge-Kuriren*, September 26, 1970. English translation on p. 360.

On Tour

On Tour

Anna Herngren
Arbetarbladet, February 25, 1971

"The function of the great modern city is to exploit the people, make them dependent and control them. The city is a monument to consumer society with banking palaces and business palaces." This message comes from the pop group Träd, Gräs och Stenar, who on Wednesday evening played at the Gävle museum for around 350 young people. Their music is sometimes melancholy like a folk song, but mostly it seems inspired by the noise of the city, drilling and heavy machinery. Together with images of a grey, cold inhumane city and filmed lyrics, their heavy music becomes nightmarishly effective.

Torbjörn Abelli:

At a gig in Gävle in the early seventies, a really pissed-off guy came up to me during the break and asked: "Why don't you agitate! You have this huge opportunity to stir up the masses, and you only sing about the moon." I tried to explain to him that we were not good agitators—we let others take care of that. At best, what we can provide is a rebellious attitude through music. It is built up by us with those present in the room—we want to formulate moods where you dare to change things. We don't have scores, we don't know where the music is going, and almost all music, even the songs you recognize, contain a certain amount of improvisation. Things go awry sometimes, but it's a gamble that we embark on. If we agitate, that is where it lies.

Previous spread: Träd, Gräs och Stenar and King Kong exploding in sound and light at the Moderna Museet in Stockholm, May 18, 1971. Photo: Morten Kjærgaard.
Left: Bo Anders Persson in Fælledparken, May 9, 1971. Photo: Morten Kjærgaard.

Blir popen folkligare?

— Av Jan-Åke Pettersson —

Träd, Gräs och Stenar höll konsert på Cue tillsammans med Fläsket Brinner i fredags. Det blev levande musik praktiskt taget hela kvällen. Med ett kort avbrott höll den på från halv nio till ett.

Det var Träd, Gräs och Stenar som inledde det hela. De hade just kommit från Köpenhamn och var på genomresa. Ingen visste att de skulle spela och det hade säkert kommit mer folk om det hade varit annonserat.

Även om många tyckte det var skönt, så var de inte själva nöjda med sin musik.

— Efter att ha vistats i Köpenhamn blir vår musik hård stadsmusik. Får vi bara komma ut på landet blir den mycket mjukare och mer harmonisk. Vi bor på landet så mycket vi hinner och har ett hus i Hälsingland. För att en grupp skall kunna fungera måste man också kunna leva tillsammans.

● SÖVANDE

Deras musik kan på det tekniska planet, karakteriseras som malande och sövande. En låt kan vara hur lång som helst. Det finns ingen begränsning i musiken, utan improvisationerna får flöda som de vill. Dessa står främst gitarristen Bo Anders Persson för.

Vad är det då de vill få fram?

— Den helhet man får fram tillsammans med människor. Kontakten med oss själva och med publiken. Vi vill försöka nå så långt in i en känsla som möjligt. Därför snackar vi lite innan vi kör låten, så publiken inte skall missuppfatta det hela och få fel känslor.

Deras stil gör att den som går in för att lyssna och få en känsla inte misslyckas. Man har gott om tid att flyta in i musiken.

Vissa personer karakteriserar deras musik som "medvetet dålig". Ju mer risit man spelar, ju större blir kontakten med publiken.

● IDÉ

— Detta är helt fel. Det är en dum uppfattning om vad ljud är. De utgår från en idé om vad som är bra och dåligt. Så kan det inte vara, för vad är det som är bra och dåligt?

— Vår musik är en stor rit där alla deltar. Om man ser det så, uppstår aldrig denna uppdelning.

Träd, gräs och stenar: »Tillbaka till naturen!«

Gräsligt på Olympia Publiken gick hem...

"Träd, gräs och stenar" underliga krumelurer på Grängesbergsscen

Närmare 360 personer lyssnade på Träd, Gräs och Stenar på museet på onsdagskvällen.

Folkfest i Gävle museum med Träd, Gräs och Stenar

Träd, gräs och stenar popgrupp med budskap:

BRUKA JORDEN!

Spelar gärna i stan men ej på diskotek

Träd, Gräs och Stenar spelar i Bollnäs
Bollnäsflicka med i deras naturkollektiv

Kringstrykande musikband:

MUSIK FÖR FOLKET SÅ ALLA BEGRIPER

Träd, gräs och stenar på Vindelälvens strand

Träd, Gräs och Stenar talade om miljövård

☐ Folk från restaurant Fröet och Träd Gräs Och Stenar bjuden på kök i Hagahusets kök.

Träd, gräs och Stenar på Hagahuset

Dom bjuder på mat, musik o. utställning

— Av Tommy Rander —
Träd Gräs Och Stenar. — Kring det namnet vilar ett skimmer av mystik. Dom var de första att börja fundera på om popen verkligen måste låte på ett bestämt sätt, då

hette dom Persson Sound. Sedan började dom kalla sig International Harvester, och bestämde sig slutligen för det nuvarande namnet. Medlemmarna har också varierat lite grand.

● Dom spelade på Hagahuset under fredagen och lördagen. Det kom mycket människor, och dom som blev hungriga blev bespisade. Träd Gräs och Stenar har nämligen med sig en grupp från "Fröet" i Stockholm som lagar mat, bestående av "vänligt" odlade grönsaker, dvs framsprungna ur jorden utan andra hjälpmedel än de naturliga.

● Förutom matgruppen ingår också en odlingsgrupp i turnén. Den i sin tur har en utställning med sig om "vänlig odling".

● För utomstående, icke förstiåsigpåare på Träd Gräs Och Stenar verkar möjligen detta något förvirrade.
Men det är det inte alls. Medlemmarna i bandet har länge på

olika sätt arbetat för alternativa livsformer. Dom vill se fler människor på landet, odlanda sin egen mat och skapande sin egen kultur.

● Vad man nu har gjort är bara att ta steget fullt ut — deras turné blir alltså en demonstration av ett alternativ. Idag spelar Träd Gräs Och Stenar på Backa Fritidsgård, dom startar tidiga morgonen och håller på hela dan.

● Det är meningen att alla kategorier människor kan vara med. Förutom musik, och bandet ser helst att publiken deltar i spelandet, finns alltså mat som restaurant Fröet står för. Samt utställning om Vänlig Odling. Ett alternativ mitt inne i stenöknen.

● Anklagelserna om lands-

bygdsromantik viftar gruppen bort. Alltefftersom tiden går står det ju allt klarare att den nuvarande tendensen mot ökad tillväxt för storstäderna och uttunnad och igenvuxen landsbygd inte kommer att hålla. Det gäller att skapa nya livsformer, menar dom.

● Träd Gräs Och Stenars musik är kraftig och stark. Den är väldigt kollektiv och tät till hela sitt väsen. Varifrån den kommer är svårt att fastslå — Bo Anders Persson menar att den å ena sidan är väldigt svensk, men samtidigt spelar dom också en del låtar av Dylan och Rolling Stones.
Men det är låtar som på något sätt är generationssånger, låtar man inte kommer ifrån därför att man levat under en viss tid.

POPGRUPPEN "Träd, gräs och stenar" från Stockholm spelade vid hembygdsföreningens annorlunda kväll vid Vindelälven. Gruppen, som spelade för full volym, väckte viss nyfikenhet bland publiken.

TRÄD, GRÄS OCH STENAR
ett annat ord för människa

Left and above: Articles by Jan-Åke Petterson, *Arbetet*, November 30, 1970, and Tommy Rander, *Göteborgs-Posten*, February 1972. Headlines from *Norrskensflamman*, November 20, 1971; *Dagens Nyheter*, February 21, 1971; *Bargslagsposten*, October 20, 1971; *Arbetarbladet*, February 25, 1971; *Västerbottens Folkbladet*, August 2, 1971; and *Ljusnan*, November 13, 1971. Articles from *Västerbottens Folkblad*, August 2, 1971; *Örnsköldsviks Allehanda*, August 2, 1971; *Grängesber*, October 14, 1971; *Norrskensflamman*, July 30, 1971; and *Norrländska Social-Demokraten*, November 30, 1971. English translations on pp. 361–363.

Gustav Lindström

Örnsköldsviks Allehanda, August 2, 1971

The performance of the music group Träd, Gräs och
Stenar in Bredbyn on Saturday evening was far from
a success and more than half of the approximately
150-strong audience left Olympia before the break
and during it an even large number disappeared, which
was perhaps what the band intended. Because the
break lasted a full forty minutes, which was probably
a bit too long if one was to stay for the entire
program. When they were asked to continue playing,
they replied that it was more pleasant to sit and
discuss with the young people who had settled down
on the floor; well then you understand what purpose
they had with their music.... Once the music got
started again, at least one of the musicians turned
their back to the audience for most of the show, even
though they said they wanted to have contact with
them. This shows how little they really could or
maybe, in reality, wanted with their performance.

Jakob Sjöholm:

We played on a slope by Vindelälven
[a large tributary river in northern
Sweden] **one summer night in 1971. It was
an almost religious moment. We were in
that famous flow where everything just is
right. Everything was ideal: the audience,
the sound, the light, the air, and the
feeling. I looked at my fingers wondering
what was happening. It was as if a force
took over the situation while I was just
a tool. You ended up just standing there
smiling like a fool, transcending to another
dimension. It felt as if I could do anything
on the guitar. Our homemade speakers
were spread out in the grass. People
danced in ecstasy.**

Torbjörn Abelli:

When we played, many just shook their heads and left after ten minutes—nothing is happening. We played in Järnvägsparken in Flen, a wonderful little stage. Really, it was too small for us. But we fit on there. An old man watched us play. Afterward, he came up to me: "It looks like you are having fun when you play, but is it music?"

Torgny Sjöstedt:

Overlapping memories and details from a gig. Early seventies, Gothenburg. The band I was in is called Love Explosion. We shared an evening with Träd, Gräs och Stenar. Hagahuset used to be called Dickinsonska folkbiblioteket [Dickinson Public Library], a gift from the merchant Dickinson to the city. The books are gone now and it's a multi-activity house. The concert space on the first floor opens up towards the large café with a balcony that wraps around two of the walls. The windows toward Nya Allén are covered in dark curtains and in front of them is the stage.

The gig hasn't started yet. The members of Träd, Gräs och Stenar are arranging their gear on stage. The pianist, Arne, sits by his electric piano—a little box with keys and a row of little short steel strings. He holds a tuning key in his hand—one of those that piano tuners use—a bent long iron stick with a hollow tip that grips the pin. Arne is pretty short, with light brown hair and a walrus mustache. He is quietly sitting on a stool, hitting the notes, listening, and turning a little with the key. It must be hard to tune a piano. I find it hard to tune a guitar. Sometimes when I play with Love Explosion I can't get it right. If one string seems to be tuned I try to stick with that string.

I talk to Bo Anders and he says that the band played in Norway and that they started a macrobiotic diet. "Macrobiotic"—I haven't heard the word before. Lots of different styles are popping up, not just in music; everything is connected. World famine, the war in Vietnam, commercialism.

The gig starts. There is the bass player, Torbjörn Abelli. He has long blond hair and smiles as if he could never get annoyed or angry. He plays his short bass riffs over and over again, without variation, serenely and seemingly content that nothing is happening. He is tall and slightly hunched over. Bo Anders tells the audience about the macrobiotic diet. Porridge of raw, untreated grains. Decoction of green leaves. He describes their breakfast and talks of macrobiotic cultivation.

Left: Träd, Gräs och Stenar, Stadsparken in Lund, May 23–24, 1970. Photo: Unknown (taken with Thomas Mera Gartz's camera).
Above: Flyer for Parkfesten in Lund, 1971. English translation on p. 363.

At one point, Mera leaves the drums and stands at the edge of the stage with his back against the wall. He plays a black violin that he holds on his forearm. He sings slowly and in unison with the violin's melody. "Svarta pärla du är så nära—gömd på botten av ett hav" ["Black pearl, you are so close / Hidden at the bottom of the ocean"]. His hair is black and curly, his face is long with a big forehead. What is this about?

It's Love Explosion's turn to play. On this particular night, there are quite a few of us in the band and things get a bit confused when we are getting up on stage and start plugging in our instruments. Bo goes up to the mic. Bo is good with words and adds pauses that make people smile and giggle.

"I want to take the opportunity to tell you what we usually eat for breakfast," says Bo. "First, we usually start by smoking one of the cigarette butts from the ashtray that we've prepared the night before. Then we continue with a class of Coca-Cola that we drink together with a couple of Brago biscuits and we finish it off with a few cheese puffs that have been stored in an opened package." Everyone in the band smiles and we start playing our first song. "Rickard Nixon han har—ett badkar för två" ["Richard Nixon / He has a bathtub for two"]. Then Träd, Gräs och Stenar returns to the stage with a long, dark, monotonous and evocative song in a minor key. Mera sways by his drums. He tilts his head back and plays rhythmic phrases that wander in semicircles above the drumkit, from the hi-hat to the largest tom-tom drum. Again and again, in a slow crescendo that never seems to climax. I'm sitting on the floor in front of the band. A lot of audience members sway to the music.

214

Bert Gren

Göteborgs-Posten, February 21, 1972

When Träd, Gräs och Stenar play, it becomes more of
an event than a concert. This was also the case in
Hagahuset this weekend. Their music is certainly
essential--but it is still only part of the larger
whole.... Macrobiotic food was available for purchase
and they showed us with various posters and leaflets
why it is better and healthier than the industrially
processed food we usually eat. They also try to
reflect the freedom you can experience in nature in
their music. It's rarely beautiful, but it's down-
to-earth and original, and if it catches fire and
they get some response from the audience, anything
can happen. Then suddenly an atmosphere arises where
everyone can feel free to do what they want. This is
what Träd, Gräs och Stenar is all about. Admit that
it is better than Concrete, Plastic, and Asphalt!

Thomas Mera Gartz:

Sometimes it wasn't as much fun to play.
It could be a late summer evening, cold and
damp, and you were only wearing sandals
and the wrong clothes. Freezing. There was
nothing to eat and no one knew where to go.
People lit up and were gone. The dark side
of drugs became apparent pretty quickly.
We were tripping, too. I thought about
smoking before I played and stuff. This was
during Träd, Gräs och Stenar. With Pärson
Sound there wasn't much of it. It wasn't
associated with that music.

Jakob Sjöholm:

I started smoking weed really early, when
I was fifteen. It was mostly about listening
to music at that time. For a period when we

Left: Bo Anders Persson doing some weeding, 1969. Photo: Thomas Mera Gartz.
Right: Jonas Wikander, Thomas Mera Gartz, Torbjörn Abelli, and Sonja Gransvik on the ferry between Denmark and Sweden, May 1971.
Photo: Jakob Sjöholm.

216

were out playing with Träd, Gräs och Stenar, all of us smoked every day for several years. It was normal to smoke grass—everyone in our social circles did, which was good and bad. When we smoked before a gig, we would be able to listen to the little things in the notes. We would become hyperfocused on different sounds. That's why it could take so long to tune everything. Smoking had significance to the band's music, it created a basic atmosphere of being open and taking stuff in.

Sonja Gransvik:

We stood out because of our choices. We lived simply while also smoking quite a bit—hash and the like—but not everyone did so. We were a mixed group of people, and not everyone was as orthodox. The hash smoking was sort of part of the ideology. It gave you another perspective on the world and it was completely separate from the

dominant alcohol tradition. However, if you got stuck in a hash addiction, you weren't very constructive.

Thomas Mera Gartz:

Bo Anders's VW bus had a sun painted on the front, right by the VW emblem. I painted the entire bus with a paintbrush and regular lacquer paint: a horizon with mountains, forests, lakes and valleys, that unite heaven and earth, a cerulean-blue day sky, greenish-brown land, and a white-orange-red sun with long rays across the front. Torbjörn's car was an old DKW painted with a landscape, trolls, mushrooms, flames, rainbows, and yin-yang. It was rotting with rust. Then Jakob arrived with a sky-blue VW bus. The engine cut the sun, the transmission in the sky. . . . The police were breathing down our necks when they saw our painted cars on the country roads; they threatened

217

Bo Anders Persson and Sonja Gransvik fixing the VW bus. Torbjörn Abelli's DKW, which was also used as a tour vehicle from 1969 to 1971, can be seen in the background, Grönås, 1970. Torbjörn Abelli: "The DKW was a two-stroker that ran on oil-mixed gas, way before anyone could spell 'catalytic converter.' The painting was done by myself, my sister, my brother-in-law, and their daughter." Photo: Torbjörn Abelli.

us, stared at us with superior grins, and checked our licenses, what we had in our pockets, and in our trunks.

At the border between Denmark and Sweden, they decided to search us and our cars every time, and it happened a few times that my naked body, asshole and underwear had every seam inspected. Eager dogs were let loose in our vehicles to sniff for substances that were more material than spiritual. That's why we never became prisoners. . . . On country roads in the middle of nowhere, police could stop our painted cars, nag and provoke us, herbal tea in a small leather bag on a belt could make things drag on for ages, dividing and squeezing us before they let us go again, while other friends and acquaintances had to sit in the slammer for their smoking stuff.

Thomas Tidholm:

Around 1967, I noticed that many young people were culturally homeless and were not doing well. They sought out new music and wanted to dance and feel free. Some of them belonged to the band or our little family. When we moved out into the country, they came to us, and many of them were worse for wear. International Harvester and our friends solely consumed cannabis. Solely! Although there was quite a lot of smoking, it was never

Left: Per Odeltorp (known as Stig Vig), Gabi Björnstrand, and Torbjörn Abelli during the Denmark tour, 1972. Photo: Jakob Sjöholm.
Above (top): Flyer for Träd, Gräs och Stenar show in Lyngby, outside of Copenhagen, May 1, 1971.
Above (bottom): Poster for Träd, Gräs och Stenar's gig in Gladsaxe, outside of Copenhagen, May 8, 1971.

Bo Anders Persson and Thomas Mera Gartz playing violin in Fælledparken, Copenhagen, May 9, 1971.
Photo: Morten Kjærgaard.

Bo Anders Persson's VW bus, which was used as a tour bus from 1968 to 1972. The painting was done by Thomas Mera Gartz. Torbjörn Abelli: "An inverted nightly landscape with a sunset in front. A commentary on the landscape we were traveling through." Photo: Torbjörn Abelli.
Right: Arne Ericsson, Fælledparken, 1971. Photo: Kostas Kakoseos.

Arne Ericsson and Jakob Sjöholm in Fælledparken. Photo: Morten Kjærgaard.

Träd, Gräs och Stenar in Fælledparken. Photo: Morten Kjærgaard.

Above: Flyer for Träd, Gräs och Stenar and King Kong at Moderna Museet, 1971. Design: Kjartan Slettemark.

a question of doing speed or dope. Not
many people were taking LSD. People
probably saw it as a kind of super hashish,
but it is not possible to have a drug like
that in society—an antisocial drug, for the
individual at his own risk. I don't think
drugs are good at all, not in the long run.

Not from a political perspective, not
if we are to hold together a functioning
society. Society is a common reference
that everyone should ideally share and
collaborate on—for or against. Our small-
est common denominator.

Michel de la Bruyere Vincent:
We started King Kong Lightgroup in June 1969 at Kunstakademiet Arkitektskole
[The Royal Danish Academy of Fine Arts]

Above: The bus parked next to the venue, Fælledparken, Copenhagen, 1971.
Right: Setlist for Träd, Gräs och Stenar and King Kong Lightgroup gigs, 1971.

in Copenhagen. It was Kjeld Christian Krarup, Steen Thure Krarup, Anne Ditlevsen, Kai Larsen and me. We became Denmark's biggest light show, and at the beginning of 1971, we were looking for a new music group to collaborate with. Kjeld Christian Krarup knew of International Harvester's records *Sov gott Rose-Marie* and *Hemåt*, and the music from the film *Misshandlingen*.

In January 1971, Kjeld Christian traveled to Stockholm to propose a collaboration with Träd, Gräs och Stenar. During a meeting with Torbjörn Abelli, they agreed to organize a tour together in Denmark and Sweden in April and May 1971. Träd, Gräs och Stenar and King Kong Lightgroup met in Copenhagen at the end of April, and rehearsed a program in the Glass Hall at Danmarks Tekniske Universitet [The Technical University of Denmark]. The performance there on May 1, 1971, and the performance at Moderna Museet in Stockholm on May 18, were the highlights of the tour.

Arne Ericsson:

During our Denmark tour, King Kong and the boys rented a house for us in Ballerup [in Copenhagen's northwest suburbs]. It was classy and we played in Fælledparken, among other places. The Danes are more open from birth than we Swedes, and we were embraced immediately.

h-jn
Information, May 10, 1971
Träd, Gräs och Stenar proved that Fælledparken in Copenhagen is lovely on a wonderful day in May with a free concert yesterday afternoon. The heavy, monotonous music is well-suited for such an occasion. There is a falling, lingering melancholy in it that

Right: The audience in Fælledparken waiting for Träd, Gräs och Stenar, Copenhagen, 1971. Photo: Jakob Sjöholm.

I have not felt anywhere else. And when someone made a goal over in Idrottsparken [stadium], the cheers and applause thundered down over the concert in a very nice way. Spring, sun and people together. "The sun is the light show today," said the group's leader, Bo Anders.

Thomas Mera Gartz:

> Our flyers had gathered a thousand people. Food, beer, and cookies, with or without pot. The atmosphere sang between bands and people. At the same time, large roars from the masses at the soccer game in the stadium close by. After that, people were drawn from there into our music, so the audience kept growing. Bands and people and air and earth were of all this. The sound grew, my arms and legs danced and moved over the drums, danced and danced.

Jakob Sjöholm:

> King Kong was a bigger collective than we were. They worked with something similar and brought a lot of energy. We had a lot of fun together and the collaboration felt like a continuation of the *International Harvester Good Luck Show*; we were developing the visuals. But it was a big ordeal. Had we continued with King Kong, we would have needed twenty more people on tour. There wasn't enough money for that.

Jan Borges
Extrabladet, May 3, 1971
The Swedes Träd Gräs och Stenar play music from a different perspective. In the old-fashioned sense, they're certainly not that good at playing their instruments, but they have something to say, and they're perfectly capable of using whatever means and abilities they have to create a big and violent

expression with it. It is amazing that they can capture you with their dark but powerful music so that you are sucked in and become one with what is happening. Contributing to this was also King Kong's lights, which in this context were just right.

Michel de la Bruyere Vincent:

For the tour, we brought two projection screens which, together, were forty meters wide and eight meters high. Before we started the collaboration with Träd, Gräs och Stenar, we had created a color system and a large number of fluid images, graphic filters, films and film loops, structured and fixed in several programs that were developed, modified, and improvised to the band's poetry and meditative music.

We had similar views on ecology and the environment, inspiration from nature, as well as a critical humanistic approach to global development in general. Artistically, both groups belonged to minimalism, with repetition as the basis for the audiovisual expression.

Reit
Sjællandstidende, May 10, 1971
There is every reason to praise the organizing group Zaratustra for the festival Earthquake in Slagelse-hallen on Friday and Saturday. Artistically, this is probably the most exciting thing on Sjælland in years.... When in two days you can gather more than 1,500 young people for such an ambitious event, it is proof of the environment's raison d'être.... The Swedish group Träd, Gräs och Stenar ... was simply not

Left: Underneath King Kong's light table. Photo: Morten Kjærgaard.
Above: Träd, Gräs och Stenar and King Kong planning the show for that evening, Moderna Museet garden. Photo: Morten Kjærgaard.

good enough, but Zaratustra could not have known that, because they had been recommended by several others. The group's strength lies in the lyrics, but it was difficult to hear them. In contrast, the Swedish group was supported exceptionally well by the King Kong light show, which used many pieces of film that were so finely composed that Träd, Gräs och Stenar almost played to the light show and not the other way around.

Jakob Sjöholm:

> We really felt at home in Christiania. That was what we were fighting for at home in Sweden, and they were already implementing it. The concert in Christiania was at the top of a house, in the attic with wooden floors and wooden beams.
>
> Our music just went on and on as people danced. It was psychedelic, several people were dancing naked, it was that kind of vibe.

Thomas Mera Gartz:

> It was Sosse-Sweden, after all. A social democratic [aka "Sosse"] society, a so-called "folkhem" [the "people's home" concept underlying the Swedish welfare state]. The Danish anarchists and hippies who became Slumstormarna [a squatter activist movement that "occupied" housing in the 1960s and early 1970s] and created Christiania and Huset [Copenhagen's multi-activity building], never had any violent confrontations with the police. There were a few riots but not much more. When we were on tour in Copenhagen in 1971–72, we lived in a house occupied by Slumsormarna. During our gig at Huset, someone told us that the police were attacking the house we were staying in. We stopped the gig and ran there with the audience. It turned out it wasn't that bad. Slumstormarna had so-called "warnings"; the alarm went off when the police were on their way. Then people gathered to be able to continue barricading these houses. The situation was in a way tougher in Copenhagen than in Sweden, although the climate was freer and people had an easier time expressing themselves.

Jakob Sjöholm unpacking Träd, Gräs och Stenar's instruments
and amplifiers in front of King Kong's big projection screen in
the large exhibition space at Moderna Museet, Stockholm.
Photo: Morten Kjærgaard.

Träd, Gräs och Stenar's bus parked at dusk in Copenhagen, May 1971.
Photo: Morten Kjærgaard.

Friendly Farming

CHAPTER 12

Friendly Farming

Jan Andersson
Aftonbladet, July 4, 1971
This summer Träd, Gräs och Stenar won't have any performances. The entire group is traveling to Värmland to grow vegetables.

Thomas Mera Gartz
Norrbottens-Kuriren, July 29, 1971
Back to nature but in a modern way.... We have to realize nature's impact on humans and learn how to live off of nature without destroying it. We are starting to lose ourselves in asphalt and chemical additives. You notice it more clearly in Stockholm today. Stockholm is shit--everyone is longing for the country.

Thomas Tidholm:

There were rumors about their commune in Värmland, that they ate biodynamic food with brown rice, brewer's yeast with a little oil on top. Then we heard that they snuck out to [the nearby town of] Likenäs and went to the café there, haha. Everyone became skin-and-bone thin; it was horrible to see them. They were clearly malnourished, since they were eating the wrong diet. But they would never admit to that. That stuff about food wasn't present during my time in International Harvester—it came later together with thoughts on biodynamics, yin and yang, very advanced stuff. I don't have anything bad to say about it, I just wasn't involved at all. We ate pretty much everything.

Previous spread: Sonja Gransvik and Bo Anders Persson mowing in Finnskogarna, west of Likenäs, 1974. After three growing seasons of communal cultivation at Anders Björnsson's place, Bo Anders and Sonja borrowed a house and land in Totjärnsberg, Nyskoga [southwest of Likenäs]. Photo: Rita Modin.

Left: Roger Gustafsson, Bo Anders Perrson, Greta Lindblom, Jon Klingberg, and Greta's son Niklas. Roger Gustafsson: "Image from May 1971, when we first arrived in Likenäs to cultivate. Photo: Sonja Gransvik.

Participants in the Vänlig odling ["Friendly Farming"] course. From left: Sten Walling, Jan Hammarlund, Åse Berglund, Lova Lindroos, and Micke Lindfield, Likenäs, 1971. Photo: Roger Gustafsson.

Bo Anders Persson:

We came to a gig in Oslo where the organizers said that they had an American who made incredible vegetarian food. It was Zen cooking, a form of meditation that entails living off of a small bowl of brown rice and meditating. You are supposed to eat what is good for the seasons and the place that you live in. It was rice and vegetable in a stew with some root vegetables and onion. We thought the food was a little under-seasoned. That's how we embarked on our vegetarian journey.

Sonja Gransvik:

Bo Anders came home [from Oslo] with a cookbook titled *Zen Cooking*, and he was almost enchanted by it. It was about

macrobiotic cooking in combination with philosophic thought. It presented an integration between food, philosophy, and life itself. That book was an eye-opener for us. After that, we started to look at food and conserving in new ways—more like what people are doing now—but at that time there were not many people who thought about organic food and about what food production looked like. Zen cooking meant that we changed our habits completely. At this time, parts of the band lived in a small commune. It was Mera, his girlfriend Ulla, and Bo Anders and me. We had an American deserter, Niel Jörgensen, living with us, and it turned out that he too had brought macrobiotic cooking ideas

Above: The Friendly Farming course, 1971. From left: Mike Lindfield, Steve Roney, Thomas Mera Gartz, Sten Bergman, and others. Photo: Roger Gustafsson.

with him from California. We rented old schools in a couple of places in Hälsingland where we spent a lot of time in both the summer and the winter. The band could then easily rehearse and we could all live there collectively.

Thomas Mera Gartz:

Some of those who didn't want to go to Vietnam and be slaughtered came to Sweden. One of them ended up in our group and launched macrobiotics, which we adopted because we realized that it was both good and cheap. It cost almost nothing compared to regular food. Vegetables and rice were our staple foods for several years. We went to Solidarisk handel [Solidarity Trading], a store in Stockholm that imported Vietnamese rice, and we bought directly from biodynamic growers from Järna. In 1969–70, a group began to buy wholesale vegetables and deliver them by car to those who ordered. It was cheap and done without profit. It was impossible to make a living off of it; it was completely idealistic.

Sonja Gransvik:

To a large extent, I think it was the zeitgeist that influenced us. It was about us wanting to bring our whole lives into what we were doing. Music, cooking, dancing, and togetherness. We saw ourselves as small parts of the larger whole that was life itself. The time was right to think about what we actually ate and consumed. What does the chain look like before the food reaches us? Together we created an ecologically conscious lifestyle.

Arne Ericsson:

Bo Anders, Mera, and Torbjörn were a kind of spearhead for macrobiotics. I got into it too, which might not have happened had I not been in the band.

Jakob Sjöholm:

I was never really as strictly into all that, but I was a vegetarian even before I joined the band, which the others weren't. But I thought it was kind of boring to just eat boiled wheat. For a period, it became almost religious and at that point I felt it was too much.

Sonja Gransvik:

Bo Anders subscribed to a magazine called *Livsmedelsteknik* [Food Technology], where you could read about all the additives, cosmetics, and chemicals that affected the longevity of food and so on. What the magazine was praising, we thought was terrible!

During the winter [1970-71], we had been on tour in Värmland with Rikskonserter [a state-run concert promoter]. Solveig Bark worked there and supported contemporary musical ideas in every possible way. On the tour, we served food—with sourdough bread and herbal tea—and we worked with a kind of all-embracing art music. We would inspire people who came there to create their own instruments and make music together.

During the tour, we visited the farmer [Anders] Björnsson, who told us about his private version of organic farming and philosophy. He spoke of American imperialism and how one instead should seek one's way back to the roots, take care of what one has, and cultivate in one's surroundings. We were inspired by his thoughts. We were ideologically on the left, just like him, but we weren't nearly as puritanical as the new left movement, and we weren't super tripped out either. There was a strong longing to return to the source and to create a better world in order to save the planet and try to stop industrialism. We thought we could change the world. With macrobiotics—which is based heavily on Zen Buddhism—came the interest in human

nature if you removed all imprints of social, hierarchical, economic and structural norms. What does life mean? What does it mean for man to have a life—if we remove all our norms? That line of reasoning has become my great curiosity, especially putting the diet in context with how we live and how we use our resources and treat animals and nature.

Bo Anders Persson:

Mera had heard a radio show with Björnsson, where he laid out the text on vegetative life and man's role in it. There was a clip of him on TV where he was laying out pieces of paper as ground cover. We first came to Värmland with a eurhythmics project for children; we would drum together and create spontaneous music with drums and flutes. When we had time off, I called Björnsson. He had this big farmer's house, but he was no builder, so it had deteriorat-

ed. Björnsson was a character in the area, that was pretty clear. He parked us on his couch and started talking. He had barely gotten started after three hours had gone by. When he started to feel tired he snuck into the kitchen for a cup of coffee and a sip of filmjölk [fermented sour milk]. He brought us a jug of cordial, and a few bread rusks so we wouldn't keel over. Then he talked for another three hours on antagonism in plant life, between the forest and the cultivated land. Industrial agriculture was the politics of death; one was to use a handheld hoe and see the plants as individuals. It was pretty far-out, alright.

I was into the idea that he should adapt his farming a little more to industrial methods, but he did not agree at all. It had to be one man and a handheld hoe. Björnsson had attended school for six years, moved around, and had an amazing ability at

250

absorbing information from people. He was around 75 when we met, and was obsessed with the idea of adapting human culture to "vegetative life," as he put it. I was at his place a lot, and when I later moved up here, I almost became like part of the family. He could be a bit macho but he had to adapt to his wife's ways; she was from around here, a sharp and talented old woman. If he ever got fed up, he exclaimed: "Haven't I always been right, perhaps?" Then his wife knew the only thing to do was give up. They probably had their discussions.

We had asked people out there about starting to farm, and there was a lot of, "Nah, it's just a lot of work." When I asked

Björnsson if we could get hold of a piece of land, he said, "No problem, I have a piece of land. Come here tomorrow and we'll get started!" Björnsson was clearly interested in getting an audience. We spread the word among our friends in Stockholm about our cultivation course, which consisted of him providing us with cultivation tasks and preaching while we hacked along. Björnsson was joyous; he was really in his element. In the beginning, there were twenty of us living in a large, ramshackle farmhouse from the eighteenth century. We tried to buy it, but it didn't work. The landlord was a large forest owner, and he didn't give a shit about us.

Left: Anders Björnsson and Bo Anders Persson talking on the porch in Likenäs on Träd, Gräs och Stenar's Värmland tour, March 1971. Photo: Jakob Sjöholm.
Above: Potato harvest, 1971. Farmer Anders Björnsson can be seen in the background, Sonja Gransvik in the foreground. Photo: Roger Gustafsson.

S.-Å.

Nya Wermlands-Tidningen, August 23, 1971
The northern Klarälv valley is currently experiencing a wave of new-farming-joy. In the midst of
an age of technology with an increased pace and the
closure of small farms, a "grower movement" has
suddenly arisen.... It is surely no coincidence
that this wave of new cultivation has started in
the northern Klarälv valley. People here have seen
farm after farm shut down. They have seen fields
grow back, and abandoned farm properties fall
into disrepair.... "Finnskogens Druva," and its
philosophical father, the cultural prizewinner
Anders Björnsson from Likenäs, have come to be at
the center of events.... In the northern Klarälv
valley alone, there are about fifty plantations with
the blackcurrants, "Finnskogens Druva." ... Since
nature-friendly farming is in vogue right now, young
people in particular have embraced these ideas. This
summer, two pop groups from Stockholm have been in
Likenäs, where, under the supervision of gardener
Anders Björnsson, they have learned how to cultivate
the right way. It is cultivation without chemical
additives, cultivation where the soil and nature do
the work. Now, no one should think that this has been
a frivolous summer adventure for the young people

Above: The Bäckström farmstead that Träd, Gräs och Stenar rented in Likenäs, 1971. Photo: Roger Gustafsson.
Right: Anders Björnsson guiding the course participants in the mysteries of cultivation, Likenäs, summer of 1971. Photo: Roger Gustafsson.

from Stockholm. Fläsket brinner [The Pork Is Burning] and Träd, Gräs och Stenar, yes, the groups are called that, have had a really busy time farming in Finnskoga-Dalby, and they have received a lot of praise from the local population for what they have achieved. The young farmers have struggled with primitive housing conditions all summer in Finnskoga-Dalby just to learn how to farm.

Peter Mosskin:

We were standing on a small plateau overlooking Klarälven. Anders Björnsson's plantations spread out and he explained that if raspberries and blackcurrants were planted too close together, they took away each other's vitality. I remember the view of the river valley and the little sinewy man's

ability to talk nonstop. I was alone and listened for a couple of hours, until hunger forced me down to Sonja and Bo Anders's kitchen where it smelled of sesame seeds, whole grains, and brown rice. On the way home, I stopped in Malung, bought a hamburger, and the next day I moved my blackcurrant bush to another part of my backyard.

Anita Livstrand:

The natural farming in Likenäs was enriching in several ways, with the collective, the practical cultivation skills, the philosophy, and the approach to life. We did a lot of loosening up of the soil, but I liked being on that plateau and we

Anders Björnsson holding a class in Friendly Farming, Likenäs, summer of 1971.
Photo: Roger Gustafsson.

Två ungdomar flydde storstadens omänsklighet
Nu satsar de sig själva i en ny tillvaro på landet

Men finns det livsbetingelser för dem i Bollnäs-byn Herte?

Finns det fortfarande plats för en levande landsbygd, nu i den tid kraven på effektivitet och produktivitet växer allt våldsammare? Ska vi även i framtiden kunna finna små röda stugor, med pelargonier i fönstren, och kanske ett par tre kor betande utanför på ängen här i Hälsingland? Än är inte vår landsbygd helt död, och kanske finns det ett hopp. I ett slags protest och aversion mot storstädernas omänsklighet har en ändring redan börjat skönjas. Ungdomar som hela sitt liv vistats i denna stenöken, söker sig ut på landsbygden.

Fyra kamrater till Thomas och Ulla har kommit upp till stugan ungdomarna hyr i Hertsjö, utanför Bollnäs. I köket samlas de och dricker en kopp kaffe, pratar och trivs. Långt från den allt omänskligare storstaden.

did it together. The spruce forest next to our fields was a bit of a problem, with turpentine soil around the spruces, which was not easy to grow anything in.

Anders Björnsson:

We have come so far that we work for the side of life, and then we can never recognize any authority that works for the side of death. If it has been proven that he does nothing, that he creates nothing, that he fights nothing, well then, despite his extraordinarily well-oiled jaw, he is on the other side, and he is against me. That's why I'm cheeky and tell everyone who asks what I think of [Georg] Borgström and [Hans] Palmstierna [well-known environmentalists of the era]—that they are just talkers. I have not seen that they have done anything, and because these people have not done anything, they are as Christ once said: they are false prophets.

Sonja Gransvik:

Those who had participated in Gärdesfesten and were in the social circle around Träd, Gräs och Stenar came here in the summer, and many stayed in our commune. Our house in Likenäs had been empty for a long time and didn't have electricity, but it had lots of rooms and mattresses. We fixed it up temporarily—the floor was broken in one place and there was some water damage. We rigged up a simple running water system for the summer and things become pretty cozy. We walked the four kilometers to Björnsson's farm every day and worked for free.

We only had the odd bike and Träd, Gräs och Stenar's VW bus, but there were too many of us to fit in that. We walked slowly. We weren't in a rush—that's what we wanted to get away from. During that first summer, there were so many people who wanted to come that we had to make lists.

Visitors could only stay for two weeks; otherwise, the house would be too full.

Above: Part of an article by Jan Edh, in *Hälsningslands Tidning*, November 15, 1969. English translation on p. 363.
Right: Sonja Gransvik testing the harvest, Likenäs, 1972. Photo: Roger Gustafsson.

VÄNLIG ODLING

JAG ÄR LIVET

JORD

FRI JORD

MANJORD

Foto: Thomas Trummig Roger Gustavsson

om en vänlig odling:

Våra förfäder hade ett talesätt: "Naturen ger alltid ett dukat bord". Våra egna liv har vi köpt utan fått gratis och runt omkring oss slösar naturen med liv i olika former; överallt i jorden ligger frön till växter som bara väntar på rätt betingelser för att gro. Men det finns många olika livsformer och människan kan inte bara ta för sig utan måste ständigt arbeta på att stödja de övriga arterna av liv som hör det mänskliga livet till. Liksom andra levande varelser måste hon för svara sin livsmiljö, både mot inre och yttre fiender. Den kampen har tagit sig olika uttryck genom historien men den har alltid kännetecknats av människans vilja till största möjliga frihet under de givna förutsättningar.

Kampen för frihet kan föras med olika grad av insikt om människans roll i naturen och universum. Någon gång dök den felaktiga tanken upp att människan kunde göra snabba framsteg genom att göra sig till herre över naturen. Så länge som hon endast hade enkla redskap till hjälp kunde hon bara åstadkomma begränsad skada, men nu när hon har till gång till kemi och teknik blir en felaktig teori ett hot både mot det mänskliga släktet och dess medvandrare på jorden. Därför är det nödvändigt att vi lär oss att skilja mellan två olika linjer för vårt arbete, en vänlig och en ovänlig.

Ingenting händer klart & det finns ett behov, varken i naturen eller i samhället. Men frågan är: Vilka eller vilkas behov är ledande för utvecklingen? Om enskilda egoistiska intressen tillåts göra sig gällande medför detta att utvecklingen följer den ovänliga linjen, med katastrofer och nöd som följd. Sådan är den utveckling vi ser omkring oss idag. Om utvecklingen skall följa den vänliga linjen måste majoriteten av människorna finna former för att genomföra ett samhälle där släktets eller helhetens behov blir ledande för utvecklingen. Och så kommer med säkerhet att ske, eftersom det blir allt svårare att få oss att anse att förstörelsen av den miljö vi lever i sker i vårt eget intresse.

För att uppnå ett gott liv i ett vänligt samhälle måste människan medvetet göra klart för sig vad av teknik, kemi och sociala organisationer hon verkligen behöver och lägga det övriga på historiens sophög. Och för att förstå vilka de verkliga behoven är måste hon utgå från materien och dess lagar? Det är helt orimligt att människan skulle kunna uppnå bättre villkor genom att skilja sitt tänkande från materien, ty materia är detsamma som liv. Livet är en materiell kraft. Vi kan se hur livet koncentrerar sig i materien, får den att utvecklas och röra sig.

Men inte heller den materia som ligger livlös och död för våra blickar är skild från livet. Allt omkring oss befinner sig i olika stadier av uppbyggnad eller nedbrytning. Det går inte att tänka sig en materia skild från livet, lika litet som liv skilt från materien. Men det som vi kallar "död materia" är för tillfället inte lika intensivt levande som t ex växter och djur, och det är naturligt för oss att lägga större vikt vid det som är "levande" utvecklas och rör sig inför våra blickar.

För att skaffa sig föda utan att åstadkomma olyckor för både det egna släktet och andra levande organismer måste människan iakttaga naturen sådan den är och bara göra sådant som innebär så små ingrepp som möjligt. Detta är grunden för den vänliga odlingen. Jorden är levande. Vi tar hjälp av livet i jorden, både av mikroliv, daggmaskar och "ogräs". Själva kan vi inte skapa det liv som skall hjälpa de ätliga växterna att växa utan vi får försöka använda oss av det liv som finns, inrikta oss på att skapa så goda förutsättningar som möjligt för de organismer som kan hjälpa oss.

Vi är inte de första att arbeta efter en sådan linje. Innan teknikens utveckling hade gett människan resurser att böka omkring i jorden ungefär hursomhelst var man helt enkelt tvungen att arbeta med naturen för att överleva. I vårt land är det i synnerhet det traditionella finska svedjebruket som visar många drag som man kan kalla rent vänliga. Det uppkom innan odlingen blivit styrd av ett så enskilda profitintressen och metafysiskt tänkande grundat ekonomiskt system. Nu liknar vår egen situation i mångt och mycket de finska invandrarnas; om vi vill överleva måste vi utgå från våra behov och försöka se på naturen med otvunglig blick.

Till en mänsklig miljö hör först och främst ren luft och friskt vatten. För att människan skall må bra krävs dessutom det gröna gräset, de "gröna" träden (ek, lind, lönn, alm och rönn) samt bärbuskar och fruktträd. Men för att en sådan miljö skall kunna uppnås måste var je enskild individ delta i kampen för den.

I vårt klimat finns två olika slags växtliv; det bruna livet (skogen) och det gröna (den odlade marken). Båda har sina typiska växter, djur och insekter som inte blandar sig med varandra hur som helst utan står i ett inbördes motsättning.

Det är i den gröna växtligheten som människan kan odla sin mat och därför måste hon hjälpa och försvara det gröna livet mot det bruna, som annars vill ta överhanden. Detta sker genom att skapa så goda förutsättningar som möjligt för de "gröna" växterna och deras mikroliv.

Genom att låta gräset växa och brytas ner till för vi jorden "gödning" utan att använda vare sig konstgödsel eller kodynga. Användandet av konstgödsel har visat sig medföra att växterna får dålig kvalitet och blir så svaga att de måste "skyddas" mot sjukdomar med olika gifter. Gifterna är självklart farliga både för oss själva och för den gröna mikroflora som skall hjälpa växterna att från mark och luft ta upp de ämnen de behöver.

Vi får inga särskilda "gröngödslingsväxter" utan använder de växter som kommer av sig själva. På så vis får vi naturen tillfälle att återställa den obalans som odlingen eventuellt kan ha medfört.

Vi använder behövde boskapen för att överleva men vi börjar känna till hur man lever gott på säd och grönsaker med bara en obetydlig konsumtion av kött, fisk och mjölkprodukter. När vi inte längre är beroende av kon blir livet enklare och vi kan leva många fler på samma markareal. Därför skall vi inte grunda odlingen på gödslingen med kodynga.

Vi gör heller inga särskilda komposter utan låter växtdelarna brytas ner i jordens översta skikt, precis som sker i naturen. Mikrofloran är inte densamma i jord utan som längre ned. Det är de översta organismerna som med hjälp av luftens fria syre skall bryta ned gräs och gamla växtdelar till växtnäring. Om vi plöjer ner dessa till 10 tums djup sker nedbrytningen långsamt och det naturliga livet i jorden motverkas. I stället måste vi bearbeta jorden från ytan t ex med hacka eller spadplog har.

Ingen teknik är en mängd detaljer och mycket återstår att undersöka. Så småningom måste en ny vetenskap med livet som grund växa fram. Men den praktik som hunnits med hittills visar att en odling enligt riktlinjerna ovan är möjlig och kan försörja många människor på en relativt liten yta.

Klart är det fortsatta arbetet inte kan ledas av ekonomiska intressen utan måste styras av vårt behov av en friskt levande föda ur en levande jord.

MER PRAKTISK INFORMATION OM ODLING i KOMMANDE HUVUDBLAD

Om någon har några synpunkter på innehållet i den här artikeln, vill vi gärna att hon eller han hör av sig. Skriv i så fall till: "Vänlig odling" Pl 168, 680 63 Likenäs eller till Anders Björnsson, Björnliden 68063 Likenäs.

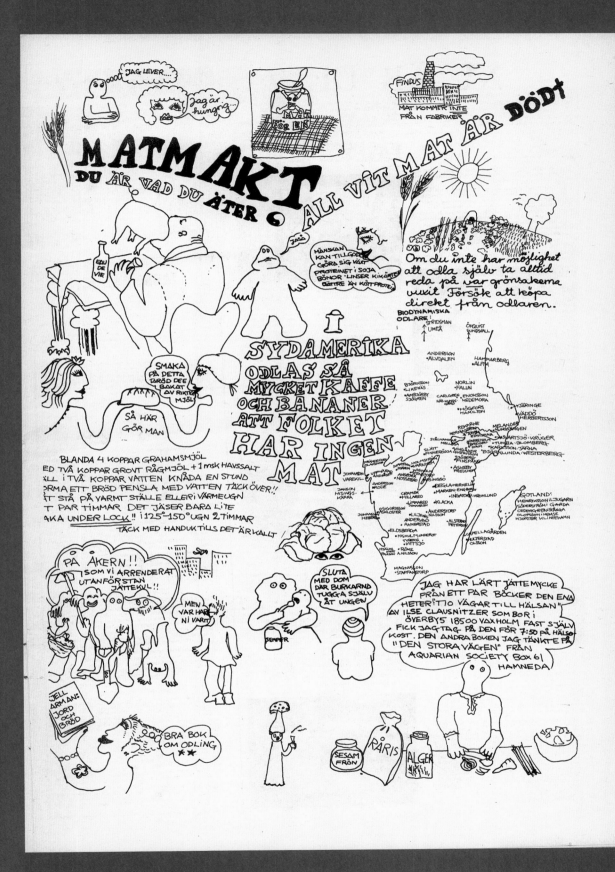

Left and above: *Huvudbladet 2*, 1972. Text by Bo Anders Persson, photographs by Thomas Mera Garts and Roger Gustafsson. English translation on pp. 364–366.

ANGREPPEN

Mot angrepp av olika slag finns en del knep man kan använda sej utav. Ett är olika örtavkok, med vilka man besprutar växterna. Genom att insekterna använder sej av luktsinnet när de angriper sjuka växter kan man på så vis lura dom. En del avkok har också en viss stimulerande inverkan på växterna.

Örtavkoken är dock bara en räddning för stunden. Det gäller hela tiden att hitta orsaken till att växten blivit sjuk och angripen samt undanröja den.

EFTERARBETET

Foto: Roger Gustavsson

SKÖRDEN

Grönsaker skördar man efterhand de mognar. Rotfrukterna ska ha varit utsatta för frost innan de skördas. Vid frostangreppen skickar de ned lagringsämnen från bladen ned i frukten, som därigenom får en högre kvalitet och mera näring samt håller sej bättre under förvaringen.

När det gäller rotfrukterna tas potatisen upp först och därefter rödbetor och kålrötter samt slutligen morötter och selleri och allra sist palsternacka. Blast och annat avfall låter man ligga kvar ute på fältet, där det får vara ytkompost.

FÖRVARINGEN

Produkterna ska förvaras så att de i största möjliga mån får samma betingelser som när de växer i jorden. Som regel kan man säga att det som växer under jorden ska förvaras under jord, t ex i jordkällare, och för det som växer ovan jord är ofta torkning en lämplig förvaringsmetod.

Efter skörden går man över fältet och jämnar till det så inga gropar och kullar finns kvar inför nästa års odling.

FÖRBEREDELSE FÖR NÄSTA ÅRS ODLING

Först och främst hackar man för nedbrytningens skull över de areaer man ska bruka nästa år. Har det hunnit bli torv eller är det ny mark som man ska förbereda för nästa år använder man den smärglade spaden till att skära av rötterna innan man hackar.

TÄCKNING

En annan metod för att bryta ny mark utan vändning av jorden och med liten arbetsinsats är att man täcker jorden med organiskt material eller kartong eller tidningspapper. Efter ett-två år har man då en odlingsbar jord.

DENNA SPADE ÄR LÄMPLIG ATT HA NÄR MAN SKALL SKÄRA AV RÖTTER UNDER MARKYTAN. DEN PASSAR ÄVEN TILL ATT GRÄVA PLANTERINGSGROPAR.

NERSMÄRGLAD KANT HELA SPADEN ÄR VÄSSAD

Vid all odling gäller det att ha ett mesta möjliga liv i jorden så att Moder Jord kan producera friska, sunda och vänliga växter åt människan. Äter människan inte produkter som är friska och sunda kan hon heller inte bli frisk och sund.

Naturen i sej är frisk och sund. Naturen tillåter ingen sjukdom hos sej. Vid odling gäller det därför att så långt det går följa naturens lagar alltså att arbeta tillsammans med naturen. Då arbetar man också för livet. Människan kan också följa andra lagar och arbeta mot naturen men då arbetar hon också mot livet.

I jorden finns ett otal olika arter av organismer, som alla har olika funktioner och också lever på olika djup och i olika miljöer nere i jorden. Varje organism är anpassad till en miljö, där den har en uppgift att fylla. En del organismer arbeta med nedbrytningen i jorden och andra arbetar med uppbyggnaden. Genom den sinnrika och helt naturliga organisation som finns av organismer i jorden stannar de nedbrytna ämnena som behövs vid ytan kvar vid ytskiktet och de ämnen som behövs längre ned i jorden forslas dit av organismer samtidigt som de ytterligare bryts ned och bearbetas och sätts ihop till nya ämnen.

Även roten är en organism och precis som alla andra organismer har rötterna utsöndringar av olika slag liknande t ex människans svettavsöndring. Dessa utsöndringar är mat för vissa bakterierkulturer, som i sin tur arbetar fram den näring som rötterna behöver. På så vis hjälper dom till att täcka varandras behov samtidigt som de fyller uppgifter för varandra. I praktiken lever de alltså i en slags symbios-samliv.

När plogen vänder jorden bringar den samtidigt kaos hos livet i jorden. Hela den sinnrika organisationen och strukturen som livet i jorden byggt upp när det fått arbeta under naturliga och vänliga förhållanden, förstörs.

De olika liven i jorden kastas huller om buller så att mikrobakterierna som hör hemma i ytan komma både en och två decimeter ned i jorden och hamna i en helt främmande miljö samtidigt som mikroliv därnerifrån hamnar i ytskiktet. På samma gång som de olika liven hamnar i helt främmande miljöer förstörs också de olika kommunikationerna mellan de olika arterna av liv. I sin främmande miljö kan de olika liven inte heller utföra sina uppgifter.

Att plöjning inte kan vara bra för jorden är helt klart när man ser på konsekvenserna för livet i jorden. Att jorden fortfarande förmår vara produktiv efter plöjning beror till största delen på den oändliga styrkan i livet självt.

För att bryta upp en gräsvall kan man använda spadrullharv.

Vi håller för närvarande på och skriver en liten stencil om Vänlig odling som vi snart är klara med.

Vänlig odling
c/o Fröet
Jakobsgatan 18
Stockholm

PLOGEN KOMMER!!

JORDEN ÄR LEVANDE JORDEN ÄR VÄNLIG OGRÄS, MASKAR OCH SMÅKRYP ÄR VÅRA VÄNNER

LITE PRAKTIK I VÄNLIG ODLING

GRÄSET ÄR GRUNDEN

SÅBÄDDEN

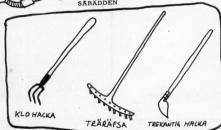

KLO HACKA TRÄRÄFSA TREKANTIG HACKA

Med klohackan jämnar man till marken så att inga gropar finns som vattnet kan samlas i. Samtidigt ristar man ur jorden ur grästorvor och hackar lätt i ytan. Denna hackning bör göras två-tre gånger innan sådden.

Sedan räfsar räfsar man ihop grästorvorna och andra svårnedbrytbara växtdelar i stängar En träräfsa är bra. Genom att dessa växtdelar samlas i sträng-

ar är det ingen risk att dom river sönder såraden vid senare hackning.

Den trekantiga hackan drar man upp sårader med. En viktig sak att tänka på är att spänna upp en lina, vilken man följer när man drar såraden. På så vis blir såraden rak, vilket underlättar vid den senare bearbetningen av jorden.

SÅDDEN

Själva sådden gör man för hand eller också använder man sej av en enkel såmaskin. Fröna myllas inte ned i jorden utan om det är en bred sårad kan man leda en skottkärra och har man en smal sårad kan man leda en cykel i själva såraden så att fröna trycks

ned i jorden. Då rotar sej fröna lättare.

Eftersom dom fröna som finns att köpa i Sverige är framodlade i varmare klimat än vi har det i det här landet bör man vänta med sådden tills vädret är varmt. Dom fröna behöver nämligen mycke värme för att kunna gro.

POTATIS

För potatissättning gräver man först med spade en fåra eller drar en fåra med trekantig hacka i marken cirka en dm djup på sin höjd. Potatisknölarna lägges i med 15-20 cm mellanrum så att groddarna pekar uppåt. Sedan fyller man igen fåran med jord och trycker till.

Potatisen kan med fördel sättas precis intill och parallelt med dom ihopräfsade strängarna. Strängarna kan man sedan kupa upp runt potatisen alltefter den växer under sommaren. Då rör man samtidigt om i strängarna så att nedbrytningen påskyndas där.

PLANTERINGEN

 — HJÄRTBLAD

Vid planteringen använder man antingen den trekantiga hackan eller den specialsmärglade spaden och gör en grop. Plantorna har man först dragit upp i drivbänk eller köpt. Vid planteringen tar man bort de två nedersta bladen, som kallas hjärtblad och -om plantan är stor- också de största bladen eftersom de kan kräva för mycket näring i det för plantan kritiska acklimatiseringsskedet. Hjärtbladen tar man bort därför att klorofyll nere i jorden inte bryts ner på vanligt vis. Istället bildas gifter.

Sedan lägger man plantan på den sluttande sidan av planterings-

gropen och täcker med jord upp till den första bladgreningen. Därefter trycker man till hårt så att plantan sitter fast ordentligt i jorden. Då ska där vara en liten grop vid själva plantan som vatten kan samlas i.

Vid den här planteringen får man en större rot och samtidigt bildar plantan ett knänär den reser på sej, vilket gör att den står stadigare.

Planteringen sker i mulet väder dels för att det då är fuktigt i luften och dels för att solstrålarna inte ska träffa plantans rötter.

OGRÄSHACKNINGEN

EN OGRÄSHACKA

Av ett gammalt sågblad, som man slipar på baksidan, kan man göra en ogräshacka. Man sätter fast sågbladet på en plåtbygel som har hållare för skaft. För att böja sågbladet värmer man det. Det är bra att ha en klack på bygeln, som sågbladet kan vila mot. Sedan sätter man fast sågbladet genom att linda ståltråd eller sätta i skruvar.

VASSAD KANT

Ogräshackningen är viktigast tiden närmast efter sådden. Man ska aldrig låta ogräsen växa så mycke att dom tar överhanden över kulturväxterna. När man hackat får ogräsen ligga kvar och tjäna som ytkompostering.

Ogräsen fyller en viktig uppgift. De är medicinalväxter som tillför vad jorden behöver av näringsämnen. Genom att ha dom som ytkompost hjälper man till att upprätthålla en riktig balans i jorden.

GALLRINGEN

Genom att vässa en matsked på ena sidan får man ett utmärkt redskap för gallring och rensning i själva såraderna.

LUCKRINGEN

Vid luckringen använder man sej av klohackan igen, som man lätt drar fram och tillbaka i själva ytan. Då kommer mer syre in i jorden och på så vis hjälps livet i jorden. Har man dåligt liv i jorden luckrar man så fort en skorpa bildats på markytan.

Left and above: *Huvudbladet* 3, 1972. Text by Bo Anders Persson, photographs and drawings by Roger Gustafsson.
English translation on pp. 367–370.

Twenty people at a time was the limit, after that, there weren't enough beds for everyone. Eventually, more communes were formed by young people who moved here.

Arne Ericsson:

A varied mix of people came to Likenäs, not just us from the band. Some did more, others did less. We had common meals with macrobiotic food. Klarälven ["the clear river," the longest in Scandinavia] was just twenty or thirty meters away, it

was great. Björnsson was an amazing guy that explained, explained, and explained: about, among other things, the turpentine that seeped into the fields from the forests and about cultivation without chemicals. He was known for his farming all over the country.

Anders Björnsson:

Man can create the highest form of freedom for himself and his kind, both for the individual and for all of humankind, if he bases his theory of development on kindness together with nature. We can never win because we are a product, a material product of the environment, of matter and all this, and we can never defeat the basic factor of where we come from and where we belong.

To be able to have the opportunity to develop a friendly society, we must move forward in a friendly manner, we must find a friendly way, ceaselessly; regardless of how development will happen, it must be friendly.

Hans-Göran Toresson:
brev till Thomas Mera Gartz, June 13, 1972
We have finished sowing everything except rutabaga, which we will do last of all. Today it is raining, otherwise, we would start planting cabbage. We are not quite done with the potato planting yet. A crisis has shaken us in recent days. It started when, without asking permission, we made two 25-liter jugs of dandelion wine with bread yeast and put them in the old cottage--and that's the same as Lura. Karin [Björnsson] got very angry because everyone is after us. When Anders [Björnsson] made real wine with wine

yeast several years ago, people reported him so he was imprisoned for several days before the police had to release him. And the fact that that day or the day before, the rumor had reached the village that the people who live in Lillängen (in the Samlevnad commune), which is on the other side of the river opposite Likenäs, have been stealing from the store. As it happened, a few of us were using the phone a lot in the greenhouse as well. All this made Karin very annoyed with us, and to save the situation, Anders gave us a serious talking to for several hours. I wasn't there then, but they said he was shaking. He talked about us having to take responsibility--he couldn't take responsibility for us. We had a serious discussion about it at the house, and then we poured out the dandelion wine.... There's a lot of intrigue going on here now. It is interesting to be here. But you have to be careful.

Thomas Tidholm:
In the summers, sometimes people from Värmland came to us in Hälsingland [northeast of Värmland]. They had been to Träd, Gräs och Stenar in Likenäs and

Left: Anders Björnsson and Jon Klingberg. Photo: Roger Gustafsson.
Above: Sowing the seed. Sonja Gransvik and Greta Lindholm sow and Bo Anders Persson and Jon Klingberg pack the soil with a wheelbarrow, while Greta's son Niklas looks on. Photo: Roger Gustafsson.

learned how to farm. It was all done according to strict principles. For example, you could cultivate crops in sand that was covered with newspapers. It was called Friendly Farming. Then they asked us what kind of farming we did. "Well, we have normal farming," we said. We learned from a farmer who was our neighbor: we plowed with horses, kept sheep, and fertilized with sheep shit. Our vegetable patch grew like hell. We lived on forest soil and at first, we had to make it more fertile, and add more fertilizer. It takes time to better soil. From what I understood they weren't allowed to use fertilizers. Why make things harder for yourself?

Torbjörn Abelli
Jönköpings-Posten, March 25, 1972
Grains and vegetables are the most important part of the diet. We think meat is unnecessary. We buy our food directly from farmers or grow them ourselves on a farm in Värmland. Our food isn't nontoxic, it cannot be achieved as the situation is now, but they are low-toxic. We have not added any toxins to it.

Smålands Folkblad, March 21, 1972
Träd, Gräs och Stenar is a somewhat different Swedish pop group. They don't just sing and play, at their performances, they also serve "friendly food," i.e., grains and vegetables that haven't been treated with nitrates.... The reason that the group wants to serve

Anders Björnsson (with pitchfork) in action in the potato field during a Friendly Farming class.

"friendly food" in connection with their gigs is that they feel that the food enhances the effect of their music. Food and music are to a large extent about the same things, they say, namely, the condition of man. The food they serve is at cost price, which rarely is over one krona.

Jakob Sjöholm:

> We brought food for our gigs. It was Sonja Gransvik and Ulla Berglund, and sometimes one or two guys that cooked, made soups and baked bread, which was part of the show. In the beginning the food was free, but we ended up running out of money, so we had to start charging cost price.

Strengnäs Tidning, June 19, 1972

Now Bo Anders has settled, together with a group of likeminded people, in the Klarälv valley in Värmland .... Everyone in the commune, around fifteen in all, is completely set on breaking the "toxic trend." They care for the crops together. But the project is still in its early days, and can't yield enough for them to make a living. That is why they have to take on more work.... Bo Anders as well as a few others in the commune are part of the pop group Träd, Gräs och Stenar, and they bring home money to the household by playing gigs. Others run a restaurant in Stockholm, where they also put their theories into practice. There are no vegetables treated with pesticides or artificially colored foods served there.

FRÖET

God, fullvärdig, billig mat

Säd och grönsaker
Hembakat fullkorns-
bröd med örtte

Naturvänligt odlat

ÖPPET vardagar 11–18
lördagar 12–15

Jakobsgatan 18

Left: Torbjörn Abelli in the vegetable garden, 1971. Photo: Roger Gustafsson.
Above: Flyer for the restaurant Fröet [The Seed], in Stockholm, 1971. Design: Sonja Gransvik. English translation on p. 370.

Participants in the Friendly Farming course on a lunch break.
Among others: Thomas Mera Gartz, Rolf Strindberg,
Lotta Lagerkrantz, Sonja Gransvik, Roger Gustafsson, and
Arne Ericsson, Likenäs, 1971. Photo: Bo Anders Persson
(with Roger Gustafsson's camera).

DE NYA UTVANDRARNA–2

Storstadsungdom blir glesbygdens bönder!

Av NIC NORBERG.   Foto: BERTIL BÄCK

Gruppen ungdomar kom från Stockholm till byn Likenäs i Värmland drivna av ett brinnande intresse, men utan kunskaper.

Above: Article from *Året Runt*, July 24, 1972. From left: Unknown, Bo Anders Persson, Peter Svernby, Sonja Gransvik, Roger Gustafsson, Anders Björnsson, Torbjörn Abelli, Nunna Ekdahl, and Isa Tibbling, in front of the Bäckström farmstead. Photo: Bertil Bäck.
English translation on p. 370.

Sonja Gransvik:

Ulla—Mera Gartz's girlfriend—and I took the initiative to start up a kitchen with vegetarian meals. Several people joined as it grew. We started Fröet the same year that we first moved to Värmland, the summer of 1971. Fröet was a logical continuation of Gärdesfesten and everything around Träden's gigs. We had already been cooking and bringing bread and herbal tea to several gigs. The food wasn't always that great. We made our own sourdough bread that turned out extremely tough, we hadn't really gotten the proofing right just yet.

But it was healthy. Jakobsgatan is a little sidestreet from Drottninggatan, not far from Rosenbad [the seat of the Swedish government] in the middle of the city. The Child Welfare Agency, which also ran the multi-activity center Gamla Bro, shut down, and we saw our chance. We had a task force after the first Gärdesfesten 1970 that could rent the space.

It was to primarily be a space for meeting and gathering, but then Ulla and I came up with the idea of Fröet, which became a permanent place for what we were doing. After that, everything happened quickly.

Above: Interior of the Bäckströmska gården. Photo: Bo Anders Persson.

273

Someone's mom worked at Gustavsberg's porcelain factory and got us plates and cups from their second sorting for free. We got a free phone, scouring soap, regular soap, and dishwashing liquid. And free rent! That's not possible today. Actually, it was quite unbelievable even then, but the counterculture could still weasel its way to the central parts of the city. Barnavårdsmyndigheten [the child welfare agency] had an idea that Fröet should be some kind of youth activity center, and for many youngsters, hippies and the like, it became a meeting place. Maybe that's why the agency helped us with equipment and finances. We had a meeting with Hälsovårdsnämnden [the board of health], and since we weren't going to use dairy, meat, or fish products, getting a permit was easy.

We had a simple kitchen, basically just a regular stove and sink. We kept the food in the cooler basement. We bought sacks of rice and vegetables, and cooked these huge stews and baked our own bread that was still rock hard. It wasn't only friends, but we had guests from Riksdagen, as well as the more tripped-out clientele, some pretty strung out. We were open from eleven to six, and the vegan lunch was central. We served simple, good food. We had Fröet from the spring of 1971 to 1973. That's when Ulla traveled to India, and when she came back Fröet was closed. When I got pregnant I couldn't work the stove anymore; I moved to Värmland permanently and we let others take over the business. The idea was that Fröet would be self-run, and that different people could work there.

Right: Bo Anders Persson weeding the crops, 1971.
Photo: Roger Gustafsson.

...Or...
...2...

...what did you
look like Torbjörn
...hmm you
looked like a
version...of
me...but with a
beard and the same
long hair...as I
have...

...but you
were a guy, and
had a FLY on
your pants....
...and you
were older...
five years...
or was it fifty...
doesn't really
matter...
anymore

CHAPTER 13

A Memory

by Kristina Abelli Elander

...men då för femtio... eller va det hundra år sen...
... gjorde det skillnad ...
...jag hatar att spela... flöjt...
...åh...det som e så roligt... det e ju grunden för.... allt musicerande...
Pffiuu...
ffiuu-
Pe...fi-
Pfiuuuu
...Du Torbjörn... VA JU STOR...å kunde... ...VÄLJA...
...jag tror att BAS passar mej...
...jag bodde i en by i Danmark... du bodde i STORSTAN...
... ett HAV... skiljde oss åt...
STHLM
SVDALA
DNMRK
...jag...
...du... ...Torbjörn
KBHVN
MLÖ
GRMNY

... me and my sister ... saw ... pictures of you guys ... in the Press ... and we were so PROUD ... for the family ... finally someone ... who was doing something ... that made sense ...

[Newspaper headlines: *Dagens Nyheter*— "The New Swedish Wave . . . Person Sound." *See and Hear* — "Royalty of the Week / Princess Desiré is a success at the court / 'My advice is to always be polite'"]

... I had a crush on Jakob Sjöholm ... at a very LARGE ... distance ...

So Jakob works at GUL&BLÅ ...

... so does EVERYONE cool ...

We had moved to Sweden now . . . to the big City . . . STHLM . . .

... let's go in ...

... are you insane ... ... that's humiliating ...

... min nya klass... humanistisk... kändes trist... jag hade ... liksom ... halkat utanför ... jag kände inte dom ... å dom kände inte mig ...
...vi drar till Corso...
...Bobadilla ikväll va´...
...STHLM i Sverige va helt annorlunda än Tommerup i Danmark ... här red man inte barbacka på grannpojkens Häst... på ÅKERN...
... vi knatar å tar en ... java å surrar lite...
...jussta rattar...
...å kollar in jussta snubbar...
Haru nån deg ra´
Äh täpp till truten va...
Tja goding Hur lirare´
..Hänkaru´ på en fika ..å ja e sugen på lite röka...
... ÄH ... tå å pys va... ...sabla dönickar...
...här fanns det UNGDOMSKULTUR ... med makt-faktor ... musiken blev en statusgrej ... vem är JAG... ...vem vill jag va...
...kolla... Beatles senaste...
Wow... juste... skaru tjacka´n..
BEATLES
...Stones e´ häftigare

... men jag visste ... jag hade iallafall en Stor-Kusin ...
... å han va BALL ..... å hans kompisar VA HELBALLA ...
... å dom e ... kända ... i Storstan ... STHLM ... jag ... e ...
..... STOLT ... över dig ..... kusin Torbjörn som ...
... spelar bas ... som har långt hår och gör ...
... som du vill ....
SOV GOTT! ROSE-MARIE
KILROY WAS NEVER HERE
HÖKEN

. . . admittedly
I was a bit more
Disco . . . but the
alternative
far-out stuff
started to slowly win
me over . . .

. . . what kind
of music do
you dig . . .

. . . um . . .
I have . . .
a broad
music taste . . .

. . . days spent
at my desk in
school were
mindnumbing . . .
I passed the
time by drawing
caricatures of the
teachers and
daydreaming . . .

. . . stop
chatting
. . . you over
there . . .

. . . it looks
like him,
doesn't it . . .

. . . for
sure . . .

...få kolla'ra' ....du ...seru' han där...han me håret å brillorna...
...tänk att nu går munnen på henne IGEN... ...koncentration... ...TACK....ja ...du ...KRISTINA...
...e' hmm...
...de e Torbjörn... ...Torbjörn Abelli... han spelar bas...
...jassåʼru'...
...Torbjörn e min mammas brors äldsta SON... Torbjörn å ja e riktiga ...släkt......
...säger du det du... Torbjörn e' faktiskt min pappas brallas äldsta son... vi ...känner varann...
...Åh... ...vi e... ...kusiner...
Träd Gräs och Stenar

...men vad har jag för minnen av dig Torbjörn å .... Träden... egentligen ...
...ska vi gå på gärdesfestivalen nu i Helgen....
...Träden spelar...
...Va spelar... ...Träden...
...Vi går dit...
...era spelningar va långa... långa... ibland flöt det... ofta brötade det ihop sig... sen rann det på fin-fint igen... för att sen komma i oflyt... folk digga å dansa... i timmar... i dagar... nätterna igenom... i månader... År... genom årtionden...
...Äh...det går faen inte att dansa till...Det Här....
....Get into The Groove... relax..... slappna av.... ta're chill....
ABBA RULES
ABBA 4-EVER

. . . then you became
. . . BIG IN JAPAN
. . . music nerds in
Osaka and Tokyo
. . . the USA
. . . had started
collecting your
records . . .

... so you're
related to Torbjörn
in T, G & S...
got any old
original records
you wanna get
rid of ...
I'll pay ...

... yeah ...
well ... no
... I gave away
all the records
... to a friend's
daughter ...

. . . you were flying
back and forth all
over the world . . .

... Whaaat!
... Träden's also
... they are
... CLASSIC

... yeah
... yes
... probably ...

...vi sågs ibland på släktens alla barnkalas... ditt hår va kortare nu... å ditt skägg mer välansat ...än sist...
...krissan... hur gåre me konsten....
...jorå... det tuffar på...
Pressbyrån
FRUÄNGEN
KEBAB
...nåra utställningar på...g...
...jorå det e Busy Bee.... för hela slanten...
...du kunde ALLT om datorer... det gjorde inte jag...
bye the Way... kan du Hjälpa mej me min gamla PC... ....den e hopplös....
...hm...jag e väl mest MAC... men visst... jag kan kolla igenom den...
...jamen... kanoners...

... en sommar i Sörmland ... hos min kusin Bissa ... ... din syster ... i Öllösa ... kom det fin-främmande ...
Bo Anders kommer över några dar ... han ska hjälpa oss med musiken till vår nya föreställning
... ojda ... hoppsan ...
... Kom Auymi vi kollar in det här gamla pianot ...
... nu ere LUNCH ...
... ta fram svartpepparn ... Bo Anders gillar svartpeppar ...

... sen spelade Bo-Anders & Auymi piano å gitarr hela veckan... jag tror Bo-Anders tyckte de va roligast att spela me Auymi... att leka å improvisera

... Nu ere' Kvällsmat...

... Tar fram Svartpeppan ... Bo Anders vill ha Svartpeppar...

... efter sommaren nådde nyheten även mina öron ...

... jodu ... Auymi har börjat spela me några kompisar... dom har... bildat band...

.. wow... vicken tuffing hon e Auymi... hon e väl bara .... tio... tolv...

...ibland stötte jag på din bandkollega... trummisen ...Thomas Mera Gark här i Tallis*...
...men gamla Krissan... vad gör DU HÄR
...jamen jag bor här... vad gör DU HÄR...
...jag jobbar här... ...me ungdomar...
...ojdå...
FB
...som en dag va Thomas inte där... på sin plats med ungdomarna...
...men var e Thomas...
...vet du inte... ...han dog... inatt...
*

CHAPTER 14

Rock för kropp och själ

Rock för kropp och själ

Stefan Kinell
Västerbottens-Kuriren, April 1, 1972
Rock för kropp och själ [Rock for Body and Soul] is
the name of Träd, Gräs och Stenar's new LP. And
it's in fact accurate. TGS plays music that goes
straight into your body, from your feet and up,
and when it reaches the brain it feels like riding
on a mighty tidal wave. You can view Träd, Gräs
och Stenar in two ways. As a regular "pop band."
As such, they are pretty bad, have no sense of
variation and are bad musicians. One can also see
them as symbols of the growing counterculture.
Then they are fantastic. [The song] "Rock för kropp
och själ," which takes up the entire B side, was
recorded in Vindeln last summer. It starts out
carefully and softly and then intensifies to then
almost fade away until it starts to swell again
becoming a huge wave that sweeps away everything
except what exists in the present.

Kjell Å
Dala-Demokraten, April 10, 1972
TGS lyrics are warm and full of humanity. They express
a kind of nostalgic despair over the disappearance
of farming culture and have an appeal: live healthy,
eat healthy, and be kind to each other. Looking at TGS
from a musical perspective they have a routine and an
interplay that over the years has been developed to
perfection. This record definitely proves that.

Jakob Sjöholm:

> The songs on *Rock för kropp och själ*
> had a more traditional structure, except
> the B side [a live recording of the title
> track] from Vindelälven. This wasn't due
> to speculative purposes, it was what we
> wanted. We played a few songs by the
> Stones and Dylan that were combined with
> our own. When we played the songs live,

Previous spread: Träd, Gräs och Stenar in Likenäs, 1971. Photo: Jonas Wikander.
Left: Artwork for *Djungelns lag*. Tall, 1972 (Tall 1). Cover: Gabi Björnstrand.

for example, "I ljuset av din dag"
["In the Light of Your Day"] it had a
certain structure, but there were always
free improvisational parts as well. That
made the songs longer and they felt
bigger. We had a hard time dealing with
the recording situation. Mera, who was a
great musician, sometimes found it hard
to record in a studio, and that went for the
rest of the band as well. It was something
about the form, that there were artistic
demands in place around the recording.
Things felt forced and we couldn't move
on. Our music is much better when we let
all of that go and a free flow is created.
That's our strength.

Anders Lind:

With *Rock för kropp och själ*, we recorded
on Katarinavägen [a street on Södermalm
island in central Stockholm] with close
mics on the instruments. Bo Anders wasn't
happy with the record for many reasons.
It didn't sound as cool, which I can agree

with. Musically, the spark was weaker. Bo
Anders also wasn't happy with the studio
situation. He realized that Träd, Gräs och
Stenar shouldn't record in a studio. Maybe
everyone else already knew that, but that's
when I discovered it. That's why the last
record, *Rock för kropp och själ*, sounds the
way it does.

If you listen to the first side, it's not
very good as far as sound engineering goes.
The sound is too dry. Decibel's studio
was soundproofed, so the album became
flat. The studio has since been rebuilt and
become much more alive.

Bo Anders Persson (Gärdesfesten 1970):

[Träd, Gräs och Stenar have just played
"In kommer Gösta," in which the titular
figure asks repeatedly for coffee] That
was a greeting to all of you from Torekov
in Skåne [a fishing village in southern
Sweden] . . . Torekov. But really, we're not
that into coffee. In song, you can allow
yourself all kinds of things.

Above and right: Front and back cover, and inner sleeve, of *Rock för kropp och själ*. Silence, 1972 (SRS 4608). English translation on pp. 371–375.

Erik Helmerson
Svenska Dagbladet, 8 mar 2010

Philemon Arthur and the Dung ... the progg band from Skåne that for 40 years has eluded the Swedish music scene. Who were/are they? Brothers Thomas and Michael Wiehe? Parts of bands like Risken Finns or Träd, Gräs & Stenar? Two completely unknown people from Skåne?

Philemon Arthur: (letter, June 2017)

It happened one cold February night at around 9 PM, Sveriges Radio played music that I thought I recognized, but I had never heard it before. It rocked and it swayed! The energy flowed to my body, and feelings of joy overtook me. They were songs from *Sov gott Rose-Marie* by International Harvester—I realized I had been waiting for this! I couldn't help but exclaim a jubilant profanity: "That was!" But I skipped over the last few words to not get any points deducted. To make a short story long, I got the LP and implemented the around-the-clock method on my outstanding (well) stereo system. The record got better and better and the stereo became worse and worse. Fan letters were written to International Harvester, who immediately changed their name to Harvester for some reason. A new letter was sent and a tape reel with nonsensical songs was enclosed. Then they changed their name to Träd, Gräs och Stenar. One can only wonder. Good name anyway! The response took a while so my tin-can colleague and I assumed that we had humiliated ourselves by sending nonsense from Skåne on tape. But it turned out to be simply the chronology that differs between Stockholm and Skåne. Finally, a letter arrived from Bo Anders Persson. He informed me that he had written a letter to me, but that he could not find it at the moment. That letter never appeared, but other letters from Persson and also Torbjörn Abelli did. We tried to meet from time to time. Without much success. It was either that I couldn't meet, or that I didn't dare to meet. Once, when Träd, Gräs och Stenar passed through the place where I was going to school, we almost saw each other. But that particular evening I was invited, yes almost forced, to play cards with "good" friends. Johnnie

Walker was also going to come. It turned out that JW and I didn't get along at all. I woke up at home with a freight train in my head, someone else's breath, and a hazy memory. The next day I found the following note in my mailbox:

"Hi. We were here but you seem to be living somewhere else (we are on our way to Gothenburg from Copenhagen), so we'll have to see you another time. Bo Anders, Thomas, Torbjörn."

Many years later, when Träd, Gräs och Stenar quit playing and then to many people's delight was resurrected, there was a short meeting after all. Abelli and yours truly had agreed via email to exchange CDs with one another when the band that I now have mentioned many times was playing at a music festival "way out south," that is, somewhere in Småland. Torbjörn brought *Pärson Sound* and I brought *Musikens historia del 1 och 2* [a 1992 album by Philemon Arthur and the Dung]. Abelli was easy to spot, tall with a white hat, and he was also, conveniently enough, just leaving the stage area. I walked up to him, nodded and handed him the CD. Abelli smiled, got his CDs out, and like two agents we swapped them quickly, looked in different directions, maybe said, "Have a good one" and went our separate ways. "We should hang out sometime," Torbjörn later said. Yes, we should have! Hugs, Philemon.

Above: Träd, Gräs och Stenar in front of the gas station in Likenäs, 1971. Photo: Jonas Wikander.
Right: Philemon Arthur and the Dung's Grammis [Swedish music award]—winning LP in the category "Group Production of the Year." Silence, 1972 (SRS 4607).

Anders Lind:

Bo Anders was crushed. He had been working and working and then these fuckers [Philemon Arthur and the Dung] **show up and do everything much better.**

Henrik Salander
Dagens Nyheter, March 21, 1972

Rock för kropp och själ contains simple music, the kind you can make yourself with a few guitars and rhythm instruments. One part is based on singalongs and repetitions; most of it is sound-engineered and recorded poorly, probably on purpose. The instruments are from pop music, but the music itself is "boundless" or unidentifiable. The lyrics are evocative in a naive way. Sure, it can be fun to play like this on your own, but on record, it's minimally interesting.

Benny Persson
Upsala Nya Tidning, April 15, 1972

When Bo Anders Persson in Träd, Gräs och Stenar declared "the music of the people," he started a musical development in Sweden that has become significant. The so-called folk-fest music has become common even on LPs. The only problem is that this kind of music with noncommercial interests relies so heavily on community experiences and active audience participation that it doesn't work very well on record. Unfortunately, this also applies to Träd, Gräs och Stenar's new LP--*Rock för kropp och själ* (Silence). For several weeks, I have tried to spend time with the music, and it's not at all the same thing as sitting in the green grass during a festival. The title track--a long piece of creeping music that takes up the entire B side--becomes dead if one can't identify with it. Naturally, this is a personal reaction that many will view as wrong. The rest of the album is more generous, although you do have to work hard.... For many people, Träd, Gräs och Stenar appear to be pure genius, while some label them as nonsense. Everyone should at least listen to them. "Ta det lugnt och lycka till" ["Take it easy and good luck"], as the record cover says.

Jakob Sjöholm:

I got to know this guy named Per Odeltorp that was renting a room up on Östermalm. When we had gotten to know each other, he moved in with me on Jungfrugatan. Per was a music nerd and asked if he could record us. I talked to the others in the band and introduced Per to them. The first time he came along was probably when we played at Medborgarhuset [a multi-activity center] **in Stockholm. Then he started recording us with his Revox tape recorder and his two silver microphones, which then became the two albums for our "Tall" label,** *Djungelns lag* **and** *Mors mors***. The others in the band weren't involved with it so much; it was mostly Per's and my project. The Tall albums have meant a lot to the band, even though many thought that it was strange that we released them ourselves—there wasn't a label behind it. They sounded like shit. That was par for the course with most of what we did.**

Anders Lind:

We were at Jungfrugatan, listening and talking. We were there to take part in all that Per Odeltorp had recorded with Träd, Gräs och Stenar. The warm and alive music is on all the Tall recordings. The first Tall record came very soon after *Rock för kropp och själ***. Per and Jakob had already started on it when we were working on the record for** [the label] **Silence.**

Träd, Gräs och Stenar är namnet på ett musiksällskap som har strukit
land och rike runt sedan hösten -69. Vi spelar elektriskt förstärkt
svensk folkrock och populärmusik, och ibland litet folkmusik efter
Joell Jansson, spelmannen. Sättningen är i regel två gitarrer, elpiano
bas och trummor.
Vi tror att Moder Jord är vår verkliga moder. Sten, vatten, luft,
"eld" (energi), jord, växter är vad våra kroppar är framvuxna ur.
Alla livsformer som frambringat oss är våra föräldrar tillsammans med
dem som frambringar oss just nu. Träd, Gräs, och Stenar är därför ett
annat namn för människor. Alla livsformer nu levande med oss i skapelsen är våra släktingar och syskon. Skapelsen är en Helhet där ingen är
herre, utan alla är levande i universom, och universum är levande i oss.

Ekonomins ägare och deras köpta hjälpredor har tvingat oss in i städerna
för att göra tjänst vid deras maskiner och kontor. För gick människorna
godvilligt med på detta men nu börjar de se att det mitt i det "demo-
kratiska samhället finns ett nytt slaveri, mitt i "välfärden" en ny
slum. Maten kommer från affärerna i livlösa förpackningar, förgiftad
av olämpliglödling och av livsmedelsindustrins behandling och ibland
stulen till vrakpriser från länder iAfrika och Asien som skulle behövt
den själva, eller behövt använda samma jord till att odla något annat.
Våra egna åkrar behandlas med biprodukter från den kemiska industrin i
Tyskland och USA och avfallet från vårt leverne förgiftar luft och vatten.
Och ändå blir det inte mycket pengar kvar när månadshyran är betald.
Ett sådant samhälle hotar till slut livet självt, både människans liv
ochlivet hos de övriga organismerna i luft, jord och vatten. I den kamp
som uppstår när vi börjar försvara vår livsmiljö måste vi lyfta bort
herrarna över våra huvuden och förändra världen för att leva med naturen
istället föratt söka behärska den. Först då kan det mänskliga vetandet
användas för att skapa ett gott liv åt människan i ett vänligt samhälle.
Traditionella kunskaper, där de inte utrotats under trycket från imperi-
alismen, kommer att användas tillsammans med de nya. Människan får medvetet ta vad hon behöver och lägga allt onödigt på historiens sophög. Allt

är inte progressivt som glimmar. En ny kultur kommer att skapas, det
är nödvändigt, tillsammans med en ny vetenskap med livet och dess villkor som grundval.

Medan kunskaperna om detta växer fram ska vi sjunga våra sånger och spela vår musik så länge det är möjligt. När tiderna blir hårda får vi
använda de kunskaper vi har för att överleva, som alla andra. Men något
stort och samtidigt mycket alldagligt sker bland människorna. Kanske
kommer vi för första gången i historien att förstå på vilka villkor man
kommer från nödvändighetens rike till frihetens. Och då är det intressant
att leva.

Träd, Gräs och Stenar

Torbjörn Abelli bas
Arne Ericsson elpiano
Thomas Gartz trummor
Bo Anders Persson och Jacop Sjöholm gitarrer

Torbjörn Abelli's speaker, 1970.

Bo Anders Persson's
homemade guitar, 1967.
The neck and body are in
one piece.

Jakob Sjöholm's homemade
electric guitar, 1969.

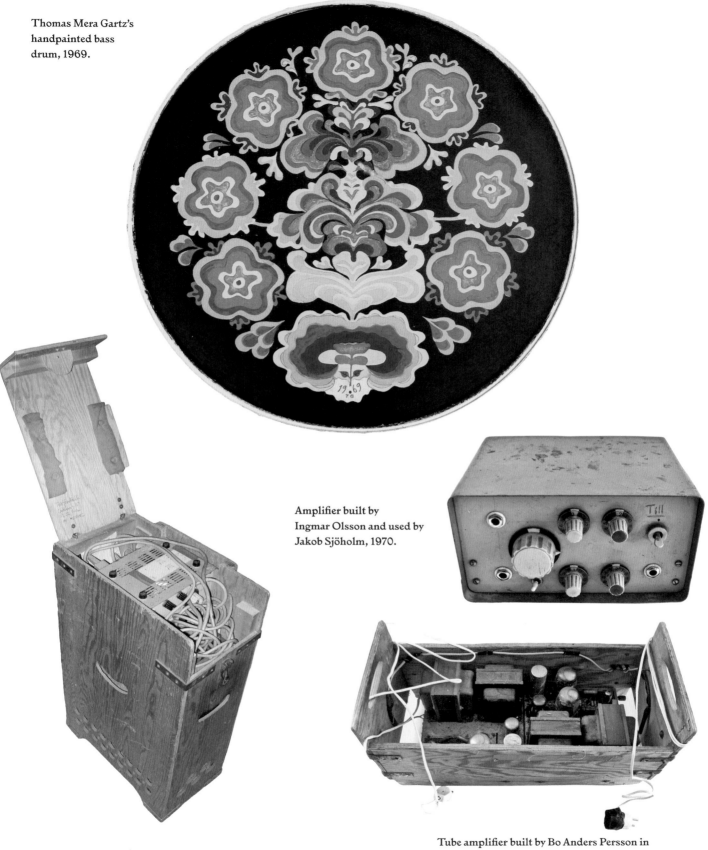

Thomas Mera Gartz's handpainted bass drum, 1969.

Amplifier built by Ingmar Olsson and used by Jakob Sjöholm, 1970.

Torbjörn Abelli's amplifier, 1970.

Tube amplifier built by Bo Anders Persson in homemade box, 1969. All photos: Håkan Agnsäter.

Sören Erlandsson
Aftonbladet, May 28, 1972

Djungelns lag [Law of the Jungle] was recorded during the group's tours last year. At the tape recorder was Per Gud. The songs on the album are pretty long, around ten minutes, sometimes well-known melodies float in where you least expect them and with no guidance from the song title such as "Drammen Export." Tidigt om Morgonen ["Early in the Morning"] is clearly the number one song. Thomas Gartz sings and it feels as if he is placing convex and concave pieces of glass in a row, tying the glasses together with the help of TGS's muffled sound, bringing out a very finely distributed spread of emotions that are present early in the morning.

Below: Träd, Gräs och Stenar playing "Hälsa Ulla" at Malmberget's youth center, 1971. Photo: Dan Engman.
Right: Front and back cover of *Mors, mors*. Tall, 1973 (Tall 2). Cover: Channa Bankier.

Jakob Sjöholm:

One evening in December, sitting in an apartment on Söder. The second Tall record, *Mors mors* [Hey Hey], was just finished, but there had been a misprint on the cover. The songs were in the wrong order, and we were rewriting and redrawing every cover by hand, about a thousand records all in all. Suddenly, I saw two men quietly sneaking into the apartment. After them five or six more followed. It turned out that we were in the middle of a police raid, because Per dealt grass, lots of grass. They turned the whole place upside down, and we were hastily driven to the jail in Sollentuna. I knew Per was a dealer, but I had nothing to do with it. I was in custody for four days at least and in the interrogations, they pressured me to confess. But it was a misunderstanding and they finally let me go. Maybe it was Per that told them how things really were. Per was convicted and went to prison—that was super hard.

CHAPTER 15

End of the Road

End of the Road

Arne Ericsson:

We became a regular band when we became Träd, Gräs och Stenar. We became so niche that those who booked us knew what they were getting. That wouldn't have been the case with International Harvester; then, there was a bit of nice unpredictability. During our shows as Träd, Gräs och Stenar, the same kind of people came, but I didn't feel the expansion to the audience. They were more just sitting down and nodding. I feel that we lost something. At the end of my time in the band, something strange happened with the music, a strange combustion. It felt as if we had reached the end of the road. "We can't give more." The playing became more forceful, but with less content. I remember that I didn't show up to a gig in Copenhagen. I was the first to leave the band. It was 1972 and I couldn't do it anymore.

Jakob Sjöholm:

Arne was on the outskirts. He was pretty quiet and shy. Suddenly he stopped coming to the gigs. We were so focused on our shows and never talked about how Arne stopped coming. It's sad and I can't really explain why it was that way. Sten Bergman joined when Arne quit. Sten lived up in the commune in Likenäs and he was there for the gigs at the UN Environmental Conference and at Gamla Bro. He didn't play like Arne, the sound was different, but he fit in well with our songs. Sten had strong opinions on how he wanted things musically, but not in an unsympathetic way. He was involved with starting Fläsket Brinner [an instrumental progg band formed in 1970], and their music wasn't far from ours. Playing with Sten was fun, but he was only in the band for a few months. We needed to change and we needed a new member.

Previous spread: Thomas Mera Gartz and Torbjörn Abelli, Northern Värmland, 1972. Photo: Okänd.
Left: Arne Ericsson and Jakob Sjöholm, Malmberget's youth center, 1971. Photo: Dan Engman.

Sonja Gransvik:

> The band could have continued to play in Värmland but it would have been all acoustic—anything else was impossible. There wasn't any electricity. We sang together, which you can hear on their last studio album. The second summer in Värmland, 1972, meant the end of Träd, Gräs och Stenar. Bo Anders was completely absorbed by farming and wanted to spend time with Björnsson. I became pregnant by Bo Anders but we had actually separated by then. That was really hard. So I decided to stay in Värmland. Bo Anders, who had gone back to the city in the fall, came back and moved in nearby.

Bo Anders Persson:

> We had our last gigs in the summer of 1972 when my daughter Klara was born. Mera was sick of everything. I had shifted my focus to farming. I thought it would be possible to combine the two but time caught up to me. We were forced to decide how we wanted to live. With having a family and all that, it became too much. We came to a mature decision.

Jakob Sjöholm:

> We felt that there were requirements from the audience and from ourselves before every gig. We wanted it to be intense, flipped out and full of ecstasy. That was exhausting. Especially for Mera, who really wanted to have that explosive experience. He was the one to say stop when he couldn't do it any longer. We used to play four to five gigs a week, and in the middle of it, Mera said that this would be the last time. A few days later it was over. There was an enormous void.

Right: Jon and Klara doing the high jump and playing out on the farmyard in Totjärnsberg, 1974. Photo: Bo Anders Persson.

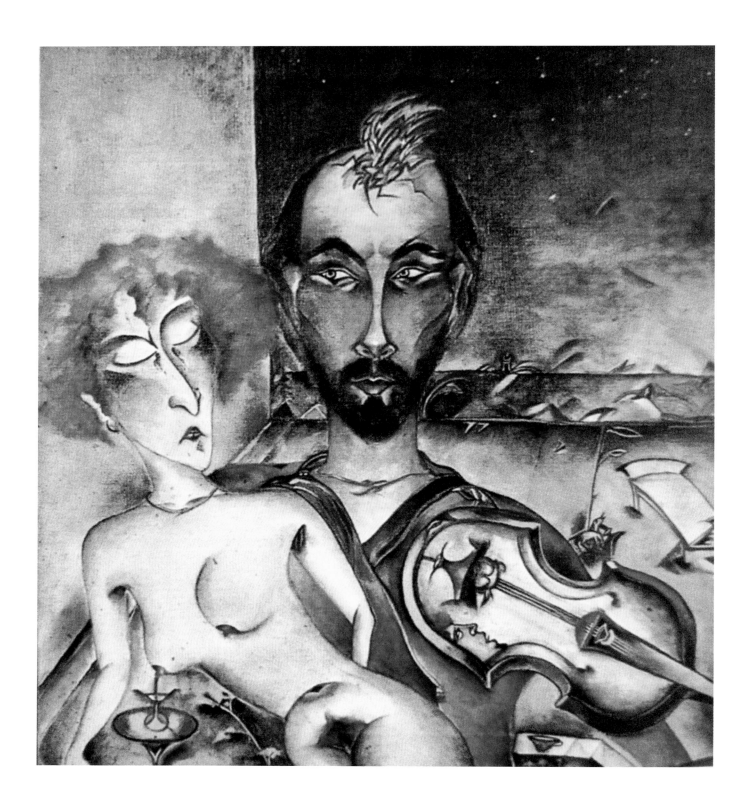

Thomas Mera Gartz:

We had more or less burned ourselves out
. . . . Working intensely for five years—
three, four, five-hour gigs several times a
week. It wasn't possible any longer.

Torbjörn Abelli:

It was like we were in a constant Saturday
bubble, from party to party, and at each
party, there was an expectation that we'd
whip up the mood further so that we would

"The band could have continued to play in Värmland but it would have been all acoustic—anything else was impossible. There wasn't any electricity."

Sonja Gransvik

lose our heads. Things should spin so you got high. It was combustive; you can't do that week after week, year in and year out. In July 1972, we stood on the gravel outside Falun prison and had finished our last gig. We made our somber goodbyes and said that we would meet again sometime.

Aftonbladet, December 27, 1972

Träd, Gräs och Stenar--which under the name International Harvester started the Swedish pop wave--is no more. Today, the guys are playing separately. Thanks for groundbreaking work and five years of good music.

Bo Anders Persson:

Even though music has its own power, that exists as a bridge between what's human and something else, and although music is an incredibly important force that has helped me to survive both physically and psychologically, it has its limitations. Getting life, music, and nature together is a vision that's hard to achieve. But visions are always hard to achieve. It's like a whisper on the horizon. It's not a demand, but more a longing. It doesn't matter that it's unclear, it is indispensable. I'm almost crying. At least there is a sense of direction, which means that a lot becomes redundant.

Page 314: Channa Bankier, *Hemifrån*, 1976.
Left: Träd, Gräs och Stenar's field in Likenäs. Photo: Jonas Wikander.

CHAPTER 16

Thanks for the Coffee

Thanks for the Coffee

Thomas Mera Gartz:

I moved in with [the painter and graphic artist] Channa Bankier on Gotland. For two years I basically didn't play at all. In 1974, I joined the band Arbete & Fritid, which led to a new era of music. It was nice because the other period had been so intense. We felt a lot of pressure to set people in motion to free themselves. It was a requirement, especially for me. In Arbete & Fritid there weren't any unwritten demands like that; it was about making good music together, while also being involved in organizing music festivals on Gotland and in Stockholm. It was a continuation of what had happened at the Gärdesfesterna and at Gamla Bro. We ran into the same people when we played. At the same time, the music movement had grown significantly, with its own culture and ideas. Everything was better organized with its own spaces, organized shows, postering, and accommodations.

Jakob Sjöholm:

Between 1972 and 1980, we basically didn't see each other, partly because Bo Anders had moved to Värmland and Mera to Gotland, and partly because all of us had family and kids. The organization "Ny kultur" was formed in Stockholm by people who were interested in music, theater, and other forms of cultural expression, to create an alternative stage. After lots of searching, we found a space in Münchenbryggeriet [a nineteenth-century brewery complex in Stockholm] that needed a complete overhaul: walls, floors, fire exits, etc. Channa Bankier, Einar Heckscher, Stefan Westlund and I worked on it for several years. For me, creating a space and stage for alternative music was a way to channel all the energy I had accumulated since we had stopped touring with the band. To raise money, we organized shows at, among other places, [the galleries / concert halls] Jarlateatern, Liljevalchs, and Folkets hus.

Previous spread: Thomas Mera Gartz and Channa Bankier on a walk along Ireviken on northern Gotland, 1974. Photo: Roger Gustafsson.
Left: Thomas Mera Gartz driving on Gotland, probably 1974. Photo: Roger Gustafsson.

I especially remember the event at Folkets hus in 1973, which was the first time that Träd, Gräs och Stenar played after disbanding. It was sold out two days in a row, with fifteen hundred people each day. Everyone worked for free, and we raised quite a bit of money for our renovations. At the same time, the city of Stockholm decided to tear down Münchenbryggeriet. Together with some of the other tenants, we managed to mobilize public opinion against the demolition, and after several years the municipality changed its decision.

So a spin-off effect of Ny kultur's painstaking work for an alternative stage is that the beautiful Münchenbryggeriet on Söder Mälarstrand remains.

Margareta Klingberg
Aftonbladet, December 23, 1973

For years, musicians of the new Swedish pop have played just for their right to continue playing. Without venues, and without a spot on the radio, they have led an itinerant existence. Helped out for free at Gärdesfester, save-the-radio festivals, freedom of speech festivals and folk festivals--all in a fight for existence. Midvinterblotet [Midwinter Sacrifice] in

Stockholm's Folkets hus was another such occasion. The proceeds, 22,000, will go to Münchenbryggeriet, the venue in Stockholm where this new music will be played on its own financial terms.... Träd, Gräs och Stenar, resurrected for a day, did not appear at all like specters but came back with both new songs and more beautiful sounds. There are several reasons to miss TG&S. I don't know any band that can play music as quietly as them--and which takes the audience with them into that quietness.

Dagens Nyheter, May 8, 1974

Hått Båjs [a Swedenized riff on "Hot Boys"] is the name of a group consisting of members of International Harvester, Träd, Gräs och Stenar, Blomkraft, Hoppets Här, Söderdårarnas spelmansgill,e etc. It's a super duper mega group, says band member Torbjörn Abelli.... It's not a coincidence if anyone thinks they sound like Schysta Schamaner or Döda Fallet. Both are synonymous with Hått Båjs.

Ingmar Glanzelius
Dagens Nyheter, June 10, 1974

Well, you can wonder about the Hot Boys, who serve up [the album] Varma Smörgåsar [Warm Sandwiches] (Silence). I can't peel back all the layers of their parodies, when they rant and rave about how the

322

Swedes used to be peasants who suddenly got herded into high-rise buildings and now only have their photo album, their surprise, their loneliness and their resignation. "The question is whether it is possible to feel so different in one and the same life," the group wonders. Thomas Tidholm has written lyrics that put odd words next to each other so that they become vigorous and spark the imagination.

"En konstig söndag tar vi vår mops, sätter oss i lilla bilen och åker ut till Obs" ["One strange Sunday we take our pug, get into the little car and drive out to Obs"]. The guy from the country who goes to Stadshotellet [a typical Swedish small town hotel] and, seduced by

"an imperial languishing foxtrot," sees only warm sandwiches before a suit of gold lamé is thrust upon him. Some of the Hot Boys have previously played in, for example, Träd, Gräs och Stenar. They make an effort to play "peasantly" and like beginners, and in any case, they do succeed. Each song is different, instruments and playing style derive character from the lyrics. A little troll forest rock, spoken nursery rhymes, children's songs. It's a fun but politically very murky record. Because it preaches hopelessness, except when it mentions the "truth", but it does not indicate in which direction we should look for it.

Front and back cover of *Varma Smörgåsar* by the Hot Boys. Silence, 1974 (SRS 4624). Cover: Anna-Clara Tidholm.
Above: A few members from the Hot Boys with friends on the square in Sala on their way to Stockholm, 1974. The Hot Boys was a constellation formed for Thomas Tidholm's recording of the album *Varma Smörgåsar*. From left: Channa Bankier, Thomas Mera Gartz, Annika Bie with child, Jakob Sjöholm, Thomas Tidholm, Eva Göransson, Torbjörn Abelli, Eva Holma with child, Sten Wallin, and Cissi Bertling. Band members missing from the photo are Bo Anders Persson and Katarina Abelli.

ROCK MOT ATOM KRAFT

PÅ KONSTFACK

FREDAG 23 NOV. KL 22.00–03.00
30:-
TRÄD GRÄS OCH STENAR
TORVMOSSEGOSSARNA
RUFF
JAJJA BAND
MIKAEL RAMEL
EBBA GRÖN
MECKI MARK MEN
NERV

LÖRDAG 24 NOV. KL 15.00–03.00
40:-
KL 15: LUPUS
BLUEGRASS SWEDES
RYKTET GÅR
CH HERMANSSON (TAL)
MARIA BERGOM-LARSSON (TAL)
DAG VAG
17 HOT SALSA
ASTON REJMERS
FUKT
ÖLSTA PROMENADORKESTER
ARBETE OCH FRITID
HAPPY BOYS BAND
SVEN ANÉR (TAL)
21 ARCHIMEDES BADKAR
ANDERS LINDER
ELDKVARN
COOL COMBO
MAGNUS LINDBERG BAND
DOKTOR ZEKE

SÖNDAG 25 NOV. KL 13.00–21.00
40:-
13 LILL LINDFORS
JANNE SCHAFFER, STEFAN
BROLUND, BJÖRN J:SON LIND
CABARET BORTKASTAT o UPPKASTAT
BYSIS
BJÖRN KJELLSTRÖM (TAL)
MÖRBYLIGAN
MARIE BERGMAN, LARS ENGLUND
ELISABETH HERMODSSON (TAL)
FLÄSKET BRINNER
CARL GUSTAV LINDSTEDT
16 OLA MAGNELL
MODERN SOUND
MAJ WECHSELMAN (TAL)
MATS GLENNGÅRD
STEAMBOAT ENTERTAINERS
LASSE TENNANDER
19 USCH
VARGAVINTER
MÖGEL

Musik från två scener,
mat & dryck i stora
matsalen
Obs, Ej förköp!

Mullkraft, Jordcirkus Konvaljen m fl, delar av Sol eller uranutställningen. All vinst från festen går till Folkkampanjen.

FOLKKAMPANJEN NEJ TILL KÄRNKRAFT–KONSTFACKSKOLAN

Above: The campaign for Nej till kärnkraft [No to Nuclear Power] at Konstfack, Stockholm, 1979. Design: Olle Berg.
English translation on p. 377.

Ingmar Glanzelius
Dagens Nyheter, June 18, 1976

Music is often used for pretending, says Thomas Mera Gartz, who has created music and lyrics for the album *Sånger* [Songs] (Silence). It becomes makeup instead of skin, just like how people become jargon instead of senses. Gartz wants to make music that grows out like branches and leaves from his own body: that's what I call honest music. Not just borrowing a passable style and then practicing until you become successful. It's a rare and nice mindset, but risky. It means that the music could come to be about how the player is feeling and not about how the world is doing. When Gartz tries to avoid music's usual game of pretend, he ends up in a new one. That is, the one about the universe: if everything is left to grow on its own, all will be good. That's what his music sounds like.... A backlit grove, you hear their silhouettes but not their core. Gartz talks about how he worked in the rat race, quit and became an anarchist. Now he sits in his arbor and thinks about how the world has a million eyes.

Sigge Krantz:

I lived in Oskarshamn [a coastal city in southeast Sweden] and saw two concerts with Träd, Gräs och Stenar. The first one was in 1970, in the school cafeteria. The second one, a music festival in Stadsparken that we organized. That time we hung out with the band and Per Odeltorp for two days, and they lived with us in our commune outside Oskarshamn. Träd, Gräs och Stenar was first and foremost about music as a state of being, and through that open state, to come into a flow. It contributed to changing my way of looking at music and playing music. Six or seven years later, I got to know Mera and Torbjörn when we played together in the fusion of Arbete & Fritid [Work and Leisure] and Archimedes Badkar [a folk-jazz fusion collaboration]. Then I came in closer contact with their thoughts on music, culture and cultivation, on their

minimalist influences as well as other influences. It turned out that we had a lot in common and had listened to one another's music. Then I met Jakob and played with him for a few years in a rock band called Jajja Band. Mera and I had a band in the middle of the eighties called Råttan Frittz. Bo Anders played with us a few times.

Per Svensson
Tonfallet, November 9, 1980

The years passed, and not until Man and Nature were on a direct collision course due to the nuclear referendum were mobilization orders issued. "Rock Mot Kärnkraft" ["Rock Against Nuclear Power"]--it was natural that Träd, Gräs och Stenar would resurrect at that moment!

Jakob Sjöholm:

At the gig against nuclear power at Konstfack in 1979, punk had arrived, so lots of punk bands played there, for example Ebba Grön. We felt closely related to punk ideologically. I don't know what they thought of our music, but it has always felt like we belonged to the same family with the same values about society.

Torbjörn Abelli:

A relapse at an anti-nuclear power gala made us want more. We played for a year and a half under the name T.GåS. There is a story behind the name. We had played at Errol's in Gothenburg, and someone on the staff said that if you've played at Errol's then you can go to an illegal club in [the Gothenburg neighborhood] Majorna. When we had packed up all our gear, we felt that the night wasn't really over yet. At the address, there was a guy at the door:
"Who are you?"
"Yeah, we just played at Errol's and. . ."
"What are you called?"
"Träd, Gräs och Stenar."
"That's your name?"

It was so dismissive; we felt completely deflated. We had serious conversations in the tour bus the day after. "We can't call ourselves that. It's too long and too far out there." So it became T.GåS instead. We tried making the music punkier and played short fast songs. That was a huge mistake, really. We weren't punk at all! So there was forced, lousy music under a contrived name for a year and a half, but we had a good time. But we hardly got any gigs—the old music venues weren't around anymore, and the new ones weren't interested in us. The pay was still stuck in the seventies but the cost of living had gone up, so we didn't have the energy to continue. I started working, and between 1984 and 1989, I had the only full-time job of my life as an uneducated childcare worker at a daycare.

The art critic Ulf Linde once gave advice to young artists: "Don't try to chase the wind." That's true for us. If you just stick to your conclusions, then you will be relevant at least a couple of times during your lifetime. Time will get in step with you, instead of trying to be in step with time. From 1967 to today, the example of 1981 shows us that there's no point in conforming; it can never be good. If we try to play some kind of punk that isn't punk, it all goes wrong. If we return to our original ideas about music, the music will become sustainable.

Bo Anders Persson
Aftonbladet, May 19, 1980
It feels like Swedish rock music died with us. We never really got any successors. Dag Vag played our song "Sanningens silverflod" and you can find traces of Träd, Gräs och Stenar in their music, but everything else is so--Americanized.

Sigge Krantz
Dagens Nyheter, May 6, 1979

There were complaints that Träd, Gräs och Stenar just
kept on playing the same song for half an hour, that
it was too far-out and slow. But that's just not true.
During that half hour, there were several parts of
passionate and expressive playing.

Jakob Sjöholm
Aftonbladet, May 19, 1980

We were the punk of that time. Same intensity.
Same social thing. Just play. Organize your own
venues. In opposition to everything.

Per Svensson
Tonfallet, November 9, 1980

It's a nasty winter's day in Malmö. No snow, but an
icy wind that gains momentum over the water and sweeps
in through streets and squares in the city. The poster
outside of Café Syd flutters: *Rock för Kropp och Själ*.
But there are no winding queues toward Västergatan.
Fifteen minutes before the show the musicians and the
café's staff outnumber the audience. I end up in the
middle of a discussion on volume since the guests of
the hotel in the same building have already complained
during the sound check. "This isn't off to a great
start," says Torbjörn Abelli, the bass player and ad-
ministrator of the group, who looks troubled. He says
that yesterday's gig in Borås at a youth center "went
ok" and that they are playing in Lund tomorrow evening.
This is the second tour of southern Sweden since their
resurrection. Further north is more problematic. Hard
to get gigs. Stockholm seems especially tough for some
reason.... "Maybe we should start now!?" Bo Anders
aims the question to the audience as much as to his
fellow musicians before he gets up on stage.

Left: T.GåS in Vitabergsparken, Stockholm, 1980.
Above: T.GåS in Vasaparken, Stockholm, 1980. Photo: Roger Gustafsson.

Then they are there again, the same old gang.... The same careful, pensive opening as I remember from Pistolteatern, Moderna Museet, or Stockholmsterassen, same old "Sommarlåten," that carefully winds its way through the venue, same old ... after five minutes I am abruptly awakened from my nostalgic dreaming when Thomas Tidholm starts singing about what can happen during a road trip to Flen. It's rock music that feels new and nice and that keeps on growing. In "Väktare med hund," all possible doubts about disturbed hotel guests and the grim Malmö winter are blown away. Mera Gartz's relentless drums and Torbjörn's swinging bass beckon Bo Anders's and Jakob's guitars, which after a while find each other and happily bounce side by side, eagerly encouraged by Tidholm's hysterical sax. This is music that goes straight into your bloodstream. The windows are fogged up, and the audience--a small one--is happy. Smiles and looks are exchanged between the stage and the audience. The ability to make contact is still there.

Jakob Sjöholm:

> In the middle of the nineties, I had moved out to Färingsö [an island in Lake Mälaren close to Stockholm], and around that same time, the band had started to meet up more regularly. I arranged it so that we could rehearse at my place. Finally, we started wanting to play out and at the same time, we noticed a growing interest in our music.
>
> During all of the eighties, it felt nostalgic when we played gigs; we were so far out on the musical periphery. T.GåS was a short period. We did two week-long tours in Skåne and up north with about ten gigs. It worked out well, everyone had had some distance from previous conflicts. It was sort of a reunion, but I have a feeling that Bo Anders wasn't having that great of a time. He still lived way up there, and I don't think he wanted to live the touring lifestyle. In the nineties, something new was happening, something that wasn't just based on the old. We got a partly new audience, to whom our music meant something else. It gave us a new way of looking at the music—our eyes and ears were changed by that.

Anders Lind:

> In 1995, we started reissuing a few Silence records on CD. Out of all the music we put out on Silence, Träd, Gräs och Stenar and Bosse Hansson were the ones that have made an impression on the world.

Jakob Sjöholm
Dagens Nyheter, December 8, 1995
This is a new phase. It's for real this time. We have written new songs and more are on their way. We are going to try and record some of them this winter.... We have met a new audience, 17-, 18-, 19- year-olds that never heard of us before, and never heard this kind of music either. That has been really fun.

Torbjörn Abelli:

> The eighties wasn't our decade. The further we got into it, the more it felt like glitter, sequins, and disco. Something different from what we stood for. In 1985, Bo Anders had ceremoniously announced on stage that "This will be our final gig." It was a dull gig and we were probably not the only ones who were out of step with the times, it was at a rather stiff party at Gärdet, which was supposed to be some kind of anniversary of the first Gärdesfesten. I was even tight-lipped about what I had done when I spoke to people. To say that I had traveled around in an old VW bus playing weird music felt as shameful as saying that I had been in the pen for fourteen years or in the madhouse. In the nineties, a barely twenty-year-old lad named Reine Fiske showed up and asked for old posters, clips, and recordings. Reine tickled us old geezers so that we started moving again. Then we suddenly got a series of gigs. It took seven years, and we almost didn't see each other that entire time. More and more bookers got in touch. In 1995, we were back at it.

Reine Fiske:

I was on labor market subsidies and got a made-up job at Rockarkivet [a Swedish rock archive dedicated to popular music and ephemera]. I came up with an idea for Krister Malm at Musikmuseet [the Stockholm music museum] to document this music, because no one had done that yet. He loved money and put me on making calls to people. Progg music, with a capital P, was tainted. It was something people were ashamed of. But I knew that I would become absorbed by whatever I found. Those hardest to find were the ones that were the least interesting to many people. They don't belong to Swedish progg, as in the political music movement. These groups were viewed as "far-out" and often played instrumental music. At the same time, their music often contained something else. The musicians had the idea of playing to reach a higher state. They were fantastic musicians and the records that were released were unique but sold badly; often they never reached beyond Sweden's borders.

Above: New member Reine Fiske. Photo: Thomas Mera Gartz.

Above and left: Summer of 1995 at Gärdet. Träd, Gräs och Stenar playing in the pouring rain. The young Reine Fiske can be seen in the bottom right image. Photo: Kristjan Aunver.

Left: Front cover of *Ajn Schwejn Draj*. Silence, 2002 (SRSCD 4758). Cover: Nino Ramsby.

International Harvester were underground when they came, and they were really important. Träd, Gräs och Stenar were also underground.

There is something special about the composition of the green album. That record is still—if I may say so—the best one they made. When Träd, Gräs och Stenar played the first Gärdesfesten—the first track on the Gärdesfesten album *12.6.1970*—it sounded like a rhythmic steamroller. When I heard that for the first time, I felt immediately that I needed to release it on record. That's a gig that gives a new perspective on what Träden sounded like. That aggressiveness hadn't come out before. It was totally new! When I hear the recording, I see an overexposed image or film clip— after spending so much time in different archives, I'm into Super 8 film. I see an image of a meadow in summer, or crops, leading down to a lake, like Siljan or Storsjön. The only problem is that the sunshine is so strong that the meadow is on fire. It's a dystopian image of the music. It goes deeper than any other music to me. There

is mourning, even though the music is also incredible. Träd, Gräs och Stenar's music was a kind of antithesis to the rest of the culture. They played urban music with one foot on a higher plane, an infinity loop that just keeps going and going. Träd, Gräs och Stenar was on my list of people to contact, but it took a while before I called. I was scared of them.

Stephen Malkmus
Pop, November 9, 1999

It seems like they had incredible contact with their audience and the photo on the cover [of Gärdet 12.6.1970] is amazing. It's hippies jamming in a garage and a blond girl dancing with her arms in the air in a tight little outfit. For some reason, Swedish hippies are better than American hippies. There is something heavy about their music.

Thomas Mera Gartz:

Music that is drawn out like rave music with that throbbing, hypnotic [quality] has become somewhat standard. Young people in the nineties understood that kind of music better than people did in 1968–69.

331

Some say that we play timeless music. In the 1990s, when we started playing again, we didn't play the old Träd, Gräs och Stenar music, we played what we were, and we have continued to do that. With Sigge [Krantz, who joined in 2010] and Reine, we play how we are together now. We are keeping that Harvester and Träd, Gräs och Stenar way of playing alive. Our music isn't looking anywhere. The pauses between the notes and beats are what make us hear a note. The space in between is now, and it is constantly being hit with a new sound. That's how we think and play. Torbjörn and I worked with those small parts in the rhythm. We fed the foundation and thought about what we were playing in the moment, not what was going to come later It helped us look toward the future and sound like the present.

Patrik Forshage
Nöjesguiden, May 13, 2017

It's impossible to imagine a Swedish psychedelic scene without Träd, Gräs och Stenar. With influences from Ornette Coleman, Grateful Dead, and Zappa, way before the Swedish avant garde had even heard of those names, Bo Anders Persson and his cronies effectively infiltrated the Swedish music movement over fifty years ago. When the band "took a break" that lasted a couple of decades, they continued to challenge music's outer and inner limits by weaseling their way into the aftermath of the punk wave with the shorter named T.GåS. Eventually, a vibrant nu-psychedelic movement emerged, and in the company of Stephen Malkmus and Dungen, they found their natural scene (and furthermore, when Bo Anders Persson retired, even an identical band member, in the shape of Reine Fiske).

Above and right: Träd, Gräs och Stenar posing for photographs for the new tour poster, "Gick för fulla hus i Ulan Bator," 1995. Photo: Janna Sjöholm.

Jakob Sjöholm:

We finally started making songs. The fact that we have had a hard time writing songs has followed us through the years. Maybe it's because improvisation was such an important part of our music. That's the cloud, or the silver lining. Mera, Bo Anders, and I wrote some songs each. We fought over the cover and the title. It was going to be called *Alla sover* [Everyone Is Asleep] after Bo Anders's song. Silence had given someone the project of making the cover art, showing someone sleeping. Suddenly, Bo Anders didn't agree to the name. It ended up being called *Ajn schvajn draj* [a play on a Germanic "one two three"], which was weird because it had nothing to do with the album. It is about everyone sleeping. *Ajn schvajn draj* was recorded here in Svartsjö in a little cubby. Everything was recorded live except for some vocal overdubs. We determined the order of the songs at Torbjörn's kitchen table. We wrote the song names on notes and each made our version of the order. It was like a family board game with those notes—it was very nice. Finally, we agreed on the album's structure. It became nominated for a Grammis in the open category; we'd never have expected that. It was a strange event, with industry people and Carola [Häggkvist, a famous singer and Euro-vision winner] and celebrities. Another world. Several of the songs were played on the radio, which we had never managed before.

Dennis Andersson
Barometern, April 24, 2002
Träd, Gräs och Stenar make music that no one else could even imagine dreaming up. Wonderfully unwieldy and impossible to be careless with. Long instrumental and hypnotic song structures. Repetitive foundations, basslines (Torbjörn Abelli) that lay down a monotonous dancing pattern, with friskily curious drums (Thomas Mera Gartz) and whis-

Träd, Gräs och Stenar playing at the opening of the
exhibition *Hjärtat sitter till vänster* [The Heart Is
on the Left], **Uppsala Art Museum, August 1998.**
Photo: Kristjan Aunver.

tling guitars (Bo Anders Persson and Jakob Sjöholm) that slowly, slowly move the course of events forward.... The band that was once called Pärson Sound, International Harvester, Harvester, and were behind the famous alternative music festivals at Gärdet at the beginning of the 1970s. That never really quit, but continued to play live. That is still at odds with society and plays developmental music for the senses that are left to save. That has found a new young audience and that has a significant supporter in, among others, Pavement's Stephen Malkmus. There might not be room for any completely tripped-out instrumental hippie madness like "Tegenborgsvalsen" or "All makt åt folket" ["Tegenborg Waltz" and "All Power to the People," both from the 1969 self-titled "green

record"] here, but it's the same kind of minimalist structures. And the instrumental suites are the basis of the record and take up the majority of it.

The sound is, of course, different and updated. But the darkness is the same. There is almost something of a doomsday feeling about some of the songs. If we ever need to portray Judgement Day, the soundtrack is already written. A song like "Elden är lös" ["The Fire Is Loose"] paints the picture of a slow, black-and-white, last dance in the ruins of existence when everything is finally crushed. *Ajn Schvajn Draj* is an album filled with noteworthy things.

Above: Bo Anders Persson in Likenäs, December 2003. Photo: Roger Gustafsson.

Torbjörn Abelli:

We came in contact with a New York band called No-Neck Blues Band, a group that was made up of equal amounts theater, performance, and music. They wanted to do a European tour with us. We didn't understand how they had even heard of us. It turned out that the European tour was too financially risky; it became just two gigs in England, in an old defunct church in London and a little hotel in Brighton. Before we went to England with No-Neck, we had never been outside of the Nordics. With their help, we got a few gigs in the USA in 2003—in New York and a few places on the East Coast, and then Minneapolis, Chicago, and Detroit. We had the finances to afford to get us there and maybe get back home again.

Bo Anders Persson:

I was on the verge of quitting the band before the USA trips, but then Jakob had put so much work into it, and I wasn't able to deal with a confrontation like that. I was a little curious too. The trips were both nice and tough, you always meet interesting people. But it's too damn easy to step on [the Americans'] toes. They can't see that they have supported shit regimes all over the world.

Jakob Sjöholm:

We played in Gothenburg, a great gig at Nefertiti [a legendary jazz club], and afterward, Bo Anders said it was his last gig. It came without warning, and then he was just gone. We had quite a few shows booked, like Primavera, a big festival in Barcelona. It would have been tough to cancel those, but we got a hold of Reine. We rehearsed and played the gigs with him.

Reine Fiske:

The members found their way back to one another. I think they liked the attention, even though not much happened. There was a revival in the mid-nineties and they wrote new songs. I often saw them play out. At the same time, I was getting to know them. Jakob got in touch—I think Mera was pressuring him when Bo Anders quit. I knew Mera pretty well and looked up to him. He was a rock'n'roll guy from Bagarmossen [a Stockholm suburb] with an interest in jazz and experimental music. Mera liked the more freaked-out, freer forms of music, and he, of course, liked John Coltrane. He saw Coltrane's quartet at Stockholm Concert Hall in 1962.

We would talk a lot about music when we hung out; naturally about Träd, Gräs och Stenar, because Mera never had trouble talking about that time. He was filled with emotions and memories. It moves me to think about him, that I had the opportunity to play with him and feel the energy that he had!

Bo Anders Persson:

I'm not involved in the production of *Hemlösa Katter* [Homeless Cats], but I play on most of it. It's the best record we made. Though, I mean, I'm not really involved at all. Maybe that says something.

Dan Backman
Svenska Dagbladet, May 6, 2009

It should really be impossible, but after forty slow years doing the work of Swedish progg-trance-rock, Träd, Gräs och Stenar is still unique and relevant. In Sweden and the world.... *Hemlösa katter*, Träden's first album in seven years, captures the band's psychedelic krautrocky soul in an even better way than the somewhat fragmented album *Ajn schvajn draj*. They have recorded most of it themselves at their practice space in Viksund, and the big, warm and elastic sound could be the best they have ever managed to get. Listen to "Folkets lok i obeveklig rörelse," "Sommardisco" and "Svärmors brudpolska" and listen to how the old guys play the Afghan Furs off of their successors.

Jakob Sjöholm:

When Bo Anders quit, there were those who thought we wouldn't call ourselves Träd, Gräs och Stenar anymore, but we wanted to wait and see what happened with the music and the band before we decided to change the name. Even though the music wasn't exactly the same without Bo Anders, it was surprisingly similar to the old Träd, Gräs och Stenar music, and we carried on the tradition. With Reine in the band, the fire was rekindled.

We had already started recording our new album *Hemlösa Katter* when Bo Anders quit. In the fall of 2009, we played in Spain and noticed that something was the matter with Tobbe [Torbjörn Abelli]. We had to stop and wait for him when we were out walking. Tobbe said that he had taken a test for Lyme disease that had been negative. We continued rehearsing, and he began to use a cane when he started to have a hard time moving and maintaining his balance. In January 2010, he said he had been in a store on Kungsholmen and suddenly passed out. He didn't know why. After that, he walked with crutches. In the spring of 2010, we went on a tour of England. Tobbe had taken a new test for Lyme disease, but they hadn't found anything at that time either. During the trip, we had to help him up on stage every night and he had a chair next to him so that he could sit down during the gigs. A week or so after we got back he said he was feeling weird. The day after he lost feeling in his legs. He called an ambulance. When I visited him in the hospital he said his arms had started to feel weird, that there was a prickly feeling in them and that it was hard to move them. Then his arms became paralyzed. That's when the doctors took a spinal tap and discovered that it was Lyme disease. But they couldn't stop the infection, and the disease spread to his lungs, and he had to breathe through a ventilator. The last time I visited him, he could only nod or shake his head. He was fully conscious, but couldn't speak. It was horrible. He died in August. It was a sad end. We arranged a memorial concert for Tobbe at Kulturhuset and it was full of friends and old musicians that performed and said goodbye.

Thomas Mera Gartz:

After Torbjörn passed, we didn't know if we should continue. There is a lot that I miss. But Jakob and I talked about it—there's nothing more fun than playing.

Jakob Sjöholm:

Both Mera and I knew Sigge Krantz from before. Sigge and I had played in Jajja Band, and Mera had played with him in, among others, Råttan Frittz. We rehearsed together and had gigs with Thomas Tidholm in 2011, but the following year we decided that we wanted to continue as Träd, Gräs och Stenar, and had gigs in Småland, Skåne, and Copenhagen. When we came home, Mera and I stood down on the street talking about how much fun it had been being on tour and that we were finally back at it. We had had so many adversities and so many depressing years. That was the last time I saw Mera.

My wife, Titti, and I were at our country house raking leaves, and it was starting to get dark when the phone rang. It was Sigge; he was crying and told me Mera had died. I couldn't believe it. I had talked to Mera the day before about the next album that we had just started working on. He died of blood poisoning. Titti and I threw ourselves in the car and got to Stockholm late that evening. I got ahold of Reine and Sigge and Steffe Stålis, our sound engineer. We met at Gullmarsplan [a square and public transportation hub in southern Stockholm] and sat dumbfounded in the car. It was horrible, a real shock. We held a memorial concert for Mera at the theater in Gubbängen with lots of friends, it was really nice. Reine, Sigge, and I found solace in one another. We moved on by doing something together; it would have been too sad otherwise. Where was I to go? Mera and I had known each other for such a long time, since the end of the sixties. Of course, I had doubts. To play music is like a free space, breathing room in the chaos of life, and I notice that I am a lot happier and friendlier when I get to play. To express oneself is important, but mostly I think I play for the community that emerges when we are enveloped by the sound and become one entity, a whole. When it goes well, it's amazing, like a religious experience.

Reine Fiske:

Playing in the remains of the band is a double-edged sword. It's tough and special. I do it because I can't stop myself. I do it for Mera and Torbjörn. I don't think they would be opposed to me being in the band. At the same time, I hear Bo Anders say: "You should put your energy into your own

projects." Because sometimes, it sounds like I'm exploring his way of playing. His style of playing is so embedded in this music that you can't remove it. I sound a lot like him. It's a declaration of love and people like it.

Sigge Krantz:

Torbjörn's passing was sad; the friendly man that had been in my musical world since the school cafeteria in Oskarshamn. A year earlier, we had had a great time at my sixtieth birthday party. I hadn't played music regularly for many years when I was asked to play bass in the band. That was probably Mera's doing. We had been playing together for ten years' time, and it was fun playing with Mera again. I also knew Jakob, but I had barely met Reine before that. I started listening to Torbjörn's playing, and learned about his approach and about Träd, Gräs och Stenar's music, which we maintain. Jakob is also important, but at the same time, new music emerges when new musicians come in. All you can do is accept that. The hard thing is to get time to play. Our living situations are so different.

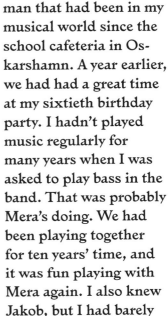

Making sound on a specific scale is maybe the most common form of music on the planet, considering the number of practitioners. Traditional music all over the world is practiced that way. There is so much groove. You can view it as clockwork: different cogs move at different speeds but display the same time. Although the music

Left: Lars Torbjörn Abelli, February 10, 1945–August 11, 2010.
Above: Thomas Mera Gartz, April 4, 1944 – April 29, 2012. Photo: Janna Sjöholm.

isn't especially outgoing, it responds to some people's need to descend into a state. The music is unassuming but can give you a lot if you just give it some time. It's exciting to hear how listeners experience our music. It can be very detailed and surprising.

Hanna Östergren:

I came in contact with Träd, Gräs och Stenar's music through my mom and friends. I've always liked the monotonous, and since I was young I've been in love with music that evolved at the end of the sixties and beginning of the seventies. I played in a band called Hills and we opened for Träd, Gräs och Stenar once. Nisse [Törnqvist] was their drummer at that time. A year or two later they called me and asked if I wanted to play with them. It was an honor to take over after Thomas Mera Gartz. That's not actually something you can do. And that's not what I have done. He had a very original way of playing. I can't play like him. I'm not a trained drummer; I started playing the drums by chance, and can't compare myself to someone who is a trained jazz drummer. I can only play as who I am. We'll see how it goes. The first time I played with Träd, Gräs och Stenar I was super nervous, which I very rarely am.

Marc Masters
Pitchfork, May 8, 2016

Träd, Gräs och Stenar's music is never a slog. It's usually easy to enter, and often downright breezy and relaxed. The band was confident enough not to force epiphanies, trusting that euphoria could grow from steady, upbeat swing. This has led some to call them Sweden's Grateful Dead, but Träd, Gräs och Stenar were more free-form, and more interested in sonic chaos. In that way, along with their status as communal outsiders, they were more like Father Yod's primitive psych-rock pioneers YaHoWha 13. The latter's delirious 3 am trips share an aura with the Träd, Gräs och Stenar songs that feature raw, seemingly-possessed singing and chanting.

One crucial difference between Träd, Gräs och Stenar and other communal collectives of the time (YaHoWha 13, Captain Beefheart and the Magic Band, the Sun Ra Arkestra) was their leaderless nature. With no particular member in charge, their music has a refreshing lack of ego; it feels like the only thing steering the ship is the momentum created by playing together. Though some guitar parts resemble solos, they rarely dominate. All the riffs merge into a multi-colored swirl, and the band digs into each repetition like coal miners chipping away in unison. Over forty years later, this all-for-one approach still resonates in the far-flung forays of collectives such as No-Neck Blues Band, Bardo Pond, Acid Mothers Temple, and Eternal Tapestry.

Reine Fiske:

The way we make a new album now is different than before. I can't help but be affected by what has been recorded, and I have probably heard more of their old music than they have themselves. Sometimes when the music is spinning around its own axis, you can't stop the energy. When I joined the band, I wanted to get there as often as possible. Mera said once after he had been playing like hell: "I can't play like that anymore. It's too intense." It's wonderful to just disappear into that feeling, where everything is released.

Hanna Östergren:

Träd, Gräs och Stenar, or Träden—we changed the name to mark the shift—builds on composition and improvisational music. It's music that's based on the interplay between the members. Playing that kind of music is the best thing I know. Getting to play the old songs is an honor. They feel more fluid, but we play our version of them.

It might have been easier for them to play before. They were all in the same place. It's not possible to get together in the same way now; I live in Gothenburg and the others live in Stockholm. And for a few years now, I've been spending more time growing crops than

"Most of our audience is men. White middle-aged and older men that collect records. Unfortunately. Not unfortunately . . . that's just how it is . . . Many of them are super nice."

Hanna Östergren

playing music, even though I'm focused on the music. I'm interested in social justice issues. But that's not anything we talk about; we don't have a pronounced ideology, like they might have had in the band fifty years ago.

During my time in Träden, we've been away abroad twice. It's been incredible! So many people have come to our gigs. It's an honor for us, while it also feels as if we are there on someone else's merits, because of what Träd, Gräs och Stenar did. Many times, we're promoted as Träd, Gräs och Stenar. But I think we should be billed as Träden while at the same time mentioning our background. We started playing at various psych festivals in Europe. Festival audiences are a specific kind of crowd, and we have had a more positive response in the USA. In Sweden and England, the audience is more standoffish. Most of our audience is men. White middle-aged and older men that collect records. Unfortunately. Not unfortunately . . . that's just how it is . . . Many of them are super nice. I think there were more women in the audience in the early days. When Sonja, Ulla, and others made food for the gigs.

Timo Kangas
Lira, 2015

A Japanese band [Kikaguku Moyo] covers a song by Träd, Gräs och Stenar--or rather, International Harvester, which they were called at the time?

Above: The new Träden in Oslo, 2017. From left: Sigge Krantz, Hanna Östergren, Reine Fiske, and Jakob Sjöholm.

Yup, Swedish hypnotic progg has spread all over the world--even to a group of former street musicians in Tokyo who now are playing the song "There Is No Other Place," written by Thomas Tidholm and the departed Torbjörn Abelli, and previously released on the LP *Sov gott Rose-Marie* in 1968.

Go Kurosawa:

Our first encounter hearing Träd, Gräs och Stenar was when Tomo Katsurada and I were hanging out with our bassist Kotsu Guy. He brought the Pärson Sound boxset and we started discovering Harvester, International Harvester, and Träd, Gräs och Stenar. Each band is totally different and we love them all. Kikagaku Moyo has been inspired by the atmosphere they create. Their melodies are sad and pastoral, but still sound ritualistic, primitive, and earthy. Their style gives an image of the woods, lakes, and a gloomy sky in Sweden—even if you've never been there. We feel like it is easier to make a "space" jam sound by using lots of effects and a few riffs. But when Träd, Gräs och Stenar jam, they maintain this earthy and primitive feeling. Not to the outer space but to the inner space. That's what we like.

Jason P. Woodbury
Phoenix New Times, February 10, 2015
Myrrors ... play into [Nik] Rayne's goal of integrating radical political ideologies into his music. The songwriter cites the philosophies of Bo Anders Persson of Träd, Gräs & Stenar, Pärson Sound, and International Harvester regarding the "stratification of western music," and a desire to break down the barriers between performer and audience.

Jed Bindeman:

The first time I heard music related to the Träd, Gräs och Stenar world was when Subliminal Sounds released the now legendary, but then totally unheard, 2CD collection from Pärson Sound, in 2001. At the time, I, like many others, used

to discover a lot of music via Aquarius Records' e-mail updates. Their description of the album sounded intriguing, so I figured I'd give it a try. When the discs showed up a few days later, I felt like I was hearing music that had been playing in my ears for years, but didn't know existed in the real world. I had no clue that my life would be forever changed from that moment on, but the second that first track started my brain fell out of my proverbial skull, dropped to the floor and became damaged in just the right way. These types of experiences happen only every so often to a devout music fan, and the impact they would have from that moment on would be profound. After several months of deep listening sessions, following their trajectory from Pärson Sound to Träd, Gräs, there was no turning back. They created the kind of music that could go on forever, somehow never getting stale, spiraling up into the sky. To sum up the feelings on my initial dive into Träd, Gräs and everything that came with them, all I could think was, "Finally, this is IT!"

As a drummer, hearing and seeing Thomas Mera Gartz play was an especially moving and inspiring experience. Thomas's playful style, together with the raw live recordings of the band, taught me that music is allowed to breathe and take its time. It's alright to loosen up (especially in terms of holding drumsticks). Sometimes there's no rush to return to the melody, but better to just allow the music to go where it needs to, and it will naturally find its way back around . . . well, most of the time! Oh, and most importantly, don't get caught up worrying about "messing up," because that happens sometimes when you're stuck in a transcendental musical state and your eyes have fully rolled into the back of your head for the past thirty minutes!

Epilogue: It's Time to Start Meeting Again

Text by Träd, Gräs och Stenar, 1972

There is nothing better than to experience the same thing, in the same room. That's how it's been everywhere, always. You gather, play and sing—together and for each other—you dance and talk, all conditions are clear, nothing is hard to understand. You share your experiences. Everything is about that which surrounds you. Then, "work" is a part of life. You know what you are doing, where everything is coming from, and where it all goes. And "free time" is not just time that is left over that has to be used for various kinds of consumption.

Then, there is nothing to be afraid of. Death is not an end; you have seen that with your own eyes. The leaves that fall in autumn rot and create new life. The rain falls, the rivers flow to the sea. The seed germinates, the plant grows, the food comes from the earth. The sun shines, all animals are siblings. We wouldn't manage without them. "Sorrow and happiness walk together side by side, success and failure here closely follow each other" [Psalm 365 of the Swedish Church Hymnal]. But the only thing we are taught is to be afraid of being together around something—other than at a distance or protected by rules and regulations, that are called "morals," "decency," or "quality." People getting together becomes a threat to order.

Consumption and production suffer when people become interested in one another. That's why there are all these obstacles to meeting others, inconspicuously built-in with the help of bureaucracy and technology. They are formulated as if they were about organization and so on, when it is actually about politics, to force people into a "productive form of life," without considering what you then have to refrain from. . . .

If everything really was normal, then people who like each other's company would be able to meet at a place where they feel at home, and don't need to be rushed by the clock or by police. Then there could be an opportunity to really start doing something together.

PS: The best music has already been made by the Rolling Stones and Joel Jansson. It's not necessary to listen to Träd, Gräs och Stenar. One can listen to children playing or a train that is about to disappear, four kilometers away on a summer night. It's no secret.

Above: Fikapause [coffee break] **at Anders Björnsson's place in Likenäs, probably 1971.**

Text Translations

P. 32   BO ANDERS PERSSON

At Ung Nordisk Music in Stockholm, 1965, a piece called "Love Is Here to Stay" was played by an unusually long-haired composer by the name of Bo Anders Persson. The piece was well received: music with a lovely flute and song loops over a fine bossanova - like rhythm. "Pretty music, a decent piece. But it's not enough to motivate my existence."

Bo Anders Persson seems to have the need to motivate his existence. He appears to have a chronically bad conscience: he speaks a lot about the starving millions, the exploitative Western world, and "global survival," and is of the opinion that it's really an unsustainable situation for him, sitting here with a mixed grill and a beer, not able to do anything about all the misery.

Born in 1937. Started with Dixieland. "It gave me a specific attitude to listening." He learned the songs by listening to the gramophone records, not by reading sheet music. However, he became an engineer, and attended Teknis [Kungliga Tekniska Högskolan, KTH] for a few years. Says that he was "tormented" by the awareness that everything he did there "was motivated by functional requirements and aimed at peak exploitation." He quit. "I should have kept going, because then I would have had the possibility of contributing to alleviating the pressure on nature." These days, all that about exploitation and the starving millions is what he calls "a side thing, but still important. About the same as being an ordinary Christian who's ashamed but still sins. But there are so many things that are totally crazy--there is solace in that. I have strong feelings about the Provie-stuff. That is BIG."

At Borgarskolan in Stockholm, he became a student of Jan Bark. "If I hadn't met him I probably wouldn't have started working with music. He excelled in open attitudes."

He started attending the Royal College of Music in 1965, in the Composition class, and then also in the Pedagogical Theory class. He is now planning to drop the composition class. "My energy is not unlimited."

You can almost hear that. "Små toner mer eller mindre" ["Small Notes, More or Less"]--a very characteristic title of a piece played by Kammar musikstudion--pretty quiet and static plucking of notes, mostly low and long. The harpist has quite a lot to do, tuning certain strings down, pounding on the strings, scraping them with their nails, playing with a bow and things like that, but other than that, the piece is anything but provocative. Its latter part uses centimeter notation rather than bar lines. "For my own convenience."

Bo Anders Persson "believes that it's probably still possible to write for regular instrumentalists." But his sights are on something else. A few years ago he wrote "Om sommaren sköna II" ["In the Lovely Summer II"] for instruments, band, and "theater stuff," and for some time he has been working on "Om sommaren sköna III," where he will use taped interviews. The interview technique doesn't only contribute words, but also a lot of atmosphere, timbre, and drama. The interviews give the music a connection to the outer world, gives it social relations. It needs it, according to Bo Anders Persson. "I think the solution is in the theater."

His interest in the Western tradition of concert and opera halls is tepid. His significant musical experiences are of pop music--the Who among others. The current "media mysticism"--the medium is the message--is something he doesn't understand. "It's too flippant. Besides, it's based on the special position of the West. However, painfully enough, I'm on my way there too."

There are plenty of consequences and contradictions with Bo Anders Persson. Another one: he cannot understand why the state and society should support him. "But of course, I gratefully accept the stipends."

GÖRAN BERGENDAL

Something happened. It took off. At Wednesday
evening's concert, at the "Jazz festival 1967"
and the venue Sju Sekler, the frenzy, the violent
volume, the tremendous investment got a meaning and a
justification. Something that is difficult to define in
a positive musical experience was present relatively
often. That which perhaps is identification with
the moment, with the executor, identification with
whatever it may be. Either way, it is quite rare, and
could be called enriching.

At similar concerts--pop or beyond pop, jazz
or beyond jazz, contemporary serious or avant-garde
musical experimentation--one too often experiences a
violent attack as a fashionable spice, superficial and
lighthearted handling with powder kegs; the executor
seems to have limited knowledge of the content and
its force of expansion. "Bo Anders Persson Sound"
reached a reality that one accepted. It was shared
honestly and without circumlocution.

The evening was divided into two compositions. Bo
Anders Persson, flute, Arne Eriksson, cello, and Thomas
Gartz, drums, played. Thomas Tidholm joined later
with the recorder. With the help of tape devices, they
played a canon with themselves. A tape echo changed the
timbre. Overlays, roundabouts, and summersaults were,
of course, part of the technical tools. Long unified
rhythmic and melodic periods were built up through
small motif cells. The rises took place in long developmental curves. The intensity was total and engaging.

The later part of the concert was initially a
medical microphonic eavesdropping of the percussion.
Metallic surfaces were scratched and listened in on
with the microphone like a stethoscope. Such studies
have been conducted before by, for example, Stockhausen, when he investigated and elicited different
sound sensations out of a gong treated with all those
kinds of instruments/tools. But nothing gets worse
by not being new. Especially when the continuation
with the flute, recorder, drums, and cello becomes
an accelerated vibrato. A strong-acting empathy and
experience. It could be perceived purely pictorially
as an attempt to fight against the world of the senses
in order to break through, if possible.

An attempt at total theater: a film of Swedish
dance hall life ran in parallel with the music. That
the result was less stimulating was perhaps due to
the small format of the screen? Perhaps the film was
less suitable, even if it was played both forwards
and backward.

None of the musicians should really be highlighted
at the others' expense. Unless Thomas Gartz was as
convincing today as at Monday night's concert in
Kungsträdgården, of his powerful talent for his
instrument.

ULLA-BRITT EDBERG

347

Krister Västlund................Bo Anders Persson
Birgitta Weisshappel............Gabi Björnstrand
Max Von Sydow...................Jakob Sjöholm
Tuttan, a poor countess.........A-C Tjerneld
Friday, a savage................Thomas Gartz
Thomas Alba Edison..............Thomas Tidholm
Rudyard Kipling.................Sonja Eriksson

Music: Jan W. Morthenson and Magnus Banck

Summary:

Earth is exuded from the sun and starts circulating around it. Eventually, it "cools" and water emerges in the cavities. Lightning strikes the water, which creates a specific kind of mucus, and in the mucus, a number of animals "develop," very small creatures but living ones nonetheless. Now things are getting started. After only a billion years, the earth is filled with herbs and ferns in crevices and the orthoceratoids crawl on the bottom of the ocean. Plants grow and become forests, and the small animals start laying eggs and procreating. The dragon lizards take over the earth. Things are looking "bad," but after a while they all die, and all that is left is a strange little "dog," the first mammal. There is a division into several species, i.e., horses and monkeys. On a sunny and warm day in June in the "area" where contemporary Johannesburg is located, a young monkey is looking for some food, and without thinking about it he grabs a stone and bashes a little hare again and again until it dies. Since that day, nothing is the same. Eventually, they learned how to make fire and wheels and build cities and houses and pyramids. "Many" cultures and civilizations saw the light of day and many were very beautiful. But suddenly, a bunch of people started gathering on a hill in the area of the Danube's source. They started singing a silly tune to always look up in the sky and not eat anything other than sweets for the rest of their lives.

A Space Odyssey

Justus Korallus................Mats Arvidsson
Uno Lamms, PhD.................Bo Anders Persson
(expert in transmission of high-voltage direct current)
A fat fool....................Oscar Hedlund
The city court/country
court and a rabulist..........Thomas Tidholm
Fia Jansson...................Christine Arvidsson
A chambermaid.................Sonja Eriksson
The Grand Vizier of
Portugal, an Envoy............Thomas Gartz
etc.

The plot is thought to take place in the center of the soloist dressing room at the Royal Opera House.

Many are probably asking themselves: Is not this liberation of youth from the past and the trust in products of their own philosophizing something good, in and of itself? I want to ask: Where in the world do they find that which is better than our own cultural tradition--what people have had larger human successes than the Western world?

DN's opinion page on October 2nd, 1968

[Pop and Dance and Cordial]

Pistolteatern: International Harvester Good Luck Show. Participants include International Harvester (previously Pärson Sound) consisting of Bo Anders Persson, Thomas Tidholm, Arne Eriksson, Thomas Gartz, and Torbjörn Abelli. Also Gabi Björnstrand, Jakob Sjöholm, Mats och Kitte Arvidsson, Anna-Clara Tjerneld, Ulla Berglund, and others.

It's for teenyboppers, evening dancers, and families.

Perhaps the fusion sounds unusual but it covers the concepts. Somewhat. There are light projections in four places. When you first get there, there are beautiful kurbits-like images, and later both films and photographs--the latter mostly of beautiful nature scenes.

When you come inside, there is aluminum foil on the stage's backdrop and birdsong in the speakers. When you leave, pop is blasting, some are dancing on the floor while others look on.

During the break, a berry cordial is served. From a big pot with a ladle. Like in the country.

And this is actually the country, at least a faraway country, a distant land, where you sit on chairs on the floor and where you are one big family in a kind of democracy where everyone seems to think alike. You are surrounded by red cabins on the walls, images that switch to summer landscapes, that switch to spring and fall and winter.

Things don't move especially quickly in this country. Everyone has time to wait for the ideas that actually never come. But you do have time to see the homemade election videos where the stage group's members pass out ballots that are anything but lists and one sees radio boss [Olof] Rydbeck [a diplomat and the Sveriges Radio chief] say with a different audio track that he likes Irish tobacco. So does [Sven] Wedén [a libertarian politician].

Then a girl stands up and starts dancing. She dances in the exact same spot for an entire half hour. She had a Native American bandana and jeans.

Bo Anders Persson draws a house. There are just pipes and wires in it. Gas, electricity, and water--and all that. He's probably doing it because he thinks that we keep forgetting that we have pipes and wires in our houses--those big houses that look so impersonal and glamorized compared to the small red houses.

Don't ask me if it's good or bad. It's actually pretty nice. International Harvester's rhythm washes over you, wave after wave.

When I leave, rhythm-surfing, I see how they are all dancing while Sweden's sheer and vernal trees, in projected slide form, are looking on smiling across all four walls.

ULLA-BRITT EDBERG

P. 77   POSTER

STOP THE FAIR!!!!--Not an öre, not a hand to luxury consumption.

P. 78   "WE WILL DO IT — WITH MUSIC"

They do it with music--socialist popband International Harvester write songs called "Ho Chi Minh" and "Ut till vänster" ["Out to the Left"]. They have many purposes, such as hastening the fall of Western culture. They are of the opinion that Western culture has always repressed people's inherent urge to be together. This fall, International Harvester has promoted community in their "Good Luck Show" that they put on at Pistolteatern in Stockholm.

P. 80   "FRONT AGAINST UPPER-CLASS CULTURE"

From start to finish, Western culture has always been a culture for the upper- classes. It has gone so far that the word "culture" now means theater or concerts or art. But we want to talk about how there once was a folk culture in this country, just like in other countries, in other words a culture that was connected to people's lives, in other words a culture that worked. During that time people were able to live one life, but now everyone is forced to become schizophrenic.

Western history has been artificiality's victory over nature. For five hundred years, people have in growing numbers been fooled to move away from their homes with the promise of money and something nice. Nature has been suppressed. So has Africa, Asia, and South America. One has struggled to achieve something nice, something nicer . . . The nicest. People have moved into the cities and got themselves holiday homes. And they have called people who want meaning in life instead of meaning in death rednecks, and then press their clothes one more time, because wrinkles also need to be suppressed.

There is talk now of spreading culture to the people. Oh really. So they have taken people's lives away, and instead of their lives they want to give them Theater, Literature, and Art. As compensation for their lives, people are offered to sit in an armchair and shut up while other people monkey around on stage, a thousand miles away from everything that is really worth something. But they aren't alive either. They are all dead.

P.81   DEAR FRIENDS

People want to gather, but those in charge do not want people to gather. Except under certain conditions: for example, you must not gather for too long or with too many people, and you must spend a lot of money when you do.

The reason that they don't think people should meet are that they suffer from fear of sex.

Money and shit is the same thing, that's scientifically proven. (By, among others, Sigmund Freud.)

They have put the police there so that people do their shopping and then go home.

This way, Sergels torg will become a playground for the commercial fascists (and the others).
"Take a day and walk around
Watch the nazis run your town."

[Stockholm Social Democratic/Liberal politicians] Hjalmar Mehr, PO Hansson, and Nils Hallerby can go and sell themselves. Either way they shouldn't participate in any discussions. The City Council is completely corrupted.

[Department store chain] Åhléns's famous potato salad has a horrible aftertaste.

The water in the fountain is more expensive than meat soup.

Stockholm Concert Hall is going to be rebuilt for 17 million. Wouldn't it be cheaper to send the [music nerds] directly to Vienna with Club 33 [a travel club for youth offering European "charter trips" to customers under thirty-three years of age].

We are nicer than they have ever been.

Go to the square on Thursday and look on when Hantverket opens its little exhibition with upper-class stuff in our café. You can't come in of course but really press your nose up against the glass and you might see a glimpse of Princess Sibylla.

Boo to the idea of Western development. Keep things open to the left.

GOOD LUCK

INTERNATIONAL HARVESTER

P.95   POSTER

".. as long as there is a single attacker left in our country, we will keep fighting to annihilate him..." Ho Chi Minh.

A couple of hundred people had arranged to meet with International Harvester at Arkivmuseet in Lund last night. It wasn't exactly an impressive audience, but probably about what was to be expected. International Harvester is an odd pop group, and their fame has not reached very far beyond our capital's limits.

When I reviewed the band's first LP a month ago, I wrote something about International Harvester in a Swedish summer meadow. There is no need to change that characterization. The sextet invited these kinds of associations by illustrating their music with landscape images.

In the ad it was called "Lightshow"--a few flickering spotlights with blinking color filters did not fit within this perhaps audience-enticing headline. Instead, it was more in line with the old silent movie theaters with a piano-playing older lady at the front. However, yesterday the order was naturally reversed--the music was illustrated with photographs and drawings, but they could almost have done without them.

It's difficult to confuse International Harvester with any other Swedish pop group. The setup is unusual, since there are two string instruments with unusual tones and shapes. The first one has a creaking sound that is difficult to define but which evokes American jug band music. On top of the full accompaniment, there is a guitar that fits well into the sound pattern.

The exact opposite of Tio i Topp ["Ten at the Top," a record chart and radio countdown]--what does that sound like? International Harvester could be one of the answers to that. You can't dance to their music; any humming and foot stomping faces obstacles. The group starts off at a low level, one by one the instruments join in, and tempo and volume rise until a compact wall of sound has been created. Around this, other notes are woven in by cowbells, bells, and flutes, all while the image of a Swedish landscape in summer emerges.

That is how I experienced International Harvester's music this time. It was fascinating in all its trying monotony, and its approach to the Swedish folk tradition is interesting. A year ago, I would surely have found this kind of music much more difficult; despite the fact that it's not especially fun to listen to, it does have a fairly inexplicable force of attraction that might come from the exaltation of the Swedish landscape.

International Harvester should absolutely not be praised to the skies--they are not worth that. But why not let the band play at schools? From time to time, Swedish musicians from classical, modernist, and jazz groups tour and play for school youth. The musicians go out to the audience. Why not let pop music do the same? Music education is stuck in old patterns and must be renewed.

OTIS

to those who organized International Harvester's
performance in Bollnäs, Feb. 10.

A special thank-you because you were brave
enough to break with the stiff convention and let
this group of incredible musicians through, in
full freedom.

International Harvester is one of a small hand-
ful of Swedish groups (also Sound of Music, Mecki
Mark Men, Hansson & Karlsson) that have managed to
throw off the heavy yoke of commercialism.

They have something significant to say, unlike
the large masses.

The distance that the audience usually feels
between themselves and the performers is completely
obliterated in International Harvester's case.
The audience is one with them through their music,
which communicates with everyone present in an
extraordinary way.

They are a collection of individualists, and
those are all too rare, not just in music, but
in all areas. It was quite significant, however,
that 99 percent of the audience was made up of
so-called "weirdos." It is regrettable that no
representatives of "ordinary people" were pleased
to attend. They might have been given food for
thought.

To everyone who for one reason or another missed
the event, and incidentally also to the crowd who
turned up, I want to say:

Buy International Harvester's LP Sov gott,
Rose-Marie. An amount of 25.00 is certainly not
much to experience a moment of evocative and
conscious music.

"THE IDIOT."

CEDERS KAFÉ
VITABERGSPARKEN
HARVESTER
IS PLAYING AND SO ARE YOU
KJARTAN [Slettemark]
WILL WALK A TIGHTROPE
JUNE 17 7:30

"SUPPORT THE FRIENDSHIP BETWEEN THE SWEDISH
AND CHINESE PEOPLE!"

Swedish/Chinese Friendship Association

VIETNAM
LUND'S STUDENT UNION'S COLLECTION FOR
HANOI'S STUDENTS 1968 · PRICE 3 kr
Postgiro 636860

Now, I'm going to try to tell you, Joel Jansson, what it was like when I heard you playing for the first time. I had found a record in a book (Jan Ling: *Nyckelharpan*), a small 45 that was tucked in the back. The first few songs sounded much like illustrations in a book.

Then when your songs came on, an actual experience came upon me, a feeling that I rarely have had in connection with Swedish folk music. First, it was the rhythm, of course, or the beat, as one says. Those goody-goody straight Swedish melodies, nothing to be afraid of, whoever you may be.

From the same place as that old dance music that you always heard and liked. But at a distance. Joy and power, delivered with the nyckelharpa's rich sound. It was the first time I heard the old-fashioned way of playing that is adapted to the instrument, with the bass and the fifth included in basically every stroke so that they feed sound into the resonant strings. A throbbing sound that endows the simplest melody with a halo of sounds.

The only thing I can compare it to is when drums, guitar, and bass sometimes come together to form one sound. And just as it all is starting to sound familiar and straightforward, I started noticing that you heard a lot better back in those days.

I mean the holes between the bowing, the big calm that makes the quick and little unruly movements, have plenty of space in all the excitement. Just what I thought I learned from the Rolling Stones and all the other black and white big city musicians who set out to penetrate all layers of ideas and abstractions to get to the body, the straight and physical. The joy of existing manifested in sound.

It was like coming home and discovering that you don't need to forget or smooth over your history, that you have a right to it, and that it is fine as a tool for the future. Even if you do want to play rock music.

I wonder how it is that I hear such unusual qualities in your playing when there is so much great Swedish folk music.

But I guess it is because you played for dancing, as long as anyone wanted to dance to the nyckelharpa, until they started feeling like its sounds were too fickle and outdated. And perhaps you weren't technically skilled enough to be appreciated at the spelman gatherings, when artists and teachers and distinguished homeland men were looking for something national to rest their ears on, something that was slick enough to pass for the people's culture to their ears.

I have great reverence for the spelmän's crooked rhythm, which constantly stops and starts back up again, and their peculiar melodies.

It feels as though the music attests to a will of high culture in the middle of the woods, a struggle against nature but on fair terms. It would be interesting to know where that music, that way of living, would have been able to go had it been given the chance to develop for a few more centuries, instead of being split by technologies and the forces of a capitalist economy.

I feel related to that music too. But it hasn't spoken to me like your playing, with its regular steady rhythm, a direct and secure impact on body and mind.

I must have arrived here when you offered me the final and conclusive proof that I had heard right. Because you did what I always thought of as the highest of some forms of rock.

I mean, to offer up the universe for free, in the midst of the simplest music. I don't want to be religious or crazy, but I don't have any other words to describe the feeling when you hear how in the middle of everything, the music rhythmically and physically stops. Yes, the beat goes on, but you have found a sound on the harp and you hold out for half a beat, or at least for a bit too long, so that you can hear your wish to leave the melody and its simple-minded niceties behind and dive right into matter.

For a second, you don't give a shit about what is up or down, and let the sound split into all its constituents. And you offer up that sensation for free, without mannerisms. I mean, Flamingokvintetten [The Flamingo Quintet] are perhaps popular because they sound nice, and Hoola Bandoola because they offer conceptual security in a compelling way.

And then there is Kebnekajse, which is trying to highlight the grandiose in the melodies of Dalarna. But if we want to fully take the step into some kind of Swedish folk rock, we don't need to stop at the average, haughty, or slightly superficial. There is something to be gleaned, even though the sources are few.

I saw you a few years ago. I hope you are well, you were about seventy-one then and you never know.

Regards
BOANDERS

P. 169 "'TRÄD, GRÄS OCH STENAR' IN SKÄRHOLMEN"

"Träd, Gräs och Stenar," a bunch of kids and wonderful noise came together this weekend at the library in Skärholmen.

It was the first in a series of family Sundays which are to be held at the library. The purpose is for all ages to actively participate and do something together.

This past Sunday it was with the motto "listen to and make music." It was no normal performance by a pop group. The program started way before the guys in the band were finished rigging their instruments and electric apparatuses. When the first drum was unpacked, the kids flocked around it, pounding.

Those who weren't helping the guys in Träd, Gräs och Stenar to create music on their instruments had brought their own simple instruments. For those who didn't have anything to blow into or bang on, simple plastic cups with rice in them were arranged. Using rice to keep time worked exceptionally well, even though the floor in some spots started to look like a rice field.

Everyone had fun, everyone was participating, and that was the whole point.

MARGARETA BOGSTRÖM

DESPITE THAT THE PARTY ON GÄRDET WILL TAKE PLACE ON FRIDAY (FROM 15:00), SATURDAY AND SUNDAY (FROM 12:00). COME AS EARLY AS YOU CAN. IF ENOUGH PEOPLE COME, THE PARTY CAN'T BE STOPPED.

Bring food and instruments and we'll show the authorities what the grass is for. We have squabbled with them about permits since February. It was about toilets, parking spaces, and worries that the lyrics would include political (!) texts. The authorities have systematically worked against us. If one does not have private contacts and an expertise in bureaucracy, it's not possible to procure all these strange permits that at least fifteen strange authorities have harassed us with. Trying to sabotage our Party.

Everyone is welcome.

At first, we wanted to be in Hagaparken. We weren't allowed.

Then we moved to Skeppsholmen.

A week ago, the Swedish Building Agency (who owns the grass) suddenly sent us information that we needed to pay 50,000 kronor, in advance, for destroyed lawns.

We don't have 50,000 kronor.

The Opera receives grants of 30 million kronor each year from taxes. Their audience consists of a small elite group. Most operagoers belong to Social Group 1 [the upper-class socioeconomic demographic]. It's their entertainment that the taxpayers subsidize.

The party at Gärdet will include pop music, folk music, jazz, old-time dance, games for everyone, film, theater, and dance for everyone. And music by everyone. Bring simple things that you can play there. The party is for people. That is why the authorities have tried to stop us. They will not succeed.

We have decided to have the party on Gärdet by Borgen. Sixty different music groups, theater groups, and singers will be participating. They are coming from all parts of Sweden, but mostly from Stockholm. Lots of people are coming from other towns.

We can't cancel this Party. Which the authorities are trying to force us to do. It would mean letting a big audience down. Most of our work has been put into this bureaucracy. We haven't been able to work as much on the music, theaters, and other practical arrangements as we would have liked. Since the bureaucrats have been holding us back the whole time. The authorities, who should have helped us, have instead sabotaged us to the best of their ability.

We don't have time for the bureaucrats anymore.

We are having our Party--Festen om Gärdet--without permits. And we hope that as many as possible come to Gärdet. It's important.

BRING YOUR OWN ACOUSTIC INSTRUMENT OR SOMETHING YOU CAN MAKE INTO AN INSTRUMENT. WE MUST BE ABLE TO PLAY, DANCE, AND MAKE THEATER UNDER ALL CIRCUMSTANCES. BRING FOOD AND A POTTY.

These groups and musicians are playing at the party on Gärdet:

Friday between 15 and 17:
Maria Jerena, Guineas, Roland von Malmborg, Sweet Bunch of Roses, an Oriental singing and dance group, Gläns över sjö och strand, Freedom Singers, Diddlers, Skäggmanslaget [The Bearded Team]

Friday between 17 and 23:
Dra till och lägg ifrån with Peps [Persson], Snabb lindring [Quick Relief], Figaro, Hackat o mallet [Chopped and Ground], Guineas, Diddlers, Skäggmanslaget, a brass band, Solen skinner [The Sun Shines], Maces Spering, Music Is Happening, Träd gräs och stenar, Bernt Rosengrens grupp, Stepmother's Blessing.

Saturday between 12 and 18:
Welcome, Charlie's Electric Band, Old Timey String Band, Det europeiska missnöjets grunder [The Foundations of European Discontent], Stepmother's Blessing, Freedom Singers, Fire, Bonnie o Blues, November, Gläns över sjö och strand, Slim Notini Blues Band, Opus 3, Terrible Ones, Herbert.

Saturday between 18 and 24:
Roland von Malmborg, Guineas, Skäggmanslaget, Diddlers, Gudibrallan, Snabb lindring, Träd gräs och stenar, Dra till och lägg ifran with Peps, Nisse Sandströms grupp, Oriental singing and dance group, Love Explosion

Sunday between 12 and 18:
Roll's Express, Hackat o malet, Peter Unge, Michelles, Bernt Staaf, Red White and Blues, Atlas, Ljudbolaget [Sound Company], Arbete och Fritid [Work and Leisure], Gunder Hägg, an Oriental singing and dance group, Johan Zetterberg, Högdalen, Fire, Träd gräs och stenar

Sunday between 18 and 22:
Herbert, Gläns över sjö och strand, Det europeiska missnöjets grunder, Blue October, Music Is Happening, Solen skinner, Turid Lundkvist, Jan Hammarlund, Atlantic Ocean, Telefon Paisa, Vetlanda Landsortsband, Blues Quality

We are making a more detailed program that will be at Gärdet.
There will, of course, be a number of changes. New groups and artists can still sign up. Or just come by and bring an instrument!

357

Sten Bergman was at the Stockholm Courthouse on
7/3 1972 and was convicted of organizing an
illegal event. The reason for the sentence was
that for any permit given, a person must be listed
as responsible according to their principles. In
our society, a group of people does not have the
opportunity to be jointly responsible for their
actions. THE VERDICT WILL BE APPEALED TO THE
COURT OF APPEAL.................

2nd PARTY AT
GÄRDET
BY US FOR US
20, 21, 22, 23 AUG.
FROM THURS. 18
PEOPLE PARTY POP
ALL MUSIC
IN THE GRASS
FREE
BRING FOOD, BLANKETS, ETC.

GÄRDET
STOCKHOLM
June 11-13 1971
Come and be as you want
Warm up your heart together
with everyone else

TRÄD, GRÄS OCH STENAR

One of Sweden's "international" pop bands has
released their third LP. It's Träd, Gräs & Stenar,
and they are "international" just because the Yanks
have started taking interest in them and since
Country Joe--from Country Joe & the Fish--once sat
in a studio and happily listened to them, surprised,
liking and concurring.

But in New Guinea's jungles, they naturally
haven't heard from them. They probably don't even
have radios or record players and definitely not
"stadiums." The best they can do is a flute, a drum,
and their own voice. It's music that is created
solitarily and simply, that is called folk music.
If the folk musicians don't listen to the pop band,
then the pop band definitely listens to the folk
music. Then new music is created, and it's "international"--not because it gets played on American
radio stations but--because it has its roots in folk
music from the whole world.

You can hear Africa's drums, India's flutes, and
Häslingland's fiddles in their music. You can hear
the humming and lalala-ing from the Rocky Mountains, but they also play like the Stones and Dylan,
because the Stones and Dylan are the folk music of
our generation, born out of a vast crowd of blues
guitarists and skiffle bands.

Träd, Gräs och Stenar tells it like it is, what
our lives are like right now. The music shows, when
it's at its hottest--when it's live, of course--that
people flow into one another, because the instruments
are as difficult to separate as the people and their
actions and vibrations. Everything becomes a song,
all people become one tribe, and thus begins a new
society with all that the tribe has in common.

They sing the Stones' song "I Can't Get No Satisfaction"--I feel dissatisfied because everything is
so "plastic," so mechanical, those in power on their
way to destroying our earth. But all is not hopeless
because someone is sitting on our back and if we get
up, he falls: help him fall. (Svarta pärla.)

Svarta pärla [The Black Pearl] is so close, even though it's on the bottom of an ocean. It is our own life when it gets to bloom in freedom. Like in the middle of the LP's fold-out, where four sitting Buddhas and two standing street sweepers share a moment of a perfect sunrise. Or as happy, liberated faces of young Chinese women, or when a naked girl gets up out of the clear water, far away from the city's poisoning usefulness. In the poster that comes with this LP as well as in the music, these are many peoples' dreams, "folksy" wishes of music of one's own (where you give "the musician" his piece of bread instead of protecting enormous record companies), of clean water, of meaningful work, clean air, unpoisoned nature, and a life close to the earth instead of a life lived in the shadows of machines. What people don't want to acknowledge is that dreams can only be realized at the price of lowered production and consumption, at the price of decentralization and lower standards.

And what is even more difficult to understand is the price that the armed Black Panther is willing to pay for agency over their own life.

But Träd, Gräs & Stenar stand in solidarity with him too, as with all oppressed people, who with or without weapons want to overthrow the monster with shovels for hands and build a new society.

What does all this have to do with music, someone asks? Entertainment and politics don't go together? If they want to change society they shouldn't waste their time on a bunch of useless music? And it's these people who ask who should listen to Träd, Gräs och Stenar. They say that there is just one human, and everyone can ask their heart for their needs. The illness is just fragmentation, not living a whole life.

To divide reality up into work and free time, seriousness and pleasure, duty and desire, when everything really should be connected, which it was once, when the harvest was a party and seriousness at the same time. At that time, you weren't able to buy happiness with your hard-earned money.

Society is everything—it's how you make music, how you love, how you talk, how you work, how you live. If you think that society is wrong, you can start anywhere to change it, change yourself. You don't need to get into politics in the narrowest sense. You can start, like Träd, Gräs & Stenar, with music.

It's possible to still end up in jail sometimes, which one of them did the other day for protesting for clean air, clean water, clean food, and more housing. It was a protest against everything that destroys us, in the way that Träd, Gräs & Stenar's music, in its most beautiful circumstances (like at Gärdet this summer) is a demonstration of everything that is good for people and that too many are missing. All that is good starts off with being together, a connection other than conversation is needed. Someone plays the drum, someone plays guitar, and someone who has never dared before sings "All Along the Watchtower," as if he wrote it all, as if he felt it all, as if he dreamt it all.

Hello my friend
So happy to see you again
I was so alone
All by myself
I just couldn't make it.

Have you heard Baby
What the wind's blowin' round
Have you heard Baby
A whole lot a people's coming right on down
Communication is coming on strong
I don't give a damn Baby
If your hair is short or long
I said get out of your grave
Everybody is dancing in the street
Do what you know, do not be slow
You got to practice what you preach
Because it is time for you and me
Come to face reality
Forget about the past Baby
Things ain't what they used to be

P. 204 <u>"MERA MUSIC"</u> [More Music] <u>(CONTINUED)</u>

Keep on straight ahead
We got to stand side by side
Send power to the people, that's what
they're screaming
Freedom of the soul
Pass it on
pass it on, to the young and the old

You got to tell the children the truth
They don't need a whole lot of lies
Because one of these days, Baby
They'll be running things

So when you give them love
You better give it right
Woman and child, man and wife
The best love to have is the love of life

Hello my friend
It's so good to see you again
I've been all by myself
I don't think I can make it alone
Keep on fighting.

Jimi Hendrix
1970

P. 205 <u>"YOUNGSTERS IN OLD SCHOOL MAKE POP OUT OF</u>
<u>FOLK MUSIC"</u>

In an old primary school, which has been closed for several years, in Grönås, Järvsö, intensive musical experimentation was conducted this summer. The extremely down-to-earth and completely Swedishized pop group Träd, gräs och stenar has realized the pricelessness of old Swedish folk music and now wants to do everything to pass it on in the way they play it. Two of the group's members interrupted their studies at the Royal Academy of Music in Stockholm in order to devote themselves to the music they believe is more important. Today, Träd, gräs och stenar is by far the most interesting group in new Swedish pop.

BY JAN-ÅKE PETTERSSON

Träd, Gräs och Stenar held a concert at Cue together with Fläsket Brinner last Friday. There was live music practically the entire evening. With a short break, it went on from 8:30 pm to 1:00.

It was Träd, Gräs och Stenar who started it all. They had just come from Copenhagen and were passing through. No one knew that they were going to play, and there would probably have been more people if they had been advertised.

Although many thought it was nice, they themselves were not satisfied with their music.

"After staying in Copenhagen, our music becomes hard city music. If we can get out into the country, it will become softer and more harmonious. We live in the countryside as much as we can and have a house in Hälsingland. In order for a group to function, one must also be able to live together."

SOPORIFIC

On the technical level, their music can be characterized as grinding and soporific. A song can be as long as you want--there is no limitation in the music, but the improvisations can flow as they wish. Guitarist Bo Anders Persson is mainly responsible for these.

What is it then that they want to achieve?

"The wholeness you get together with people. Contact with ourselves and with the audience. We want to try to reach as far into a feeling as possible. That's why we talk a little before we play the song, so the audience won't misunderstand the whole thing and get the wrong feelings."

Their style means that those who go for listening and getting a feeling will not be disappointed. You have plenty of time to flow into the music.

Some people characterize their music as "deliberately bad." The lousier you play, the greater the contact with the audience is.

IDEA

"This is completely wrong. It's a stupid idea of what sound is. They start with an idea of what is good and bad. It can't be like that, because what is good and bad?

"Our music is a big rite in which everyone participates. If you look at it that way, this division never occurs."

P. 210 CLIPPINGS

Träd, gräs och stenar: "Back to nature!"

Awful at Olympia
The audience went home...

"Träd, gräs och stenar" strange squiggles on the
Grängesberg stage

Träd, gräs och stenar
A pop group with a message:
FARM THE LAND!

Folk fest at Gävle museum with Träd, Gräs och Stenar

(Image caption: Close to 300 people listened to
Träd, Gräs och Stenar at the museum on Wednesday
evening)

Träd, Gräs och Stenar play in Bollnäs
Bollnäs girl is part of their nature commune

P. 211 CLIPPINGS

Music band on the prowl:
MUSIC FOR THE PEOPLE
SO EVERYONE UNDERSTANDS

Träd, gräs och stenar on the Vindel River's beach

Träd, Gräs och Stenar
spoke on environmental protection

THE POP GROUP "Träd, gräs och stenar" from Stockholm
played at the local history society's unusual
evening by the Vindel River. The group, who played
at full volume, aroused some curiosity in the
audience.

TRÄD, GRÄS OCH STENAR
another word for human

P. 211 "TRÄD, GRÄS OCH STENAR AT HAGAHUSET:
THEY GIVE OUT FOOD, MUSIC AND AN EXHIBITION"

BY TOMMY RANDER

Träd Gräs Och Stenar--A shimmer of mystery exists
around that name. They were the first band to start
thinking about whether pop really has to sound a
certain way. They were called Persson Sound at that
time. Then they started calling themselves International Harvester, and finally decided on the current
name. The members have also varied somewhat.

They played at Hagahuset on Friday and Saturday.
Many people came, and those who got hungry were
fed. Träd, Gräs och Stenar had brought a group from
"Fröet" in Stockholm who prepare food, consisting of
"friendly" farmed vegetables, i.e. sprouted from the
earth without any aids other than the natural ones.

In addition to the food group, a cultivation
group is also included in the tour. It, in turn, has
brought an exhibition about "friendly farming."

For outsiders, those who don't get Träd, Gräs Och
Stenar, this may seem somewhat confusing.

But it is not at all. The members of the band have
long worked in different ways for alternative forms
of life. They want to see more people in the countryside, growing their own food and creating their own
culture.

What they've done now is just take the plunge--
their tour will thus be a demonstration of an alternative. Today, Träd, Gräs Och Stenar are playing at
Backa Fritidsgård. They start early in the morning
and go on all day.

The intention is that all categories of people
can participate. In addition to music, and the
band prefers that the audience participate in the
performance, there is food that the restaurant
Fröet is providing. As well as an exhibition on
Friendly Farming. An alternative in the middle of
the stone desert.

The group brushed away any accusations of rural
romanticism. As time goes on, it is increasingly
clear that the current tendency towards increased
growth for the big cities and a thinning and over-
grown countryside will not last. It is about creating
new forms of life, they say.

Träd Gräs Och Stenar's music is powerful and strong. It is very collective and compact in its whole being. Where it comes from is difficult to determine--Bo Anders Persson believes that on the one hand, it is very Swedish, but at the same time they also play some songs by Dylan and the Rolling Stones.

But they are songs that somehow are generation-songs, songs you can't escape because you lived at a certain point in time.

P. 213 FLYER

PARKFEST in Stadsparken
Everyone can come and everything is free

Cordial and cinnamon rolls, boxcars, kites, soccer, games and music:

Saturday TRÄD GRÄS o STENAR play from 13:00
Sunday ARBETE o FRITID play from 13:00 with a break for NATIONALTEATERN'S children's play "JUBEL I HOLKEN" [JOY IN HOLKEN] at 15:00 (all times are estimates) there will also be music all around the park: AGENTEN also Hiss Cosmo Planning, GRUS i DOJAN, violins and YOU

MISCELLANEOUS:
Saturday at 20 in AF's grand hall.
LUMINOUS LIGHT SHOW
With King Kong from Denmark and Träd, gräs och stenar
Tickets at entrance 5 kr
Sunday at 20 and 22 at Lilla teatern, Sandg. 14
Nationalteatern will play LEV HÅRT - DÖ UNG
[LIVE HARD – DIE YOUNG]

Arranged: Studentaftonutskottet [The Student Evening Committee] and Lilla teatern

P. 258 "TWO YOUNGSTERS FLED THE BIG CITY'S INHUMANITY NOW THEY ARE INVESTING THEMSELVES IN A NEW EXISTENCE IN THE COUNTRY"

But are there living conditions for them in the Bollnäs-village Herte?

Is there still room for a living countryside, now when demands on effectiveness and productivity grow all the more violent? Does the future in Hälsingland hold red cabins, with geraniums in the windows, and maybe a couple of cows grazing in the meadow? The countryside is not completely dead yet, and perhaps there is hope. As a kind of protest and aversion against the inhumanity of the big cities, a change is starting to become discernable. Youngsters who have lived their entire lives in these stone deserts are moving out into the countryside.

FRIENDLY FARMING FREE EARTH MAN EARTH

On friendly farming:
Our ancestors had a saying: "Nature always provides a set table." We have not bought our own lives, but given them for free, and all around us nature is generous with life in various forms: everywhere in the earth are the seeds of plants that are just waiting for the right conditions to germinate. But there are many different forms of life and man cannot just take for himself, but must constantly work to support the other species of life that belong to human life. Like other living creatures, she must defend her habitat, both against internal and external enemies.

That struggle has taken various forms throughout history, but it has always been characterized by man's will for the greatest possible freedom under the given conditions.

The fight for freedom can be waged with varying degrees of insight into man's role in nature and the universe. At some point, the erroneous idea arose that man could make rapid progress by making himself master of nature. As long as he only had simple tools to help him, he could only do limited damage, but now that he has access to chemistry and technology, a flawed theory becomes a threat to the human race and its companions on Earth. Therefore, it is necessary that we learn to distinguish between two different lines of our work, one friendly and one unfriendly.

Nothing happens without a need, neither in nature nor in society. But the question is: whose needs are guiding the development? If individual ideological interests are allowed to assert themselves, this means that development follows the unfriendly line, with disasters as a necessity and consequence. Such is the development we see around us today. If development is to follow the friendly line, the majority of people must find ways to implement a society where the needs of the family or the whole become the guide for development. And so it will certainly happen, as it becomes increasingly difficult for us to consider the destruction of the environment we live in as being in our own interest.

In order to achieve a good life in a friendly society, man must consciously make clear to himself what technology, chemistry, and social organizations he really needs and put the rest on the garbage heap of history. And to understand what the real needs are, he must start with matter and its laws. It is completely unreasonable that man could achieve better conditions by separating his thinking from matter, because matter is the same as life. Life is a material force. We can see how life concentrates in the matter, causing it to develop and move.

But even the matter that lies lifeless and dead to our gaze is not separated from life. Everything around us is in various stages of building up and breaking down. It is not possible to imagine matter separated from life, any more than life separated from matter. But what we call "dead matter" is currently not as intensely alive as, for example, plants and animals, and it is natural for us to place more importance on what is "alive," developing and moving before our eyes.

In order to obtain food without causing accidents to both his own kind and other living organisms, man must observe nature as it is and only do things that involve as little intervention as possible. This is the basis of friendly farming. The earth is alive. We take help from life in the soil, both from micro-life, earthworms, and "weeds." We ourselves cannot create the life that will help the edible plants to grow, but we must try to make use of the life that exists, directed at the organisms that can help us.

We are not the first to work along such lines. Before the development of technology had given man the resources to rummage around the earth at will, you simply had to work with nature to survive. In our country, it is especially the traditional Finnish way of slash-and-burn agriculture that shows many traits that can be called downright friendly. It arose before cultivation was governed by an economic system based on individual profit interests and metaphysical thinking. Now our own situation is in many ways similar to that of the Finnish immigrants: if we want to survive, we must start with our needs and look at nature with undistracted eyes.

The human environment primarily includes clean air and fresh water. In order for humans to feel good, green grass, "green" trees (oak, linden, maple, elm, and rowan), as well as berry bushes and fruit trees, are also required. But for such an environment to be achieved, every single individual must participate in the struggle.

In our climate zone, there are two different kinds of plant life: the brown life (the forest) and the green life (the cultivated land). Both have their typical plants, animals, and insects that do not mix with each other in any way but stand in mutual opposition.

It is in the green vegetation that man can grow his food, and therefore he must help and defend the green life against the brown, which otherwise wants to take over. This happens by creating the best possible conditions for the "green" plants and their micro-life.

By allowing the grass to grow and decompose, we add "fertilization" to the soil without using either artificial fertilizers or cow manure. The use of cow dung has been shown to cause the plants to be of poor quality and become so weak that they have to be "protected" against diseases with various toxins. The poisons are of course dangerous for both us and for the green microflora which should help the plants to absorb the substances they need from the soil and air.

We do not sow special "green fertilizer plants" but use plants that come naturally. In this way, nature gets the opportunity to restore the imbalance that cultivation may have brought about.

Our ancestors needed cattle to survive, [but] we are beginning to know how to live well on grains and vegetables with only an insignificant consumption of meat, fish, and dairy products. When we are no longer dependent on the cow, life becomes easier and we can feed many more people off the same area of land. Therefore, we should not base the cultivation on fertilization with cow dung.

We also do not make special composts, but allow plant parts to break down in the top layer of the soil, just as it does in nature. The microflora is not the same on the soil surface as further down. It is the top organisms who, with the help of the air's free oxygen, must break down grass and old plant parts into plant nutrition. If we plow these down to a depth of 10 inches, the decomposition is slow and the natural life in the soil is hindered. Instead, we have to work the soil from the surface, for example with a hoe or knife harrow.

The cultivation also consists of many details and much remains to be investigated. Eventually, a new science based on life must emerge. But the practice that has been done so far shows that cultivation according to the guidelines above is possible and can support many people in a relatively small area.

It is clear that the continued work cannot be guided by financial interests, but must be guided by our need for healthy living food from a living earth.

If anyone has any comments on the content of this article, we'd love to hear from them. In that case, write to:

"Friendly Farming" PI 168, 680 63 Likenäs or to Anders Björnsson, Björnliden 68063 Likenäs

MORE PRACTICAL INFORMATION ON CULTIVATION IN AN UPCOMING ISSUE OF *HUVUDBLAD*

P. 261 *HUVUDBLADET, 2*

I am alive...
I'm hungry...
Food does NOT come from the factory

MATMAKT DU ÄR VAD DU ÄTER
[FOOD POWER YOU ARE WHAT YOU EAT]

ALL VIT MAT ÄR DÖD
[ALL WHITE FOOD IS DEAD]

HUMANS CAN ABSORB THE PROTEIN IN SOYBEANS, LENTILS,
CHICKPEAS BETTER THAN MEAT PROTEIN

If you don't have the opportunity to grow your own,
always find out where the vegetables were grown. Try
to buy directly from the grower.

IN SOUTH AMERICA THEY GROW SO MUCH COFFEE AND
BANANAS THAT THERE ISN'T ENOUGH FOOD FOR THE PEOPLE

(Map of biodynamic farmers in Sweden and their
locations)

TRY THIS BREAD, IT'S BAKED WITH REAL FLOUR
THIS IS HOW YOU MAKE IT

MIX TWO CUPS OF GRAHAM FLOUR WITH TWO CUPS OF COARSE
RYE FLOUR + 1 TBSP SEA SALT
POUR IN TWO CUPS OF WATER AND KNEAD FOR A BIT
SHAPE INTO A LOAF AND BRUSH WITH WATER. COVER!!
LET SIT IN A WARM SPOT OR IN A WARMING OVEN FOR A
FEW HOURS. IT WILL RISE JUST A LITTLE.
BAKE UNDER A LID!! AT 125°-150° IN AN OVEN FOR TWO HOURS
COVER WITH A TEA TOWEL UNTIL COMPLETELY COOLED

WHERE HAVE YOU BEEN?
IN THE FIELD!! THAT WE ARE LEASING OUTSIDE THE CITY.
SUPER FUN!!

KJELL ARMANS JORD OCH BRÖD
[GOOD BOOK ON FARMIN"]

QUIT USING THOSE JARS AND CHEW THE FOOD FOR THE
KID INSTEAD

(Items on the counter: Sesame seeds, Brown rice,
Seaweed)

I'VE LEARNED A LOT FROM A COUPLE OF BOOKS. THE FIRST
ONE IS CALLED "TIO VÄGAR TILL HÄLSAN" ["TEN PATHS
TO HEALTH"] BY ILSE CLAUSNITZER WHO LIVES IN
ÖVERBYS 185 000 VAXHOLM BUT I GOT IT FOR 7:50 AT THE
HEALTH FOOD STORE. THE OTHER BOOK I WAS THINKING
OF IS "DEN STORA VÄGEN" ["THE GREAT ROAD"] FROM
AQUARIAN SOCIETY, BOX 61 HAMNEDA

ATTACKS

Against attacks of various kinds, there are a number of tricks you can use. One is different herbal decoctions, with which you spray the plants. By using the insects' sense of smell when they attack sick plants, you can thus deceive them. Some decoctions also have a certain stimulating effect on the plants.

However, the herbal decoction is only a temporary rescue. It is always important to find the cause of the plant becoming sick and infested and eliminate it.

HARVEST

Vegetables are harvested as they ripen. The root vegetables must have been exposed to frost before they are harvested. During frost attacks, they secrete substances from the leaves into the fruit, which thereby gets a higher quality and more nutrition and keeps better during storage.

When it comes to root vegetables, potatoes are taken up first, followed by beets and turnips, and finally carrots and celery, and last but not least, parsnips.

Greens and other waste are left outside in the field, where they can become surface compost.

STORAGE

The products must be stored so that they, to the greatest extent possible, experience the same conditions as when they grow in the soil. As a rule, you can say that what grows underground should be stored underground, for example in an underground cellar, and for what grows above ground, drying is often a suitable storage method.

FINISHING WORK

After the harvest, you go over the field and level it so that there are no pits left for next year's cultivation.

PREPARATION FOR NEXT YEAR'S CULTIVATION

First of all, for the sake of decomposition, the areas to be farmed next year are hoed. If the surface has become peat or one is working on new land that is being prepared for next year, use a sharpened spade to cut off roots before doing the hacking.

THIS SPADE IS CONVENIENT TO HAVE WHEN CUTTING ROOTS BELOW THE SOIL SURFACE. IT IS ALSO SUITABLE FOR DIGGING PLANTING HOLES.

SCALLOPED EDGE --> THE ENTIRE SHOVEL IS SHARPENED

COVERING

Another way of breaking new ground without turning the soil, with little effort, is to cover the soil with organic material or cardboard or newsprint. After one or two years, you then have arable land.

LITE OM LIVET I JORDEN
[A BIT ON LIFE IN THE EARTH]

In all cultivation, it is important to have as much life as possible in the soil so that Mother Nature can produce healthy, hearty, and friendly plants for humans. If people do not eat products that are healthy and hearty, they cannot become healthy and hearty either.

Nature in itself is healthy and hearty. Nature does not allow any disease. When cultivating, it is therefore important to follow the laws of nature as far as possible, i.e., to work together with nature. Then you are also working for life. Man can also follow other laws and work against nature, but then he is also working against life.

In the soil, there are countless species of organisms, all of which have different functions and live at different depths and in different environments down in the earth. Each organism is adapted to an environment, where it has a task to fulfill. Some organisms work with the breakdown in the soil and others work with building it up. Through this ingenious and completely natural organization found in organisms in the soil, decomposed substances needed at the surface remain at the surface layer and the substances needed further down in the earth are transported there by organisms at the same time as they are further broken down, processed, and assembled into new substances.

The root is also an organism and just like all other organisms, the roots have secretions of various kinds similar to, for example, human sweat secretion. These secretions are food for certain bacterial cultures, which in turn produce the nutrients that the roots need. In this way, they help cover each other's needs at the same time as they complete tasks for each other. In practice, they thus live in a kind of symbiosis.

PLOGEN KOMMER!! [THE PLOW IS COMING!!]

When the plow turns the soil it simultaneously creates chaos to life in the soil. The entire intelligent organization and structure that life in the earth has built up when it was allowed to work under natural and friendly conditions, is then destroyed.

The different life forms in the soil are tossed about all topsy-turvy so that the micro-bacteria that belong in the surface layer come one and two decimeters down into the soil and end up in a completely foreign environment at the same time as micro-life from below ends up in the surface layer. At the same time the different lifeforms end up in completely alien environments, the different communications between the different species of life are also destroyed. In their alien environment, the various lives can also not perform their tasks.

It's obvious that plowing isn't good for the earth when one looks at the consequences for life in the soil. That the soil is still able to be productive after being plowed is largely due to the infinite strength of life itself.

To break up a grass bank, you can use a knife harrow.

At the moment we are writing a little pamphlet on Friendly Farming that we will be done with shortly.

Friendly Farming
% Fröet
Jakobsbergsgatan 18
Stockholm

THE EARTH IS ALIVE
THE EARTH IS FRIENDLY
WEEDS, WORMS AND CRITTERS ARE
OUR FRIENDS

FRIENDLY FARMING IN PRACTICE
THE GRASS IS THE FOUNDATION

[Drawings of tools: cultivator, wooden rake, triangle hoe]

THE SEEDBED

With a cultivator, you level the ground so that there are no pits that the water can collect in. At the same time, you shake the soil out of tufts of grass and lightly hoe the surface. This hoeing should be done two or three times before sowing.

Then tufts of grass and other hard-to-degrade plant parts are raked together in rows. A wooden rake is fine. By gathering these plant parts in rows, there is no risk of them tearing the seedbeds later during hoeing.

The triangular hoe is used to make seed rows. An important thing to remember is to stretch a piece of string, which you follow when you make the seed row. In this way, the row becomes straight, which facilitates the cultivation of the soil.

SOWING

The sowing itself is done by hand or by using a simple seed planter. The seeds are not covered, but if it is a wide seed row, you can push a wheelbarrow over them, and if you have a narrow seed row, you can lead a bicycle in the seed row itself so that the seeds are pressed into the soil. Then the seeds will take root more easily.

Since the seeds you can buy in Sweden are cultivated in a warmer climate than we have in this country, you should wait to sow until the weather is warm. Those seeds need a lot of heat to germinate.

POTATOES

For planting potatoes, you first dig a furrow with a spade or drag a triangular hoe in the ground about a decimeter deep at most. The potatoes are placed at 15-20 cm intervals with the sprouts pointing upwards. Then you fill the furrow with soil and tamp it down.

The potatoes can be advantageously placed right next to and parallel to the rows with raked grass and weeds. The rows can then be cupped up around the potatoes as they grow during the summer. Then at the same time, you move about the rows of compost so that the decomposition is accelerated there.

[Illustration: Cotyledon]

PLANTING

When planting, use either the triangular hoe or the sharpened spade and make a pit.

The plants have first been purchased or cultivated in a cold frame. When planting, remove the two bottom leaves, which are called cotyledons, and--if the plant is large--also the largest leaves, as they may require too much nutrition in the plant's critical acclimatization stage. The cotyledons are removed because chlorophyll doesn't break down in the soil in a beneficial way. Instead, toxins are formed.

Then you place the plant on the sloping side of the planting hole and cover it with soil up to the first leaves. Then you tamp down hard so that the plant is firmly stuck in the soil. Then there should be a small pit around the plant where water can collect.

With this planting technique, you get a bigger root and at the same time, the plant forms a "knee" as it grows, which makes it stand more firmly.

Planting takes place in cloudy weather partly because the air then is moist and partly because the sun's rays should not hit the plant's roots.

P. 263 *HUVUDBLADET, 3 (CONTINUED)*

WEEDING
A WEEDING HOE

AN OLD SAW BLADE, SHARPENED ON THE BACK, CAN BE MADE
INTO A WEED HOE. YOU FIRST PLACE THE SAW BLADE ON
A METAL BRACKET THAT HAS A HOLE FOR THE SHAFT. TO
BEND THE SAW BLADE, YOU HEAT IT. IT IS GOOD TO HAVE A
LEDGE ON THE BRACKET THAT THE SAW BLADE CAN REST UP
AGAINST. THEN THE SAW BLADE IS SECURED BY WRAPPING
STEEL WIRE OR INSERTING SCREWS.

Weeding is most important in the time immediately after sowing. Weeds should never be allowed
to grow so much that they take over the cultivated
plants. When weeded, the weeds can remain on the
ground to serve as surface composting.
Weeds play an important role. They are medicinal
plants that supply nutrients to the soil. By using
them as surface compost, you help to maintain a
proper balance in the soil.

THINNING

By sharpening a tablespoon on one side, you get an
excellent tool for thinning and clearing the seed row.

LOOSENING THE SOIL

When loosening the soil, you use the cultivator
again, which you easily drag back and forth on the
surface itself. Oxygen then gets into the soil and
in this way, life in the soil is helped. If you have
poor life in the soil, you need to loosen it up as
soon as a crust forms on the surface.

P. 269 FLYER

FRÖET
Tasty, sound and cheap food
Grains and vegetables
Home baked whole grain bread with herbal tea
Nature-friendly farming

OPEN Weekdays 11-18
Saturdays 12-15

Jakobsgatan 18

P. 272 CLIPPING

The group of youngsters came from Stockholm to the
village of Likenäs in Värmland driven by a burning
interest, but without any knowledge

P. 299 ALBUM COVER

I.
I LJUSET AV DIN DAG
[IN THE LIGHT OF YOUR DAY]

In the light of your day
Do what you like
In the dark of your night
Do what you like

Everyone needs their food
Come one let's make it together
You are a child of the universe
So are all of us

The man wants you in his hand
But he knows nothing of this beautiful land
We must find a true way to go
Open your door and let the sun shine on

Let the bird out
A bird like a sun
Let her be free
And never hold her down
Let her be free
Let her fly
Let her burn

Hear her sing:
Come come together

Give more life!

VÅRAN VILA
[OUR REST]

In the light of the sunset
Your eye was so grey
When I upon you think
I know what I have
Out of the deep and from high above
I call out to you
And if you don't respond
I won't get upset

By my ancestors' skies
Your belly was so nice
It lived in my hands
It was our evening prayer
In the grass under the sky
Where life is born
Where the ground moves slowly
While time stands still

We were going to make things good
Yes, hand in hand
But we saw the smoke approaching
It drifts from land to land
It's capitalism's lackeys
That are pushing their game
When a few bags of money
Is the difference between right and wrong
On their poisoned meadows
We were to build our home
A place where their machines
Were our only inheritance

I so vividly remember that time
When things were too much for me
Everyone was in the square
And no one was having fun
The police were driving their car
The sky was yellow
I said, the fruits have ripened now
That were planted by my great great-grandfather
I said, the air is clear and the water is clean there

371

For each and every one
I said, the garden behind the wall
Who has the key to it
You said, Olle swallowed it yesterday
It's shit now
Come with me to the store
They have three flavors left
Yellow, green and white

I want to find rest now
For both you and i
We have to believe in our senses
If we like it or not
In the great storm
While the wind is changing

Arne: electric piano, Bo-Anders: guitar,
song (Våran vila), piano, Jakob: guitar, song,
Thomas: drums, song (I ljuset av din dag),
Torbjörn: bass, song, Ulla: tambourine

"Rock för kropp och själ" is recorded in Vindeln on a beautiful Friday evening in July 1971. A local home association in an old miller's residence which now is a café. We stood on the grass right next to the roaring Renfors. Fires were lit and while darkness and dew fell people danced to this song which was the next to last one that evening. Then came Gösta. Per Gud recorded it all.

"Solen går upp, solen går ner" is recorded at Bäckströms gård in Likenäs on a Saturday evening in September 1971, before we were leaving for the people's park. We had our first "lura party".

And were having a great time. And you can hear that. We have to have been about 20 or so.

The other songs are recorded at Decibel Studio by Anders Lind on 29 and 30 of January 1972.

Philemon Arthur and the Dung have come up with "Gösta."

Jonas in SEPÅ has photographed the pictures on the cover, Eva did the drawings, Thomas fixed up the sleeve, and many others as well ...

Perhaps alcohol isn't to be recommended but if you use it sometimes, there is this brew from Värmland called lura.

How to make it: mix 1 hg yeast, 1 kg sugar--or better 1,5 kg syrup or brown sugar--and 5 liters water. Add ca 1 kg berries, fruit, cider, or cordial. (black currants, red currants, apples (cut up), raisins, figs in different variations, possibly spices --cinnamon, cloves, or ginger--give good flavor)

Let it sit in a warm spot (ca 25°) for a week. Stir occasionally. The fermentation is stopped when no new bubbles are forming. Then you strain the lura and bottle it. The yeast will settle on the bottom. Let it stay there, it's not good for your stomach. Don't shake the bottles. The lura will be about 15--20% alcohol. Take it easy and good luck.

Per Gud is going to release an album with live shows from our trips during 1971. It's called "Djungelns lag" on the label Tall nr:1. Get the album from Per Gud % Sjöholm, Jungfrugatan 22, 11444, Sthlm (08/606554)

II.

A little wood mouse sits on a mountain and sniffs the air. The stars are reflected in his eyes, and he looks out over the wooded lands and ridges, and the years pass. The forest's trees grow and grow old and fall to the ground with great crashes in the silence. While new trees grow, the fallen trees disappear into the ground and are melted by the teeming belly of the earth, which pushes up more new trees that will all die and be melted too. And the sun rises, and the sun sets.

Sometimes, quite rarely, some people come through the forest hunting, dressed in hides and thick fabrics. But one day some of them settle down at the northwestern edge of the lake, and sweat and toil until they have a couple of fields to cultivate. And the moon rises, and the moon sets and the stars are reflected in the eyes of the mouse.

But soon some people come wearing "nice" clothes, speaking a language that sounds as if they were reading from a book. Lots of commotion ensues. They point and command and threaten them with their soldiers, and the people toil like never before. Now they don't work for themselves but for others. The fields get bigger while the forest gets smaller and soon a large mansion stands where the log cabin once stood. At the edge of the forest, the paupers live and in the evenings you can hear mouth harps and fiddles and laughter, while a spinet plinks and someone sings in French at the manor amid distinguished murmurs and clinking glasses. And on the mountain, the smoke rises from the mines where Samí people and other slaves toil their lives away.

The mouse brushes his whiskers and the moon, the stars, and the smoke are reflected in his eyes. He blinks and the years pass. When he opens his eyes again, the forests rumble with giant machines eating their way with sharp saw like teeth. Clear-cuts spread like big sores, and the trees turn into *Veckorevyn* [a young women's magazine], candy wrappers, and shit paper. The mansion has been turned into a big smelly oil refinery. Out of the fields, big blind concrete boxes sprout up and form a suburb, and across the lake small metal beetles hum on the highway that winds through the country towards the horizon like a dead river of metal and asphalt. The lichens on the trees die out even far away from here. The mouse stares wide-eyed, and what is reflected in his eyes is the same thing that we see every day. He feels worried. He should probably leave.

But he sees the people at the hot dog stand outside the subway station, and the blue-white flickering TV light from tens of thousands of windows, and thinks, "At first I was maybe a little jealous, but this is too much. I wonder if I'm not the one living a good life, and that it is the people who I should feel sorry for." Horrible and mysterious scents accompany the winds from the horizon and make his fine whiskers shiver and curl up, and it makes the trees die and the mouse's eyes water.

For a short moment, he is seized with melancholy and thinks: "Imagine if people's knowledge could be used for their own good, for the good of everything, in a society where neither is considered the best and no one is the last or worst. Who really knows if not first is last and best is worst? What if they could pick out the kinds of organizations, technologies and ways of life that they really needed for a meaningful and pleasant life together with all other beings and lifeforms like me, and throw the rest away on the garbage heap of history."

The smoke and the stars are reflected in the mouse's eyes and in his wide ears the highways roar louder than the sea. Then he thinks: "They will probably let themselves be fooled for a while longer, let themselves be bought off by promises of their very own seat at the table, even though they no longer seem to have any influence over its content. There are not many who can choose where they want to live and work, even once."

Suddenly the mouse sees that the lake looks dead. The lake is dead! Then a couple of fighter jets burst through the sky with a hellish roar. A clumsy tin can tumbles to the ground. It tries to look like a bush. But there are antennas on it and a text note on it that says: "Transmits data on anything that moves, sweats, smells, is hotter or colder than its surroundings, to the data center for further action."

The mouse can't read, but he can really see, and he thinks: "It's not easy to understand who invented all

this and why. But they must at least know that they
need fresh air, living soil and living water to live.
And trees, green trees. There are so many remarkable
things that have been invented, but who wants them
to be used in this way? Now they must come together
and defend their living space, against whomever. By
taking care of themselves and their grandchildren. At
least I would. But I must go now, otherwise, you never
know what might happen to me."

But the mouse remained for a while and, vibrating
in his whole body, he took one last look out over the
lands. Then he quickly disappeared into the night,
among the heather and rocks.

Then a lot of voices were heard from the city
shouting to each other and people ran between the
houses. There was a lot of murmuring and musical
instruments clattering. Like bubbles rising from
the bottom of the sea, cries rose to the sky: "Let's
Remove the Masters Over Our Heads! Let's Become
Classless Masters Without Slaves! Let's Change the
World WITH Nature! Lower Energy Consumption! No to
EEC [European Economic Community]! USA Out of Asia!
USA Out of Sweden! Capital to the People! Let the
Workers Out of the Factories! Let All the People Out
of All Kinds of Prisons! Live on Swedish Food! Don't
Support Food Imperialism! Live on Grain and Vegeta-
bles! Let the Animals Out of the Animal Factories!
Open Doors and Gates! Loosen the Moorings! Open Eyes
and Ears! Tear Down the Fences! Fire in the Mountain!
Look Out! Blow the Horns and Beat the Drums! Let the
Songs Out of the Mouths and Let the Souls Bloom! Come,
Let's Start the Whirling Dance!"

In the midst of the shouting and murmuring, a song
was heard rising and falling again, and again, and
again: "The sun is our mother, round and warm and
good. The earth is our father, round and good and
happy!"

Träd, Gräs och Stenar.

If anyone is interested in knowing a little about
grains and vegetables as food, we have a pamphlet
that can be sent for at Träd, Gräs och Stenar c/o
Abelli Geijersvägen 46, 11244 Sthlm (tel: 500432)
send with 1 krona in stamps. Feel free to write
regular letters and tell us something. Bye!

Text in the illustration in the right margin:

CHOOSE YOUR OWN SAUSAGE
A RED OR A BLUEBERRY FLAVORED GRAY

HAHA BLABLA
THE PRINCESS HAS NAILS
NIXON DONATED TEN MORE
PALME SAID THANK YOU
WE ARE BROTHERS

HIGHER
GRADES
CERTIFICATE
PAPER

BUY
WORK
BUY
WORK
BE QUIET

LOWER
HALL

Text in the illustrations on the right margin:

THE ELECTION PARTY
THE SAME SHIRT IN FIVE COLORS!
Choose today
or you will have to wait another three years
UNTIL THE NEXT DEMOCRACY DAY

RATATATATATATAT
DIE DIE DIE DIE DIE DIE

EXPERT IN DIFFERENT SUBJECTS
DIFFERENT BOOTH
FRAGMENTATION
MONOPOLY
GOD
HIGHEST HIGH
BEST

WHERE ARE YOU HERE I AM
HELLO HI
COME HERE
GET IT TOGETHER
HOO HO
HELLO
HELP HAHAH
HOW SHALL WE...
THIS IS HOW WE DO IT

HEY YOU! WAKE UP YOU'RE GOING TO SCHOOL WORK CON-
SCRIPTION
THE FACTORY, THE POINT
BE QUIET SLEEP AWAKE
COME HERE GO THERE HERE I DECIDE

Träd, Gräs och Stenar is the name of a music community that has been on the prowl all over the country since fall of '69. We play amplified electric Swedish rock and popular music, and sometimes a little folk music after Joel Jansson, the spelman. The setup is usually two guitars, electric piano, bass, and drums.

We believe that Mother Nature is our actual mother. Stone, water, air, "fire" (energy), earth, and plants are what our bodies have grown out of. All lifeforms that have created us are our parents together with that which creates us right now. Thus Träd, Gräs, och Stenar is another name for humans. All life forms living with us now in creation are our relatives and siblings. Creation is a Whole where no one is master, but everyone is living in the universe, and the universe is living in us.

The owners of the economy and their bought auxiliaries have forced us into the cities to serve at their machines and offices. In the past, people willingly agreed to this, but now they are beginning to see that in the middle of "democratic society," there is a new slavery, and in the middle of the "welfare" a new slum. The food comes from the shops in lifeless packaging, poisoned by inappropriate farming and by the treatment of the food industry and sometimes stolen at scrap prices from countries in Africa that would need it themselves, or need to use the same soil to grow something else. Our own fields are treated with byproducts from the chemical industry in Germany and the USA and the waste from our lives poisons the air and water. And yet there is not much money left when the monthly rent is paid. Such a society ultimately threatens life itself, both human life and the life of the other organisms in the air, soil, and water. In the struggle that occurs when we begin to defend our habitat, we must lift away the masters over our heads and change the world to live with nature instead of seeking to dominate it. Only then can human knowledge be used to create a good life for man in a friendly society. Traditional knowledge,

where it hasn't been extinct under pressure from imperialism, will be used together with new knowledge. Man will consciously take what he needs and put everything unnecessary on the garbage heap of history. All that glitters isn't progressive. A new culture will be created; it's necessary, together with new science with life and its conditions as the foundation.

While the knowledge of this grows, we shall sing our songs and play music as long as possible. When times get tough, we have to use the skills we have to survive, like everyone else. But something big and at the same time very mundane is happening among people. Perhaps for the first time in history we will understand the conditions under which one comes from the realm of necessity to the realm of freedom. Then it is interesting to live.

Träd, Gräs och Stenar

Torbjörn Abelli	bass
Arne Ericsson	electric piano
Thomas Gartz	drums
Bo Anders Persson	
and Jacop [*sic*] Sjöholm	guitars

P. 324 POSTER

ROCK AGAINST NUCLEAR POWER
AT KONSTFACK
FOLKKAPANJEN NEJ TILL KÄRNKRAFT – KONSTFACKSKOLAN
[FOLK CAMPAIGN AGAINST NUCLEAR
POWER – UNIVERSITY OF ARTS, CRAFTS AND
DESIGN]

FRIDAY NOV. 23 22:00-03:00
30 KR
TRÄD, GRÄS OCH STENAR
TORVMOSSEGOSSARNA
RUFF
JAJJA BAND
MIKAEL RAMIL
EBBA GRÖN
MECKI MARK MEN
NERV

SATURDAY NOV. 24 15:00-03:00
40 KR
LUPUS
BLUEGRASS SWEDES
RYKTET GÅR
CH HERMANSSON (SPEECH)
MARIA BERGOM-LARSSON (SPEECH)
DAG VAG
HOT SALSA
ASTON REJMERS
FUKT
ÖLSTA PROMENADORKESTER
ARBETE OCH FRITID
HAPPY BOYS BAND
SVEN ANÉR (SPEECH)
ARCHIMEDES BADKAR
ANDERS LINDER
ELDKVARN
COOL COMBO
MAGNUS LINDBERG BAND
DOKTOR ZEKE

SÖNDAG NOV. 25 13:00-21:00
40 KR
LILL LINDFORS
JANNE SCHAFFER, STEFAN BROLUND, BJÖRN J:SON LIND
CABARET BORTKASTAT o UPPKASTAT
BYSIS
BJÖRN KJELLSTRÖM (SPEECH)
MÖRBYLIGAN
MARIE BERGMAN, LARS ENGLUND
ELSABETH HERMODSSON (SPEECH)
FLÄSKET BRINNER
CARL GUSTAV LINDSTEDT
OLA MAGNELL
MODERN SOUND
MAJ WECHSELMAN (SPEECH)
MATS GLENNGÅRD
STEAMBOAT ENTERTAINERS
LASSE TENNANDER
USCH
VARGAVINTER
MÖGEL

Music on two stages, food and drink in the big
dining hall. No advance ticket purchases!

Cast of Characters

Torbjörn Abelli
Born in Stockholm in 1945, died in 2010. Musician, architect, electric bass, upright bass, vocals. Played with the Hot Boys, Arbete & Fritid, Blomkraft, and Elektriska Linden.

Sten Bergman
Born in Stockholm in 1942, died in 2015. Musician and composer. Organ, flute, and clarinet. Educated at the Royal Academy of Music in Stockholm. Played with Atlantic Ocean and Fläsket Brinner. Released the solo album *Lyckohjulet* in 1974.

Arne Ericsson
Born in Bollnäs in 1942. Musician. Cello, electric cello, electric piano/clavichord.

Reine Fiske
Born in Saltsjö-Boo in 1972. Guitarist and music archaeologist. Guitarist in Träden and Dungen, but also in bands such as Paatos, Landberk, The Amazing, Elephant9, Morte Macabre, The Guild, and Svenska Kaputt.

Thomas Mera Gartz
Born in Linköping in 1944, died in 2012. Drums, violin, and vocals. Also played with Mecki Mark Men, the Hot Boys, Råttan Frittz, Bitter Funeral Beer Band, and Arbete & Fritid.

Sigge Krantz
Born in Partille in 1949. Musician, songwriter and music producer. Bass player after Torbjörn Abelli's death. Has played with Stockholm Norra, Archimedes Badkar, Råttan Frittz, Jajja Band, and Bitter Funeral Beer Band.

Bo Anders Persson
Born in Stockholm in 1937. Musician, music teacher. Guitar, vocals. Has played with the Hot Boys.

Jakob Sjöholm
Born in Stockholm in 1950. Musician, teacher. Guitar, vocals. Has played with the Hot Boys and Jajja Band.

Thomas Tidholm
Born in Örebro in 1943. Writer, poet, musician, photographer, playwright and translator. Vocals, saxophone, flute. Has played with Arbete & Fritid and the Hot Boys.

Nisse Törnqvist
Born 1981 in Gävle. Musician. Played drums in TGS after the death of Thomas Mera Gartz. Plays with Amazon, among others.

Urban Yman
Born in Helsingborg 1939, died 2020. Musician, music therapist. Electric violin, flute. Also played with Tjalles Horisont, Sound of Music, Gunder Hägg and Blå Tåget.

Hanna Östergren
Born in Borås 1982. Drummer in Träden. Member of Hills, the children's music duo Hanna & Axel, and the solo project Laughing Eye.

Kristina Abelli Elander
Born in 1952. Artist, writer, costume designer, and production designer.

Ingemar Alserud
Born in 1954, died in 2020. Journalist at *Oskarshamns-Nyheterna*.

Dennis Andersson
Journalist at *Barometern*.

Jan Andersson
Journalist at *Aftonbladet*.

Leif J Andersson
Born in 1941, died in 2009. Journalist at *Arbetarbladet* and *Göteborgs-Posten*.

Philemon Arthur
The one member of the anonymous music group Philemon Arthur & The Dung from southern Sweden. The group's members have still not been revealed.

Mats Arvidsson
Born in 1944 in Stockholm. Art critic and culture journalist at Sveriges Radio.

Dan Backman
Born in 1955. Author, freelance journalist, and culture writer at *Svenska Dagbladet*.

Lester Bangs
Born in 1948, died in 1982. American music critic in *Rolling Stone* from 1969 to 1974.

Channa Bankier
Born in 1947. Visual artist, author, and writer. Was part of the artist collective Folkets Ateljé 1968-1969.

Barbara
Writer at *Dagens Nyheter*.

Bengt Berg
Born in 1946. Writer, translator, editor, and politician.

Olle Berg
Born 1953 in Stockholm. Comic book creator, illustrator, animator, and teacher. Was involved in starting the adult comic magazine *Galago*.

Göran Bergendahl
Writer for *Nutida Musik*.

Tore Berger
Born in 1938. Artist, singer and composer. Has played with Tjalles Horisont, Sound of Music, Gunder Hägg, Blå Tåget, and Stockholm Norra.

Jed Bindeman
Drummer in the band Eternal Tapestry.

Anders Björnsson
Born in 1902, died in 1986. Farming philosopher who started "Friendly Framing" in Likenäs.

Margareta Bogström
Journalist at *Söderposten*.

Jan Borges
Danish music journalist and musician.

Carl Johan De Geer
Born 1938 in Montreal. Artist, writer, filmmaker, musician, designer, culture journalist, photographer, actor, and production designer.

Michel de la Bruyere Vincent
Born in 1946. Architect, inventor, and designer. Member of King Kong Lightgroup.

Anna-Lisa Bäckman
Born in 1941. Journalist, writer, and playwright. Participated in 1971 on the album *Sånger om kvinnor*.

Charlie
Writer for northern *Västerbotten*.

Ulla-Britt Edberg
Born in 1928, died in 2020. Author, journalist, and editor.

Th. Edman
Writer for *Bohusläningen*.

Iwan Erichsson
Critic at *Gefle Dagblad*.

Bengt Eriksson
Born 1947. Culture journalist, writer and musician. Formed the band Låt Tredje Örat Lyssna In and Tredje Benet Stampa Takten. Also one of the founders of the magazine *Schlager*.

Sören Erlandsson
Born 1945, died 2010. An initiator of the first Gärdesfest in 1970. Writer.

Patrik Forshage
Born 1965. Music writer and high school director.

Eva af Geijerstam
Born in 1945. Journalist and author.

Kjell E Genberg
Born in 1940. Author and critic in *Nöjes Aktuellt*. Was also the manager of bands such as the Panthers, the Lee Kings, and Slam Creepers.

Ingmar Glanzelius
Born in 1927, died in 2021. Jazz musician, music writer, and playwright.

Sonja Gransvik
Born 1946. Worked with Friendly Farming in Likenäs and started the restaurant Fröet in Stockholm. Runs Hälsokällan in Torsby.

Bert Gren
Born in 1946, died in 2020. Music journalist at *Göteborgs-Posten* 1969-1996, author and psychologist. Played keyboards in the band Dom Smutsiga Hundarna.

Gunnar
Writer at *Sundsvalls Tidning*.

Erik Helmerson
Born in 1967. Journalist at *Dagens Nyheter* and author.

Anna Herngren
Journalist at *Arbetarbladet*.

H-JN
Writer at the Danish magazine *Information*.

Björn Håkansson
Writer at *Svenska Dagbladet*.

Timo Kangas
Born in 1968. Writer at the music magazine *Lira*.

Roland Keijser
Born in 1944, died in 2019. Saxophonist in Arbete & Fritid and Blå Tåget.

Stefan Kinell
Writer for *Västerbottens-Kuriren*.

Kjell Å
Writer for *Dala-Demokraten*.

Jon Jefferson Klingberg
Born 1968. Son of Bo Anders Persson and Margareta Klingberg. Author, rock musician, and journalist. Played with Celeborn, Whale, and Docenterna.

Margareta Klingberg
Born 1942. Visual artist in text, photo and textile. Works and lives in Junsele and Stockholm. Journalist at *Aftonbladet* during the 1960s and 1970s.

Go Kurosawa
Drummer in the Japanese band Kikagaku Moyo.

Per Kågesson
Born 1947. Author, researcher, debater and consultant in the environmental field.

Anders Lind
Born 1946. Sound engineer. Recorded International Harvester and Harvester's two albums, as well as several of Träd, Gräs and Stenar's records. Started Silence Records in 1970 together with Eva Wilke and Joseph Hochhauser.

Gustav Lindström
Writer for *Örnsköldsviks Allehanda*.

Anita Livstrand
Born in 1953. Musician, singer and composer. Played with Ett minne för livet, Vargavinter, Turid, Archimedes Badkar and Bitter Funeral Beer Band. Her own LP is titled *Mötet*. Appeared on Thomas Mera Gartz's *Sånger* as well as *Tjejclown* and *Bara brudar*.

Stephen Malkmus
Born in 1966. American musician, singer, guitarist and songwriter for Pavement.

Runar Mangs
Born in 1928, died in 2003. Composer and music critic in *Dagens Nyheter*.

Marc Masters
Born in 1969. American music journalist writes for Pitchfork, *The Village Voice*, and *The Washington Post*, among others.

Peter Mosskin
Born in 1945. Author, journalist and musician in Gläns Över Sjö & Strand, among others.

Hans-Jörgen Nielsen
Born in 1948. Writer
for *Dagens Nyheter*.

Jan Nordlander
Writer for *Svenska
Dagbladet.*

Håkan Nyberg
Born 1938 in Nykarleby,
died in 2013. Visual
artist and illustrator.

Leif Nylén
Born in 1939, died in
2016. Author, literary
and art critic,
songwriter, and musician
in Tjalles Horisont,
Sound of Music, Gunder
Hägg, Blå Tåget, and
Stockholm Norra.

Mats Olsson
Born 1949. Journalist,
author, sports columnist
and rock writer. Was
awarded the Stora
journalistpriset in 2002.

Oscar
Writer for *Dagens
Nyheter*.

Otis
Writer for *Sydsvenska
Dagbladet.*

Benny Persson
Writer for *Upsala
Nya Tidning*.

Jan-Åke Pettersson
Writer for Arbetet.

Folke Rabe
Born in 1935, died in
2017. Composer, jazz
musician, music writer
and program director
at Rikskonserter.

Tommy Rander
Born in 1946. Musician,
journalist and writer.
Singer in the band
Shakers and one of
the initiators of the
magazine Musikens Makt
and the record company
Nacksving.

Ludvig Rasmusson
Born in 1936. Author,
freelance journalist,
speaker and lecturer.
Participated in
organizing the first
Gärdesfesten.

Reit
Writer for the Danish
paper *Sjællanstidende*.

Urban von Rosen
Born in 1944, died
in 1974. Copywriter
and critic in *Svenska
Dagbladet.*

Henrik Salander
Born in 1945. Musician
and diplomat. Was a
member of the group
The Hounds in the 1960s.

Håkan Sandblad
Born in 1942, died
in 2016. Journalist,
author, playwright, and
radio producer. Worked
at Sveriges Radio in
Gothenburg. Editor-in-
chief at the newspaper
Musikens Makt from
1973 to 1975.

Torgny Sjöstedt
Born in 1952. Songwriter,
author and teacher.
Member of the band Love
Explosion.

Kjartan Slettemark
Born in 1932, died
in 2008. Artist and
sculptor, known for his
political art during the
1960s and 1970s. Worked
with concept art, video
art, and happenings.

Pär Stolpe
Born 1943. Author and
social debater. Has
worked at the Modern
Museum and National
Exhibitions.

Per Svensson
Writer for Tonfallet.

Piero Tartagni
Documentary filmmaker
and TV producer in Italy.
Wine grower.

Anna-Clara Tidholm
Born in 1946. Writer
and illustrator.

Hans-Göran Toresson
Born in 1949. Course
participant in Friendly
Farming in Likenäs in
1971.

Björner Torsson
Born in 1937, died in
2020. Poet, architect,
and teacher at the School
of Architecture at KTH in
Stockholm.

Jason P. Woodbury
Music writer for
Phoenix New Times.

Lars Åberg
Born in 1950. Journalist
and author.

Discography

Pärson Sound

Pärson Sound, 2xCD, tillindien/
Subliminal Sounds, (TILCD 02),
2001

Pärson Sound, 3xLP, tillindien/
Subliminal Sounds,
(SUB-073-LP-BOX), 2010

International Harvester

Sov gott Rose-Marie, LP,
Love Records (LRLP 1005), 1968

Sov gott Rose-Marie, LP,
Silence (SRS 4690), 1984

Sov gott Rose-Marie, CD,
Silence (SRSCD 3614), 2001

Remains, 5xLP,
Silence (SRSBX 3500), 2018

Harvester

Hemåt, LP,
Decibel (DRS 3701), 1969

Hemåt, CD,
Silence (SRSCD 3616), 2001

Träd, Gräs och Stenar

Träd, Gräs och Stenar, LP, Decibel
(DRS 3702), 1970

Träd, Gräs och Stenar, CD,
Silence/Resource Records
(SRSCD 3602), 1995

Rock för kropp och själ, LP,
Silence (SRS 4608), 1972

Djungelns lag, LP,
Tall (TALL 1), 1972

Djungelns lag, CD,
½ Special (HALV 1-2), 2002

Mors Mors, LP,
Tall (TALL 2), 1973

Mors Mors, CD,
½ Special (HALV 2-2), 2002

Gärdet 12.6.1970, CD,
ti`llindien/Subliminal Sounds
(TILCD 01), 1996

Gärdet 12.6.1970, 2xLP,
Subliminal Sounds (SUB-075-LP),
2011

Ajn Schvajn Draj, CD,
Silence (SRSCD 4758), 2002

Live 1972, LP,
½ Special (HALV 2-1), 2003

Träd, Gräs och Stenar

Japan Tour 2007, CD, Acid Mothers
Temple (AMTCD 019), 2007

Live från Möja till Minneapolis,
DVD BY Mikael Högström, Gåshud
(G2007-1), 2007

Hemlösa Katter, 2xLP, Subliminal
Sounds (XMLP-SUB 32), 2009

Hemlösa Katter, CD,
Gåshud (G 2009-2), 2009

Träd, Gräs och Stenar, 6xLP,
Anthology Recordings
(ARC 013), 2016

Träd, Gräs och Stenar, 3xCD,
Anthology Recordings
(ARC 013), 2016

Tack för kaffet, 2xLP,
Gåshud/Subliminal Sounds
(G2017-3V, SUB-118-LP), 2017

Tack för kaffet, CD,
Gåshud/Subliminal Sounds
(G2017-3CD, SUB-119-CD), 2017

Träden

Träden, 2xLP, Gåshud/Subliminal
Sounds (SUB-127-2LLP), 2018

Träden, CD, Gåshud/Subliminal
Sounds (SUB-128-CD), 2018

Bo Anders Persson/Folke Rabe
Was?? / Proteinimperialism, LP,
Wergo (WER 60047), 1970

The Hot Boys
Varma smörgåsar, LP,
Silence (SRS 4624), 1974

Thomas Mera Gartz
Sånger, LP,
Silence (SRS 4635), 1975

Bröderna Lönn
Säg det i toner…, LP,
Musiklaget (MLLP 12), 1980

Thomas Mera Gartz
Luftsånger, LP,
Silence (SRS 4687), 1984

Thomas Tidholm
Obevakade Ögonblick,
LP, Silence (SRS 4697), 1985

Thomas Tidholm
*Ett jobb för Jacko och Jims
vinter*, Cassette, Gammafon
(ISBN 9177125029, 1988

Thomas Tidholm/Jonas Knutsson
Himlen har inga hål, CD,
Paraphon (PPCD 03), 2007

Bo Anders Persson
Love is Here to Stay,
2xLP, Subliminal Sounds
(SUB-086-LP), 2014

Bo Anders Persson
Love is Here to Stay,
CD, Subliminal Sounds
(SUB-087-CD), 2014

Thomas Tidholm/Jonas Knutsson
Orsa by Night, CD,
Country & Eastern (CE 35), 2015

International Harvester

Sov gott Rose-Marie (1968)

Harvester

Hemåt (1969)

Träd, Gräs och Stenar

(1970)

Träd, Gräs och Stenar

Rock för kropp och själ (1972)

Träd, Gräs och Stenar

Djungelns lag (1972)

Träd, Gräs och Stenar

Mors Mors (1973)

The Hot Boys

Varma Smörgåsar (1974)

Träd, Gräs och Stenar

Gärdet 12.6.1970 (1996)

Pärson Sound

(2001)

Träd, Gräs och Stenar
Ajn Schvajn Draj (2002)

Träd, Gräs och Stenar
Live 1972 (2003)

Träd, Gräs och Stenar
Japan Tour (2007)

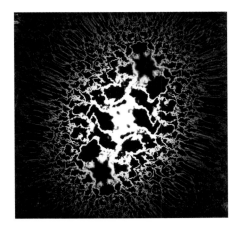

Träd, Gräs och Stenar
Hemlösa Katter (2009)

Träd, Gräs och Stenar
USA-box (2016)

Träd, Gräs och Stenar
Tack för kaffet (2017)

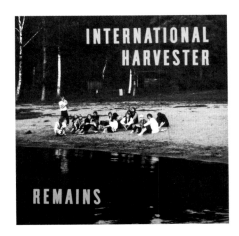

International Harvester
Remains (2018)

Träden
(2018)

Performances 1967–2019

<table>
<tr><td>1967</td><td>Pärson Sound</td></tr>
<tr><td>4/7</td><td>Stockholm, Djurgården, at Karin and Sven-Gunnar Lidmar's home</td></tr>
<tr><td>4/29</td><td>Stockholm, Pistolteatern</td></tr>
<tr><td>5/17</td><td>Stockholm, Moderna Museet (ballet with Greta Lindholm)</td></tr>
<tr><td>7/19</td><td>Stockholm, Sju sekel</td></tr>
<tr><td>8/31</td><td>Stockholm, Filips (with Bengt Berger on drums)</td></tr>
<tr><td>9/1</td><td>Stockholm, Filips (with Bengt Berger on drums)</td></tr>
<tr><td>9/10</td><td>Recording, Lidingö</td></tr>
<tr><td>9/16</td><td>Radio recording, Hörröh.</td></tr>
<tr><td>9/20</td><td>Stockholm, Filips (with Janne "Loffe" Carlsson, drums)</td></tr>
<tr><td>9/21</td><td>Stockholm, Filips</td></tr>
<tr><td>9/23</td><td>Stockholm, Filips (with Bengt Berger on drums)</td></tr>
<tr><td>9/26</td><td>Radio recording, Den tänkande mikrofonen</td></tr>
<tr><td>10/13</td><td>Stockholm, Filips (with Bengt Berger on drums)</td></tr>
<tr><td>11/9</td><td>Radio recording</td></tr>
<tr><td>12/2</td><td>Stockholm, Hotell Anglais, Svenska Slöjdföreningen (with Bengt Berger and Håkan Agnsäter on drums)</td></tr>
<tr><td>12/11</td><td>TV taping Efter föreställningen (broadcast 12/16)</td></tr>
<tr><td>12/21-22</td><td>Radio recording, Nattstudion (broadcast 1/4/68)</td></tr>
</table>

<table>
<tr><td>1968</td><td>Pärson Sound</td></tr>
<tr><td>1/31</td><td>Stockholm, Kåren</td></tr>
<tr><td>2/9-10</td><td>Stockholm, Moderna Museet, Andy Warhol exhibition (with Björn Fredholm on drums)</td></tr>
<tr><td>2/17</td><td>Stockholm, Konstfack [University of Arts, Crafts and Design]</td></tr>
<tr><td>2/25</td><td>Stockholm, Moderna Museet, Andy Warhol exhibition (with Björn Fredholm on drums)</td></tr>
<tr><td>3/8</td><td>Stockholm, Moderna Museet, Andy Warhol exhibition (with Björn Fredholm on drums)</td></tr>
<tr><td>3/13</td><td>Stockholm, Kärrtorps läroverk [Kärrtorp's Secondary School]</td></tr>
<tr><td>3/28</td><td>Täby, Tibbleskolan [Tibble School]</td></tr>
<tr><td>4/25</td><td>Göteborg, Konsthallen</td></tr>
<tr><td>4/26</td><td>Göteborg, Globe Club</td></tr>
<tr><td>5/?</td><td>Stockholm, Skrubba skolhem (with Kjell Westling, saxophone)</td></tr>
<tr><td>5/11</td><td>Helsingfors, Polli</td></tr>
<tr><td>5/12</td><td>TV taping, Helsingfors, Klubb 68</td></tr>
<tr><td>5/26</td><td>Recording, Huddinge</td></tr>
<tr><td>5/30</td><td>Finland</td></tr>
<tr><td>6/15</td><td>Lund, Akademiska föreningen, Athen</td></tr>
</table>

<table>
<tr><td>1968</td><td>International Harvester</td></tr>
<tr><td>8/10-12</td><td>Recording of Sov gott Rose-Marie, Nacka aula [Nacka Auditorium]</td></tr>
<tr><td>9/20</td><td>Stockholm, Konserthuset (with the Doors) [Stockholm Concert Hall]</td></tr>
<tr><td>9/23</td><td>Stockholm, Pistolteatern, Good Luck Show</td></tr>
<tr><td>9/25</td><td>Stockholm, Pistolteatern, Good Luck Show</td></tr>
<tr><td>9/27</td><td>Stockholm, Pistolteatern, Good Luck Show</td></tr>
<tr><td>10/2</td><td>TV taping, Pop colour (Broadcast 22.11)</td></tr>
<tr><td>10/14</td><td>Stockholm, Pistolteatern, Good Luck Show</td></tr>
<tr><td>10/18</td><td>Stockholm, Moderna Museet, Modellen</td></tr>
<tr><td>10/21</td><td>Stockholm, Pistolteatern, Good Luck Show</td></tr>
<tr><td>10/23</td><td>TV taping, rehearsal show</td></tr>
<tr><td>10/28</td><td>Stockholm, Pistolteatern, Good Luck Show</td></tr>
<tr><td>11/2</td><td>Stockholm, Stockholmsterrassen, Aktion stoppa mässan</td></tr>
<tr><td>11/4</td><td>Stockholm, Pistolteatern, Good Luck Show</td></tr>
<tr><td>11/9</td><td>Stockholm, Konstfack, Aktion stoppa mässan [University of Arts, Crafts and Design]</td></tr>
</table>

<table>
<tr><td>11/10</td><td>Södertälje, Ronna fritidsgård [Ronna Youth Center]</td></tr>
<tr><td>11/11</td><td>Stockholm, Pistolteatern, Good Luck Show</td></tr>
<tr><td>11/18</td><td>Stockholm, Pistolteatern, Good Luck Show</td></tr>
<tr><td>11/30</td><td>Stockholm, Konstfack [University of Arts, Crafts and Design]</td></tr>
<tr><td>12/8</td><td>Nyköping, Nicolaiskolan [Nicolai Secondary School]</td></tr>
<tr><td>12/14</td><td>Stockholm, Hötorget, Alternativ jul</td></tr>
<tr><td>12/21</td><td>Stockholm, Kafé Marx</td></tr>
<tr><td>12/25</td><td>Stockholm, Café Mejan, Alternativ jul</td></tr>
<tr><td>12/25</td><td>Stockholm, Konstfack, Alternativ jul</td></tr>
<tr><td>12/26</td><td>Stockholm, Sunside, Alternativ jul</td></tr>
</table>

<table>
<tr><td>1969</td><td>International Harvester</td></tr>
<tr><td>2/4</td><td>TV taping, Forum (broadcast 12.2)</td></tr>
<tr><td>2/5</td><td>Gävle, Stadsbiblioteket [Gävle City Library]</td></tr>
<tr><td>2/7</td><td>Skellefteå, Pansalen</td></tr>
<tr><td>2/8</td><td>Umeå, Stadsbiblioteketet [Umeå City Library]</td></tr>
<tr><td>2/9</td><td>Sundsvall, Stadsmuseet [Sundsvall City Museum]</td></tr>
<tr><td>2/10</td><td>Bollnäs, Folkets hus [People's House]</td></tr>
<tr><td>2/12</td><td>Sundbyberg, Lärkan</td></tr>
<tr><td>2/14</td><td>TV taping, Narrenteatern, Number 9 (broadcast 2/17)</td></tr>
<tr><td>2/14</td><td>Uppsala, Norrlands nation [Student Society]</td></tr>
<tr><td>2/24</td><td>Lund, Arkivmuseet</td></tr>
<tr><td>2/25</td><td>Lund, Akademiska föreningen [Academic Forum]</td></tr>
<tr><td>3/23</td><td>Stockholm, Fyrans ungdomsgård [Fyran's Youth Center]</td></tr>
<tr><td>3/29</td><td>Stockholm, Fyrans ungdomsgård</td></tr>
<tr><td>3/30</td><td>Stockholm, ABF Björkhagen (with Kjell Westling, electric violin)</td></tr>
<tr><td>4/12</td><td>Stockholm, Stadsmuseet musikfest [Stockholm City Museum's Music Festival]</td></tr>
<tr><td>4/20</td><td>Kumla fängelset [Kumla Prison]</td></tr>
<tr><td>4/23</td><td>Stockholm, Fyrans ungdomsgård</td></tr>
<tr><td>5/1</td><td>Stockholm, Kafé Marx (Danish TV were filming)</td></tr>
<tr><td>5/6-11</td><td>Recording of Hemåt, Stockholm, Kafé Marx</td></tr>
<tr><td>5/24-6/1</td><td>Exhibition, Stockholm, Galleri Observatorium</td></tr>
<tr><td>5/26</td><td>Stockholm, Kafé Marx</td></tr>
<tr><td>5/30</td><td>Borlänge</td></tr>
<tr><td>6/2</td><td>Recording of Hemåt, Stockholm, Vitabergsparken</td></tr>
<tr><td>6/15</td><td>Film shoot, Du gamla, du fria, Stockholm, Centralbadet</td></tr>
<tr><td>6/18</td><td>Stockholm, Vitabergsparken, Ceders kafé (Thomas Tidholm quits)</td></tr>
<tr><td>6/25</td><td>Linköping, Lunnevads folkhögskola [Lunnevad's Folk High School]</td></tr>
<tr><td>6/26</td><td>Norrköping, by the art museum</td></tr>
</table>

<table>
<tr><td>1969</td><td>Harvester</td></tr>
<tr><td>7/7</td><td>Leksand, Gropen</td></tr>
<tr><td>7/10</td><td>Bjurås, Dössberget</td></tr>
<tr><td>7/11</td><td>Falun, closed Folkets park [The People's Park]</td></tr>
<tr><td>8/12</td><td>Stockholm, Stockholmsterrassen</td></tr>
<tr><td>8/17</td><td>Bollmora, Centrum</td></tr>
<tr><td>9/19</td><td>Stockholm, Långbro sjukhus [Långbro Hospital]</td></tr>
<tr><td>9/26</td><td>Uppsala, v-Dala nation [v-Dala Student Society]</td></tr>
</table>

<table>
<tr><td>1969</td><td>Träd, Gräs och Stenar</td></tr>
<tr><td>9/29-10/5</td><td>Oslo Tverkunstnerisk seminar [Interdisciplinary Seminar]</td></tr>
<tr><td>10/1</td><td>TV taping, Oslo, Studio 69</td></tr>
<tr><td>10/3</td><td>Oslo, Club 7</td></tr>
<tr><td>10/4</td><td>Radio Oslo</td></tr>
<tr><td>10/5</td><td>Oslo, Club 7</td></tr>
<tr><td>10/6-7</td><td>Göteborg, Avenyn 18 (Urban Yman quits)</td></tr>
<tr><td>10/9</td><td>Kumla, fängelset (3 shows)</td></tr>
<tr><td>10/10</td><td>Kumla, biblioteket [Library]</td></tr>
</table>

11/11	Södertälje, Konsthallen
11/15	Stockholm, Stockholmsterrassen
11/20	Stockholm, Skärholmen
11/21	Stockholm, Gamla Bro
11/24	Sundsvall, Wiwex
11/25	Sollefteå
11/26	Hoting, Folkets hus
11/27	Härnösand, Sjöbefälsskolan [The Maritime Academy]
11/28	Kramfors, Folkets park
11/29	Sundsvall, Sidsjöns sjukhus [Sidsjön's Hospital]
12/9	Recording of music to the film Grisjakten (opened March 1970)
12/12	Hampetorp
12/15	Stockholm, Moderna Museet
12/17	Stockholm, Haninge
12/18	TV taping, Liv (broadcast 12/20)
12/27	Lidingö, Käppala
12/28	Stockholm, Gamla Bro

<u>1970</u> <u>Träd, Gräs och Stenar</u>

2/14	Stockholm, Musikhögskolan, Ung nordisk musik [Royal College of Music, Young Nordic Music]
2/15	Jakobsberg, Fågelsången
2/18-19	Oskarshamn, folkhögskola (förskola) [Folk High School Daycare]
2/21	Stockholm, Moderna Museet
2/22	Stockholm, Gamla Bro
2/25-26	Oskarshamn, folkhögskola (förskola)
2/28	Stockholm, Moderna Museet Black Panther
3/8	Stockholm, Moderna Museet Black Panther
3/18	Falun, Stadsbiblioteket [Falun City Library]
3/19	Skinnskattebergs folkhögskola [Skinnskatteberg's Folk High School]
3/21-24	Nacka aula, recording of the green album and music for the film Du gamla, du fria
4/3	TV taping, Trunken (broadcast 4/5)
4/8	Stockholm, Gamla Bro
4/13	Jakobsberg, Kvarnskolan [Kvarn Elementary School]
4/18	Örebro, Power House
4/21	Uppsala, V-Dala
4/22	Bålsta, Biskops-Arnö folkhögskola [Biskops-Arnö Folk High School]
4/23	Stockholm, Rålambshovs sjukhus [Rålambshovs Hospital]
4/25	Stockholm, Abrahamsberg, Black Panther [Abrahamsberg's Youth Center]
4/27	Stockholm, Bromma läroverk [Bromma Secondary School]
4/29	Stockholm, Moderna Museet Galleriet (acoustic)
5/8	Inspelning, Nacka aula
5/16	Stockholm, Gärdet, Drakfest (afternoon) [Kite Festival]
5/16	Stockholm, Konstfack (evening)
5/18	Stockholm
5/23-24	Lund, Stadsparken (afternoon)
5/23	Lund, Arkivmuseet [Archive Museum]
5/25	Kalmar, Falkenbergsskolan VCO
5/29	Lidingö
6/2	Åmål, Stadsbiblioteket [Åmål City Library]
6/3	Katrineholm, Stadsparken
6/4	Oxelösund, Cupol (Folkets hus)
6/5	Flen, Stadsparken
6/6	Stockholm, Moderna Museet
6/7	Mariefred, ungdomsfängelset [Youth Prison]

6/8	Stockholm, Pistolteatern (support for Gärdesfesten)
6/10	Uppsala, ungdomsfängelset
6/12-14	Stockholm, Festen på Gärdet (three gigs)
6/18	Bollnäs folkhögskola
7/7	Rättvik, Folkets park
7/8	Leksand, Trädgårdsvillan
7/8	Leksand, Gropen
7/10	Södertälje, fängelset Hall [Hall Prison]
17/11	Stockholm, Stockholmsterrassen
7/12	Kumla, fängelset [The prison]
8/14	Uppsala, Stadsträdgården Parksnäckan [City Garden Parksnäckan]
8/15	Oskarshamn, Stadsparken, free party
8/20-23	Stockholm, Second party on Gärdet
9/26	Dalarö folkhögskola [Dalarö Folk High School]
9/28	Ljungskile, Lyckornas havsbad [Lyckorna's Beach]
9/29	Göteborg, Konsthallen
10/5	Tidaholm, Rikskonserter Spela själv
10/6	Vedum, Rikskonserter Spela själv
10/7	Nossebro, Rikskonserter Spela själv
10/8	Floby, Rikskonserter Spela själv
10/9	Falköping, Rikskonserter Spela själv
10/10	Falköping, Rikskonserter Spela själv
10/11	Mariestad, Rikskonserter Spela själv
10/21	Stockholm, Spånga gymnasium [Spånga High School]
10/23	Stockholm, Gamla Bro (ockupation) [Gamla Bro Youth Center (Occupation)]
10/25	Stockholm, Skärholmen biblioteket [Skärholmen's Library]
10/28	Stockholm, Gamla Bro (ockupation)
11/18	Stockholm, Liljevalchs, 3rd party
11/20	Lund, Smålands nation [Småland's Student Society]
11/21	Malmö nation, Pireus [Malmö Student Society]
11/22	Lund, Arkivmuseet
11/24-25	Köpenhamn, Huset
11/27-28	Göteborg, Cue Club
12/3	Göteborg, Hagaslottet
12/4	Göteborg, Experimentgymnasiet [Experimental High School]
12/5	Göteborg, Hagahuset
12/17	Stockholm, Bandhagens gymnasium [Bandhagen's High School]
12/18	Stockholm, Fyrans ungdomsgård
12/19	Västerås, Idrottshallen (Jakob Sjöholm's first gig) [Västerås Sports Center]
12/24	Södertälje, fängelset Hall
12/26	Stockholm, Fyrans ungdomsgård

<u>1971</u> <u>Träd, Gräs och Stenar</u>

1/24	Västerås Öppet hus Stadsparken [Open House Stadsparken]
1/30	Lindesberg, Rikskonserter Spela själv
1/31	Hinseberg, Rikskonserter Spela själv
2/1	Tibro, Rikskonserter Spela själv
2/3	Molkom, Rikskonserter Spela själv
2/4	Ekshärad, Rikskonserter Spela själv
2/5	Torsby, Rikskonserter Spela själv
2/7	Sysslebäck, Rikskonserter Spela själv
2/9	Karlstad, Rikskonserter Spela själv
2/11	Kumla, Rikskonserter Spela själv
2/13	Saltsjöbaden, Rikskonserter Spela själv
2/18-21	Rehearsal Nyboda
2/24	Gävle Museum
2/26	Falun, Dalarnas museum
3/1	Stockholm, Gyllene cirkeln

3/5	Stockholm, Rinkeby skola [Rinkeby Elementary School]
3/6	Bålsta, Biskops-Arnö folkhögskola [Biskops-Arnö Folk High School]
3/8	Stockholm, Sveahof
3/16	Radio recording, Stockholm, Gig in Studio 2 (with folk musicians Påhl Olle, Nils Agenmark, Alm Nils Ersson and Pontus Berggren(broadcast 8/22)
3/19	Stockholm, Vendelsömalmsskolan [Vendelsömalm Elementary School]
3/21	Stockholm, Midsommargården
3/27	Laxå, Folkets hus
3/28	Karlstad, Studentkåren [Student Union]
4/2	Sunne
4/4	Borlänge, Allhuset [All-Activity House]
4/14	Stockholm, Gamla Bro
4/15	Stockholm, Medborgarhuset [All-activity Citizen's House]
4/19	Solna, Statens Biblioteksskola (film, food, talks, acoustic) [The State's Library School]
4/21	Karlshamn, Käpphästen
4/22	Lund, Skandiabiografen [Skandia Movie Theater]
4/23	Lund, Akademiska föreningen
4/24	Malmö, Scaniabiografen
4/24	Köpenhamn, Christiania
4/26-30	Rehearsal with King Kong Lightshow, Köpenhamn Polyteknisk Læreanstalt, Lyngby
5/1	Köpenhamn, Lyngby Polytekniska (with King Kong Lightshow)
5/2	Köpenhamn, Hvidovre Isstadion (with King Kong Lightshow)
5/6	Århus, Stakladen (with King Kong Lightshow)
5/7	Slagelse, Slagelsehallen (with King Kong Lightshow)
5/8	Köpenhamn, Gladsaxe Beatforum (with King Kong Lightshow)
5/9	Köpenhamn, Fælledparken
5/13	Malmö, fängelset (with King Kong Lightshow) [Prison]
5/14	Malmö, Form Mässhallarna (with King Kong Lightshow)
5/15	Lund, Stadsparken (afternoon)
5/15	Lund, Akademiska föreningen the grand hall (with King Kong Lightshow)(evening) [Academic Forum]
5/18	Stockholm, Moderna Museet (with King Kong Lightshow)
5/21	Stockholm, Fyrans ungdomsgård
6/4-5	Stockholm, Fregatten
6/9	Stockholm, Higgins
6/11-13	Stockholm, 3rd Festen på Gärdet
7/18	Åsele, Hembygdsgården (fiddle music)
7/19	Åsele, Hembygdsgården
7/22	Långträsk, Lillpite daghem (afternoon) [Daycare]
7/22	Långträsk, Logen (evening)
7/23	Altersbruk, Arnemarks daghem (afternoon) [Daycare]
7/23	Altersbruk, Logen (evening)
7/24	Piteå, Parken
7/28	Luleå, Nya Örnässkolan [Örnäs Elementary School]
7/30	Vindeln, Hembygdsfest at the old miller house [Local Association]
7/31	Örnsköldsvik, biblioteket
7/31	Bredbyn, idrottshall [Sports Center]
8/2	Gävle, bibliotek
9/6-9	Rehearsal, Stöllet, Nystugan
9/11	Likenäsparken
9/14-17	Oslo, Club 7, seminarium
9/17	TV taping, Oslo
9/17-18	Oslo, Club 7
9/20	Drammen, Capodasten
10/12	Grängesberg, Cassels donation
10/13	Ludvika, Folkets hus
10/14	Nyhammar, Folkets hus
10/21	Västervik, Rikskonserter Spela själv
10/22-23	Ankarsrum, Rikskonserter Spela själv
10/24-27	Kalmar Skälby gård, Rikskonserter Spela själv
10/30-11/1	Säffle Medborgarhuset, Rikskonserter Spela själv
11/5	Stockholm, Fregatten
11/12	Storvik, Västerbergs folkhögskola [Västerberg's Folk High School]
11/14	Bollnäs, Torsbergsgymnasiet [Torsberg's High School]
11/15	Bollnäs, Torsbergsgymnasiet
11/18	Umeå, Östra gymnasiet [Östra High School]
11/19	Skellefteå, Pansalen
11/22	Boden, Korpenskolan [Korpen Elementary School]
11/23	Malmberget, fritidsgården [Youth Center]
11/24	Kiruna, Hjalmar Lundbohmsskolan [Sjalmar Lundbohm's Elementary School]
11/25	Haparanda, Tornedalsskolan [Tornedal's Elementary School]
11/26	Kalix, fritidsgården
11/30	Arvidsjaur, gymnasium och högstadium [High School and Junior High]
12/1	Storuman, Folkets hus
12/2	Vilhelmina, fritidsgården
12/3	Lycksele, Medborgarhuset [Citizen's House]
12/4	Umeå, Centralgården
12/6	Strömsund, Pelarsalen
12/10	Östersund, Free
12/13	Stockholm, Gamla Bro
12/22	Örebro, Idrottshuset
<u>1972</u>	<u>Träd, Gräs och Stenar</u>
1/27	Lidingö, Nyckelviksskolan maskerad (acoustic) [Nyckelviksskolan's Masquerade]
1/29-30	Recording of Rock för kropp och själ, Stockholm, Decibel Studio
2/6	Stockholm, Moderna Museet's branch (acoustic, food)
2/9	Recording of Rock för kropp och själ, Stockholm, Decibel Studio
2/15	Tillberga fängelse (acoustic)
2/18-19	Göteborg, Hagahuset (food, exhibition)
2/20	Göteborg, Backa fritidsgård (food, exhibition)
2/24	Göteborg, Hagahuset
2/26	Malmö, Moriska paviljongen
2/27	Rudkøbing, folkfest
2/29-3/1	Köpenhamn, Rainbow Room
3/3	Köpenhamn/Albertslund, Kongsholmsskolen
3/4	Köpenhamn, Dagmar
3/8-9	Radiointervju med Erik Kramshøj, Köpenhamn
3/10	Köpenhamn, Politiets Ungdoms Klub, Amager (Arne Ericsson quits)
3/11	Köpenhamn, Christiania Multimediehuset
3/15	Lund, Smålands nation, Korpamoen [Småland's Student Society]
3/16	Lund, Akademiska föreningen, Athen
3/17	Kalmar, Stagneliusskolan [Stagnelius Secondary School]
3/18	Oskarshamn, Valhallaskolan [Valhalla Elementary School]
3/21	Gamleby, fritidsgården
3/22	Linköping, Arbis fritidsgården [Arbis Youth Center]
3/24	Jönköping, Bacchi lyra (acoustic, food)
3/25	Norrköping, Djäkneparksskolan [Djäkneparks Secondary School]
3/30	Stockholm, Fregatten
4/1	Stockholm, Gamla Bro (Sten Bergman's first gig)
4/7	Stockholm, Moderna Museet
4/8	Västerås, Skiljebogården (acoustic)
4/16	Oslo, Chateau Neuf
4/18	Skien, Idrottshallen
4/19	Oslo, Hausmannsgate, ockupation
4/22	Oslo, Chateau Neuf, DNS-möte

4/24	Oslo, Chateau Neuf, Solidaritetsmöte Vietnam [Vietnam Solidarity meeting]
5/8	Uppsala, Universitet, Solidaritetsmöte Eritrea [Eritrea Solidarity meeting]
5/10	Södertälje, Fritiden
5/11	Stockholm, Gamla Bro
5/13	Örebro, Power House
5/19	Ludvika, Aveny
5/20	Uppsala, Slottsbacken folkfest
5/25	Stockholm, Gamla Bro
6/2-3	Karlstad, Solporten
6/4	Karsuddens sjukhus [Karsudden's Hospital]
6/10	Norrköping, folkfest
6/11	Linköping, Folkets park
6/12	Finspång
6/16	Stockholm, Rålambshovsparken
6/16	Stockholm, Skarpnäcksfältet [UN's Environmental Conference 1972]
7/8	Rättvik, Bleckogården
7/9	Östersund, Jamtli
7/18	Sundsvall, Sidsjöns sjukhus [Sidsjön's Hospital]
7/19	Hudiksvall, Köpmansberget
7/20	Falun, fängelset [prison]

<u>1973</u>	<u>Träd, Gräs och Stenar</u>
12/22	Stockholm, Folkets hus, Midvinterblot (with Catarina Abelli, violin)

<u>1974</u>	<u>The Hot Boys</u>
3/3	Bollnäs
4/12	Stockholm, Jarlateatern
5/3	Göteborg, Sprängkullen
5/4	Göteborg, Sprängkullen
5/9	Helsingborg
5/10	Kalmar
5/11	Lund
5/12	Lund

<u>1979</u>	<u>Träd, Gräs och Stenar</u>
11/22	Stockholm, Mariahissen
11/23	Stockholm, Konstfack, Rock mot atomkraft [University of Arts, Crafts and Design, Rock Against Nuclear Power Benefit]

<u>1980</u>	<u>Träd, Gräs och Stenar</u>
4/11	Stockholm, Birkagården, Stödfest för Birkagårdsbarnens rättegång mot avgaser och buller [Benefit for Youth Center Birkagården's Court Trial Against Pollution Traffic Noise]
4/25	Uppsala, Musikforum
4/26	Örebro, Rockmagasinet
4/27	Växjö, Folkets park
4/29	Lund, Lilla Teatern Musikpakten
4/30	Malmö, Café Syd
5/1	Malmö, Café Syd
5/2	Borås, Musikhuset Allégården
5/3	Göteborg, Errols
5/6	Arvika, Kulturkafé
5/7	Karlstad, Musikkafé
5/8	Linköping, Musikforum Arbis
5/9	Stockholm, Rock Palais
5/10	Stockholm, Musikverket
6/15	Stockholm, Vasaparken (with Tord Bengtsson and Sigge Krantz)
6/25-28	Rehearsal Götgatan
10/17-18	Rehearsal Götgatan
11/30-12/2	Rehearsal Gränsgården
12/3	Östersund, Musikforum Gamla Teatern
12/4	Strömsund, Pelarsalen
12/6	Örnsköldsvik, Musikhuset
12/7	Umeå, Dragonskolan [Dragon Secondary School]
12/9	Fränsta, Ålsta folkhögskola [Ålsta Folk High School]
12/10	Härnösand, Lärarhögskolan [Institute of Education]
12/11	Hudiksvall, Läroverket [The Secondary School]
12/13	Bollnäs, Odenskolan [Oden Elementary School]
12/19	Visby, Solbergaskolan [Solberga Elementary School]
12/20	Visby Solbergaskolan, Spela själv [Solberga Elementary School]

<u>1981</u>	<u>T.GåS</u>
1/22	Rehearsal, Stockholm,
1/23	Stockholm, Bryggeriet
1/25	Rehearsal, Stockholm,
2/20	Göteborg, Renströmska sjukhuset [Renströmska Hospital]
2/23-24	Rehearsal, Göteborg, Renströmska sjukhuset
2/25	Ljungby, ungdomsgården
2/26	Malmö, Café Syd
2/27	Lund, Pub Sparta Folk å Rock
2/28	Borås, Musikhuset
5/26	Rehearsal, Stockholm
5/27	Rehearsal, Stockholm
5/29	Rehearsal, Stockholm
5/30	Stockholm, Långholmsparken
5/31	Örebro
6/23	TV taping, Bokkafét (with Ove Karlsson)
11/23-27	Rehearsal

<u>1982</u>	<u>T.GåS</u>
3/8-11	Rehearsal, Stockholm

<u>1985</u>	<u>T.GåS</u>
8/12-14	Rehearsal, Stockholm, Kapsylen
8/17	Stockholm, Gärdet
<u>1992</u>	<u>Träd, Gräs och Stenar</u>
6/6	Uppsala, Barowiak, Musikforum 20 Years

<u>1993</u>	<u>Träd, Gräs och Stenar</u>
8/21	Stockholm, Gärdet

<u>1994</u>	<u>Träd, Gräs och Stenar</u>
5/7	Stockholm, Hg 5

<u>1995</u>	<u>Träd, Gräs och Stenar</u>
5/12	Stockholm, Studion S:t Eriksgatan
5/25	Stockholm, Studion S:t Eriksgatan
5/26	Stockholm, Studion S:t Eriksgatan
6/10	Färingsö, Ölsta
8/5	Torsby, Scensommarrock
10/27	Stockholm, Kafé 44
11/4	Stockholm, Kafé 44
12/8	Uppsala, Rackarbackspuben
12/9	Solna, Apromus
12/13	Stockholm, Kulturhuset

<u>1996</u>	<u>Träd, Gräs och Stenar</u>
6/15	Stockholm, Kungsträdgården, The Museum of Music
8/8	Sysslebäck, Lyran
8/10	Emmaboda, festival
8/17	Orsa, Hansjögården
11/22	Stockholm, Mosebacke

<u>1997</u>	<u>Träd, Gräs och Stenar</u>
2/8	Stockholm, Postrestaurangen
7/25	Öland, Mellstaby, Kulturnatten [Culture Night]
8/16	Orsa

9/20	Uppsala, Bror Hjorths hus [Bror Hjort's House]
9/27	Färingsö, Ölsta Folkets hus, Bo Anders 60 år [Bo Anders's 60th birthday]
10/25	Göteborg, Göteborg Art Rock Förening
11/8	Stockholm, Etnografiska museet, Klubb Filips 30 år [Museum of Ethnography, Klubb Filip's 30-Year Anniversary]
12/5	Oslo, Chateau Neuf

1998   Träd, Gräs och Stenar

5/15	Stockholm, Judiska teatern, Beatkvällar [The Jewish Theater]
5/16	Stockholm, Judiska teatern, Beatkvällar
5/30	Göteborg, exhibition Hjärtat sitter till vänster ["The Heart Is on the Left" Exhibition]
8/29	Uppsala, vernissagefest Hjärtat sitter till vänster ["The Heart Is on the Left" Opening]
8/29	Uppsala, vernissage Hjärtat sitter till vänster
8/29	Uppsala, vernissagefest Hjärtat sitter till vänster
11/13	Stockholm, Tantogården
11/14	Stockholm, Tantogården
12/15	Stockholm, Sture Film festival, Med pupillerna i kosmos
12/16	Stockholm, Sture Film festival, Med pupillerna i kosmos

1999   Träd, Gräs och Stenar

8/31	Stockholm, Tantogården, Underground Will Take Over
11/4	Stockholm Kafé 44
12/27	Stockholm, Kolingsborg, The Happening

2000   Träd, Gräs och Stenar

1/29	Stockholm, Kafé 44
4/1	Stockholm, Liljeholmen Kulturfabriken, Samma mark - Samma rymd
4/6	Göteborg, Jazzhuset Klubb Lolita
5/1	Kalmar, Ung Vänster
5/13	Stockholm, Kafé 44
5/20	Stockholm, Drakfesten på Gärdet [Kite Festival on Gärdet]
6/18	Tanum, Kampetorp
6/27-29	Recording at Jakob's place
7/31-8/4	Recording at Jakob's place
8/18	Stockholm, Arkitekturmuseets trädgård, Festen på Gärdet Skeppsholmen [Museum of Architecture's Garden]
9/2	Riddarhyttan, Motståndsfestivalen (for the first time in the band's history TGS had to cancel the show due to an accident)
10/6	Umeå, Studion Folkets hus
10/7	Skogsnäs, Kulturhuset
12/8	Stockholm, Kafé 44

2001   Träd, Gräs och Stenar

2/2	Västerås, Village
2/28	Lund, Smålands nation [Småland's Student Society]
3/2	Hässleholm, Perrong 23
3/3	Ängelholm, Gottwalds café
3/23	Stockholm, Fylkingen (Release party for the Pärson Sound CD)
4/13	Torna Hällestad, Kafé Tolvan
4/14	Sölvesborg, Kartago
4/15	Malmö, Möllevångsgården Inkonst
4/24	Stockholm, Göta Källare - opening for Stephen Malkmus
4/25	Göteborg, Jazzhuset - opening for Stephen Malkmus
5/17	Norrköping, Popstopp
6/2	Lund, Bananfesten
6/3	Malmö, Möllefesten
7/14	Arvika, Arvikafestivalen Apolloscenen
7/26	Nyskoga, Hembygdsgården
7/28	Ransbysätern, Utmarksmusiken
7/29	Ängelholm, Tullakrok

8/3	Stockholm, Skeppsholmen, Krockfest (together with The Latin Kings)
8/18	Eskilstuna, Stadsparken, Sommarens sista suck
10/6	Uppsala, Grand, Förbundet Djurens Rätt and De Hemlösas Förening [Animal Rights Association and Homeless Association Benefit]
11/25-26	Rock at Sea (music cruise, roundtrip Stockholm-Åbo)
12/14	Stockholm, Kafé 44

2002   Träd, Gräs och Stenar

1/24	Malmö, Kulturbolaget
1/25	Helsingborg, The Tivoli
1/26	Kristianstad, Barbacka
4/5	Göteborg, Vågen Psynk
4/25	Stockholm, Kolingsborg Psynk
4/26	Eskilstuna, Memento, Blå
4/27	Uppsala, Katalin
5/25	Stockholm, Pop Dakar
6/12	Västerås, Vasaparken, Arosfestivalen
6/29	Delsbo, Ljusbacken, Rumble in the Jungle
7/19	Skellefteå, Trästockfestivalen
8/7	Norrköping, Skulpturparken
8/31	Stockholm, Kulturhusets tak, After shopping
9/20	Katrineholm, Inferno (festival för kultur och demokrati) [Festival for Culture and Democracy]
9/28	Brösarp, Neon Gallery
10/12	Stockholm (birthday party for Torbjörn's neighbor Bengt)
11/22-23	Stockholm, Rock at Sea, Svenska Höjdare (music cruise, roundtrip Stockholm-Åbo)
12/13	Västerås, Taj Mahal
12/14	Eskilstuna (40th birthday party)

2003   Träd, Gräs och Stenar

4/5	Stockholm, Gustav Vasa kyrka (Benefit for children living on the street in Addis Ababa)
4/8	Stockholm, Lava Kulturhuset (opening for Cul de Sac and Damo Suzuki)
4/17	Göteborg, Gump Jazzhuset
5/20	TV recording Stockholm, TV4 Nyhetsmorgon (live broadcast) [Morning TV show]
5/21	London, 291 Gallery
5/22	Brighton
5/28	Västerås, Taj Mahal
7/12	Brösarp, Neon Gallery
7/16	Norberg, Kärrgruvans Folkets park
7/19	Möja, dansbanan [Dance hall]
9/5	Stockholm, Gustav Vasa kyrka [Gustav Vasa Church]
9/20	Västerås, Taj Mahal
10/2	Chicago, Empty Bottle
10/3	Detroit, Majestic/ Magic Stick
10/4	Madison, Wisconsin
10/5	Minneapolis, Fine Line Music Café
10/7	New York, Tonic
10/8	Radio WFMU, WNYU, and the shop Other Music, New York
10/9	New York, Hinthouse
10/10	Philadelphia, Khyber Pass
10/11	New York, Tonic
10/12	Providence, Rhode Island, AS220
10/13	Madison, Connecticut, The Saturnalia 4 Festival
10/15	San Francisco, Bottom of the Hill
10/17	Seattle, The Crocodile Cafe
10/18	Portland, Crystal Ballroom/Lola's Room
11/22	Kiruna, Malmia (Benefit for Hopp för barn i Etiopien) ["Hope for Children in Ethiopia"]
11/30	Stockholm, Debaser
12/13	Stockholm, Kafé 44

2004	Träd, Gräs och Stenar
3/20	Borås, Musikhuset Rockborgen
4/2	Rye, England, festival All Tomorrow´s Parties
5/7	Lund, Smålands nation
6/5	Skövde, Klubb Utopi
6/19	New York, Tonic
6/20	Philadelphia, Khyber Pass
6/22	Fort Worth, Texas, Wreck Room
6/23	Austin, Texas, Emo`s
6/24	San Diego, 4862 Voltaire
6/25	Los Angeles, Knitting Factory
6/26	San Francisco, Hotel Utah
6/28	Oregon, Berbatis Pan
6/29	Portland, Jackpot Records (acoustic with mouth harps, rubber bands, and violin)
6/29	Seattle, Neumo´s
7/1	Baltimore, Talking Head
7/2	New York, Tonic
7/3	Boston, TT the Bear
7/17	Falun, Folkmusikfestivalen Magasinet
7/31	Ödeshög, Kvarnen i byn Boet
10/1	Kalmar, Palace
10/7	Stockholm, Debaser
12/10	Stockholm, Kafé 44

2005	Träd, Gräs och Stenar
2/25	Göteborg, Nefertiti
2/26	Köpenhamn, Christiania, Byens Lys
3/12	Hasselt, Bryssel, Belgien, KRAAK Festival
4/20	Pori/Björneborg, Finland, Club 19
4/21	Helsingfors, UMO Jazzhus
4/23	Moskva, Na Brestskoi
4/24	St. Petersburg, Segei Kurvokhin International Festival
5/12	Stockholm (Torbjörn's birthday party)
10/23	Stockholm, Färgfabriken, Playing the Building
11/25	Stockholm, Rock at Sea, Svenska Höjdare [Music Cruise on the Baltic Sea]
12/9	Stockholm, Kafé 44.

2006	Träd, Gräs och Stenar
3/1	Varberg, Caprinus
3/2	Göteborg, Jazzhuset
3/3	Skövde, Klubb Utopi
3/4	Oslo, SpasiBar
6/3	Lidingö (birthday party)
6/10	Stockholm, Tantogården, Kaskelotfestivalen
6/17	Färingsö, Ölsta Rockfest
7/23	Ängelholm, Tullakrok
10/17	Stockholm, Big Ben
10/20	Stockholm, Galleri Loyal
12/8	Västerås, Taj Mahal
12/9	Tranemo (50th birthday party)

2007	Träd, Gräs och Stenar
2/23	Stockholm, Kafé 44.
2/28	Kobe, Helluva Lounge
3/1	Nagoya, Tokuzo
3/2	Tokyo, Doors
3/3	Osaka, Bridge
5/8	Stockholm, Fylkingen
7/6	Norrköping, Folkets Park, Alternativfestivalen
7/7	Öllösa (birthday party for Torbjörn's sister Bissa)
7/20	Gotland, Hellvi, Kanela Kultur.
7/21	Gotland, Eke, Suder Country
8/11	Tromsø, Karlsøyafestivalen
8/24	Ronneby, Karön, Proggfest
8/25	Hässleholm, Perrong 23, Sommarfest

9/21	Paris, Point Ephémére, SOWIESO #1
9/22	Hasselt, festivalen (K-RAA-K)3
9/23	Tilburg, festivalen ZXZW
9/25	Haag, Helbaard
9/26	Antwerpen, Hof ter Lo
9/27	Rotterdam, WORM
11/17	Stockholm, Långholmen (wedding)
11.20	Stockholm, Debaser, Slussen
11/21	Malmö, Debaser

2008	Träd, Gräs och Stenar
1/26	Göteborg, Nefertiti (Bo Anders Persson quits)
5/15	Stockholm, Landet, Groddar och Gräsrötter (Reine Fiske's first gig)
5/16	Stockholm, Mosebacke Etablissemang, Ugglan-festivalen II
5/30	Barcelona, Primavera Sound Festival 2008
6/7	Karlstad, Värmlands museum, museiparken, Guest: Bo Anders Persson
8/30	Uppsala Parksnäckan, Stadsträdgården, 2008 - A Space Rock Odyssey
10/4	Västerås, Taj Mahal

2009	Träd, Gräs och Stenar
4/25	Göteborg, Angered, Blå Stället
5/6	Stockholm, Hornstull Strand (release party for *Hemlösa katter*)
5/16	Jönköping, Kulturhuset
7/31	Gotland, Eke, Havdhem, Suder Country
8/1	Gotland, Hellvi, Hide kalkbrott
9/12	Stockholm, Nordiska museet, exhibition Proggens Affischer [The Nordic Museum, "The Posters of Progg" Exhibition]
9/18	Köping, Ögir
9/19	Hammenhög, Garaget
9/30	Barcelona
10/2	Madrid
11/7	Stockholm, Rock at Sea
12/12	Haag, Koorenhuis Theater, State-X New Forms Festival

2010	Träd, Gräs och Stenar
2/20	Stockholm, Crystal, vernissage Tracy Nakayama (acoustic)
4/28	Glasgow, CCA
4/29	Newcastle, The Cumberland Arms
4/30	London, The Luminaire
5/1	Brighton, The Engine Room
5/2	Penryn, Miss Peapod´s Kitchen Café (Torbjörn Abelli's last gig)
11/19	Stockholm, Kulturhuset (memorial concert for Torbjörn Abelli)

2011	Träd, Gräs och Stenar
6/10	Stockholm, Orionteatern (with Thomas Tidholm, Sigge Krantz's first gig)
7/3	Skattungbyn, Inspirationsfestival (with Thomas Tidholm)
12/6	Stockholm, Kafé 44 (with Thomas Tidholm)

2012	Träd, Gräs och Stenar
2/3	Stockholm, Strand (with Thomas Tidholm)
2/4	Göteborg, Nefertiti Jazz Club (with Thomas Tidholm)
2/5	Malmö, Inkonst (with Thomas Tidholm)
3/29	Växjö, Kafé de Luxe
3/30	Malmö, Babel.
3/31	Köpenhamn, Christiania, Loppen (Thomas Mera Gartz's last gig)
8/1	Dala-Floda, Hagenfesten (with Bengt Berger, drums)
11/24	Stockholm, moment:teater (memorial concert for Thomas Mera Gartz)

2014	Träd, Gräs och Stenar	4/24	Seattle, Sunset Tavern
3/16	Ulvsunda, private party (Nisse Törnqvist's first gig)	4/26	Marfa, Texas, Marfa Myths Festival
6/13	Växjö, Psykjuntan	4/27	Marfa, Texas, Marfa Myths Festival
11/27	Stockholm, Kafé 44	4/28	Austin, Texas, Barracuda
12/17	Stockholm, Rönnells Antikvariat (with Torkel Rasmusson)	4/29	New York, Rough Trade
		5/8	Stockholm, Rönnells antikvariat, Jazz är farligt 9 år!
2015	Träd, Gräs och Stenar	8/2	Falun, Grönbo
3/31	Stockholm, Riche, Jazz är farligt [Jazz Is Dangerous]	8/3	Delsbo, Ljusstöparbacken
4/24	Eskilstuna, Royal Kulturhus	8/23	Tjärö, Blekinge skärgård, PLX festivalen
4/25	Göteborg, Folk	9/6	London, Troxy
4/28	Stockholm, Haninge Kulturhus	9/7	Sheffield, Dina
4/29	Stockholm, Södra Teatern, Kägelbanan	11/8	Utrecht, Nederländerna, the festival Le Guess Who

2016   Träd, Gräs och Stenar
9/9   London, Café Oto (with Tom Watts, drums)
9/10   London, Café Oto (with Tom Watts, drums)

2017   Träd, Gräs och Stenar
2/18   Stockholm, Fylkingen (Hanna Östergren's first gig)
4/26   Göteborg, Folk
4/27   Oslo, BLÅ
4/28   Malmö, Folk å Rock
4/29   Köpenhamn, Jazzhouse
5/18   Stockholm, Under Bron (release party for Tack för kaffet)
6/11   Solna, Kulturgården, Goodville Festivalen
6/16   Veberöd, Mossagårdsfestivalen
6/17   Hammenhög, Garaget
9/9   Lissabon, Reverence Santarém 2017
9/19   London, Café Oto
9/20   London, Café Oto
9/22   Liverpool, Liverpool International Festival of
        Psychedelia

2018   Träden
1/18   Stockholm, Under Bron
1/19   Helsingfors, G Livelab
1/20   Tampere, Progenuary/Olympia
7/7   Oslo, Kafe Hærverk, Motvind 2018
7/21   Alvesta, Blädinge, Tyrolen, Progg and Visfestivalen
7/24   Sandviken, Musik i Bruksmiljö
8/15   Göteborg, Liseberg, Jazz är farligt
8/25   Hammenhög, Garaget
8/26   Malmö, Far i hatten
9/1   Stockholm, Fasching
9/21   San Francisco, The Chapel
9/23   Big Sur, Henry Miller Library
9/24   Los Angeles, Zebulon
9/25   Los Angeles, Zebulon
9/26   Los Angeles, Zebulon
9/28   New York, Music Hall of Williamsburg
9/29   Greenfield, Massachusetts, Root Cellar
9/30   Philadelphia, Boot and Saddle
10/1   Washington DC, DC9 Night Club
10/3   Columbus, Ohio, Wexner Center
10/4   Chicago, Hide Out
10/5   Louisville, Kentucky, Cropped Out Festival
11/1   Göteborg, Stigbergets bryggeri
12/15   Uddevalla, Rock the Kasbah

2019   Träden
1/30   Göteborg, Folk
1/31   Göteborg, Folk
2/1   Oslo, Kafé Haerverk
2/2   Oslo, Kafé Haerverk
2/3   Stavanger, Rimi/Imir Scenkunst
3/21   Stockholm, Årsta Folkets Hus
4/23   Portland, Liqour Store

Sources

INTERVIEWS

Abelli, Torbjörn. Interview by Lars Kaijser. Stockholm, March 12, 2010.

Ericsson, Arne. Interview by Jonas Stål. Eskilstuna. September 9, 2016.

Fiske, Reine. Interview by Mats Eriksson Dunér. June 8, 2017.

Gartz, Thomas Mera. Interview by Jonas Stål. Stockholm. February 22, 2012.

Gransvik, Sonja. Interview by Mats Eriksson Dunér. November 14, 2016.

Krantz, Sigge. Interview by Mats Eriksson Dunér. April, 2020.

Lind, Anders. Interview by Mats Eriksson Dunér, Håkan Agnsäter, and Jakob Sjöholm. May 20, 2017.

Persson, Bo Anders. Interview by Jonas Ståhl. Likenäs. March, 21, 2012.

Persson, Bo Anders. Interview by Eriksson Dunér. April 21, 2017.

Sjöholm, Jakob. Interview by Jonas Stål. Svartsjö. October 14, 2016.

Tidholm, Thomas. Interview by Mats Eriksson Dunér. September, 2016.

Yman, Urban. Interview by Mats Eriksson Dunér. September, 2016.

Östergren, Hanna. Interview by Mats Eriksson Dunér. April, 2020.

CONTRIBUTED TEXTS

Backman, Dan

Berger, Tore

Bindeman, Jed

Bruyere Vincent, Michel de la

Klingberg, Jon Jefferson

Klingberg, Margareta

Kurosawa, Go

Livstrand, Anita

Mosskin, Peter

Philemon Arthur

Sjöstedt, Torgny

Tidholm, Anna-Clara

Torsson, Björner

BIBLIOGRAPHY

Bankier, Channa. Mordet på konsten [The Murder of Art]. I Schyberg, Dick (ed.) Elektriska drömmar [Electric Dreams]. Stockholm: Schlager/Rockmani, 1982.

Berg, Bengt. Mellan bark och betong [Between Bark and Concrete]. I Schyberg, Dick (ed.) Elektriska drömmar. Stockholm: Schlager/Rockmani, 1982.

Böcker, writings

Gartz, Thomas Mera. Rapport från en musikhink [Report from a Music Bucket].

Meyer-Hermann, Eva (ed.) Andy Warhol: en guide till 706 föremål på 2 timmar 56 minuter [Andy Warhol: A Guide to 706 Items in 2 Hours 56 Minutes]. Rotterdam: NAi Publishers, 1997. 11.

Persson, Bo Anders. Tradition som radikalt alternativ - i Stockholm och Budapest under 1970-talet. Uppsats för tre poäng vid kursen "Folkmusik i världen" [Tradition as a Radical Alternative — in Stockholm and Budapest During the 1970s. Essay for three points in the course "Folk Music in the World"]. Falun/Borlänge: Dalarna University, 1992. 16.

SOU 2002:91. Hoten från vänster. Säkerhetstjänsternas övervakning av kommunister, anarkister m.m. 1965-2002 [Threats from the Left: The Security Services' Surveillance of Communists, Anarchists, etc., 1965–2002]. http://www.regeringen.se/rattsdokument/statens-of-fentliga-utred ningar/2002/01/sou-200291/

FLYERS, PAMPHLETS, DOCUMENTATION, LETTERS

Det exploderande hjulet / Det är dags att börja träffas igen [The Exploded Wheel / It's Time to Start Dancing Again]

Folk vill träffas [People Want to Meet]

Front mot överklasskulturen [Front Against the Upper-Class Culture]

Fåren får både vara och skita på Gärdet [The Sheep Can Both Be and Shit at Gärdet]

Persson, Bo Anders. Något om musikfester och livets gång [Something About Music Festivals and the Course of Life]

Rock för glatta livet [Rock for Happy Life]

Toresson, Hans-Göran. Letter to Thomas Mera Gartz, June 13, 1972.

Träd, Gräs och Stenar är namnet på ett musiksällskap [Träd, Gräs och Stenar Is the Name of a Music Company]

NEWSPAPERS AND MAGAZINES

Alserud. "Ny Oskarshamnsförening ordnade folkrockkonsert." Oskarshamns-Nyheterna. March 20, 1972.

Andersson, Dennis. "Hypnotiskt och unikt." Barometern. April 24, 2002. http://web.comhem.se/t.m.gartz/ajnrec.htm (20180302)

Andersson, Jan. "Träd, Gräs och Stenar, Samla Mammas Manna, Gudibrallan ... Får ett popband heta vad som helst?" Aftonbladet. July 4, 1971.

Andersson, Leif J. "International Harvester i Gävle." Arbetarbladet. February 6, 1969.

Backman, Dan. "Hemlösa katter: Elastiskt, varmt och uråldrigt." Svenska Dagbladet. May 6, 2009. https://www.svd.se/elastiskt-varmt-och-uraldrigt (20180302)

Bangs, Lester. Rolling Stone. No. 67, 1970.

Bankier, Channa och Gartz, Thomas Mera. "Varför ere så tråkigt." Musikens Makt. No. 8, 1973.

Barbara. "Sexton skolband i tävlan om bästa jazzorkestern." Dagens Nyheter. March 24, 1962.

Bergendahl, Göran. "Bo Anders Persson." Nutida Musik. No. 8, 1966-67.

Bogström, Margareta. "'Träd, gräs och stenar' i Skärholmen." Söderposten. October 28, 1970.

Borggren, Ingrid. "Poetiska proggare för öppna sinnen." Dagens Nyheter. December 8, 1995.

Borges, Jan. "Weekend beat." Extrabladet. My 3, 1971.

Bäckman, Anna-Lisa. "En gång hovkonditori. Nu ett ställe med 'Freak out.' Musik som spränger." Dagens Nyheter. October 22, 1967.

Charlie. "Expolaris gav popare samvetsnöd." Norra Västerbotten. February 8, 1969.

"De vill leva giftfritt." *Strengnäs Tidning*. June 19, 1972.

Edberg, Ulla-Britt. "Bo Anders Persson Sound." *Svenska Dagbladet*. July 21, 1967.

Edberg, Ulla-Britt. "Pop och dans och saft." *Svenska Dagbladet*. September 25, 1968.

Edh, Jan. "Två ungdomar flydde storstadens omänsklighet. Nu satsar de sig själva i en ny tillvaro på landet - Men finns det livsbetingelser för dem i Bollnäs-byn Herte?" *Okänd tidning*. November 15, 1969.

Eliza. "'Hår'-regissör Fränckel till Malmö. Visfestival ombord på Storken." *Svenska Dagbladet*. September 23, 1968.

Erichsson, Iwan. "Popmusik okonventionell." *Gefle Dagblad*. February 6, 1969.

Erlandsson, Sören. "Djungeln lag som rock." *Aftonbladet*. May 28, 1972.

Eriksson, Bengt. "Den svenska popens revolt." *Aftonbladet*. July 4, 1970.

Forshage, Patrik. "Träd Gräs och Stenar - Tack för kaffet." *Nöjesguiden*. May 13, 2017. *https://ng.se/recensioner/musik/trad-gras-och-stenar-tack-for-kaffet (20180302)*

Fredriksson, Svante. "Musikrörelsens 'pensionärer på Sverigeturné'." *Arbetet*. April 15, 1980.

"Fullt hus på konsert. Krav på större lokal." *Västerbottens-Kuriren*. February 10, 1969.

"Förvirring om Harvester." *Aftonbladet*. February 23, 1969.

Geijerstam, Eva af. "Den nya popen: Till kamp mot Coca-Cola kulturen- Träd, Gräs och Stenar popens spelemän." *Dagens Nyheter*. February 21, 1971.

Geijerstam, Eva af. "Många nya grupper och få bra musiker." *Dagens Nyheter*. August 24, 1970.

Geijerstam, Eva af. "50 000 kronor tvingar Skeppsholmspopen flytta." *Dagens Nyheter*. June 10, 1970.

Genberg, Kjell E. "Apropos DOORS-konserten." *Nöjes-Aktuellt*. October, 1968.

Glanzelius, Ingmar. "Gartz - vila för desperata." *Dagens Nyheter*. June 18, 1976.

Glanzelius, Ingmar. "Ofarligt och bondskt." *Dagens Nyheter*. June 10, 1974.

Glanzelius, Ingmar. "Är människan ej längre viktig?" *Göteborgs-Posten*. April 21, 1968.

"Gratis popfolkfest med teater och gammeldans." *Dagens Nyheter*. May 22, 1970.

Gren, Bert. "Gård i Värmland inspirerar Träd Gräs och Stenar." *Göteborgs-Posten*. February 21, 1972.

Gunnar. "Träd, Gräs och Stenar." *Sundsvalls Tidning*. November 26, 1969.

Gustafsson, Mats and Jackson, Lee. "For fans of seriously damaged psychedelic excess only: Pärson Sound." *The Broken Face*. No. 15, 2003. *http://web.comhem.se/t.m.gartz/prsintbf.htm (20180301)*

Halo. "Träd, Gräs och Stenar talade om miljövård." *Norrskensflamman*. July 30, 1971.

Hambræus, Bengt. "Nya skivor - elektrisk blockflöjt, virtuos cembalo, fransk högtalarkonst och en del annat också." *Nutida Musik*. No. 13, 1969-70.

Helmerson, Erik. "Popens största gåta (nästan) löst." *Svenska Dagbladet*. March 8, 2010.

Herngren, Anna. "Folkfest i Gävle museum med Träd, Gräs och Stenar." *Arbetarbladet*. February 25, 1971.

h-jn. "Svenskrock - danskrock." *Information*. April 26, 1971.

Håkansson, Björn. "Träd gräs och stenar - Ett skämt?" *Svenska Dagbladet*. November 16, 1969.

"Hått Båys." *Dagens Nyheter*. May 8, 1974.

Idestam-Almquist, Dick. "Narrspel på Narren." *Dagens Nyheter*. May 27, 1966.

Idioten. "Oändligt tack." *Ljusnan*. February 15, 1969.

International Harvester. "Bekämpa inte narkomanerna!" *Aftonbladet*. April 12, 1969.

International Harvester. "International Harvester." *Paletten*. No. 4, 1968.

"International Harvester - Samhällets huvudvärk." *Bildjournalen*. No. 14, 1969.

"International Harvester 'umgicks' ungt på museet." *Sundsvalls Tidning*. February 10, 1969.

Jison. "'Träd gräs och stenar' underliga krumelurer på Grängesbergsscen." *Grängesberg*. October 14, 1971.

Kangas, Timo. "Psych-prog riktad mot den uppåtgående solens hjärta." *Lira*. June 1, 2015. *http://www.lira.se/psych-progg-riktad-mot-den-uppatgaende-solens-hjarta/ (20180302)*

Keijser, Roland. "Organiserat ljud och oorganiserat." *Uppsala Nya Tidning*. July 21, 1967.

Keijser, Roland. "Människofest." *Upsala Nya Tidning*. September 29, 1969.

Kinell, Stefan. "Träd, gräs och stenar: Rock för kropp och själ." *Västerbottens-Kuriren*. April 1, 1972.

Kjell Å. "Rock för kropp och själ." *Dala-Demokraten*. April 10, 1972.

Klingberg, Margareta. "De hittar påtusen sätt att demonstrera." *Aftonbladet*. December 1, 1968.

Klingberg, Margareta. "Svensk pop klarar sig utan kilowatt." *Aftonbladet*. December 23, 1973.

"Kom till Gärdet!" *Aftonbladet*. June 11, 1970.

"Kringstrykande musikband: MUSIK FÖR FOLKET SÅ ALLA BEGRIPER." *Norrländska Social-Demokraten*. November 30, 1971.

Kågesson, Per och Stolpe, Pär. "Antimässan ett alternativ." *Dagens Nyheter*. November 6, 1968.

Lahger, Håkan. "Skivor i stället för diktsamlingar." *Dagens Nyheter*. May 6, 1979.

Landskapsposten, October, 1969.

Laurin, Knut-Urban. "Träd, Gräs och Stenar spelar i Bollnäs: Bollnäsflicka med i deras naturkollektiv." *Ljusnan*. November 13, 1971.

Levy, Madelaine. "Pavement." *Pop*. No. 9:2, 1999. *https://popviminns.wordpress.com/2014/07/19/pavement/ (20180302)*

Lindström, Gustav. "Gräsligt på Olympia. Publiken gick hem ..." *Örnsköldsviks Allehanda*. August 2, 1971.

"Lite om livet i jorden, lite praktik i vänlig odling." *Huvudbladet*. No. 3, 1972.

"Lyssna på." *Tidningen Vi*. No. 8, 1969.

Mangs, Runar. "Ett inslag övertygade på Akademins elevkonsert." *Dagens Nyheter*. May 23, 1967.

Masters, Marc. "Träd, Gräs och Stenar - Djungels lag." *Pitchfork*. May 8, 2016. https://pitchfork.com/reviews/albums /21704-trad-gras-stenar-djungelns -lagmors-morskom-tillsammans/ (20180302)

"Mera musik." *Huvudbladet*. June, 1971.

"Mat och musik på visklubb." *Jönköpings-Posten*. March 25, 1972.

Mosskin, Peter. "Sov gott Rose-Marie!" *Expressen*. January 7, 1969.

Mosskin, Peter. "Hemåt med Harvester." *Expressen*. September 17, 1969.

"Musikhögskolan tog in 140." *Dagens Nyheter*. September 9, 1965.

"Musik på museum." *Bildjournalen*. No. 17, 1969.

Nielsen, Hans-Jörgen. "Konsten är strunt!" *Dagens Nyheter*. May 2, 1969.

Nilsson, Lennart. "Kalldusch inför invigningen: Bryggeriet rivningshotat!" *Dagens Nyheter*. December 19, 1974.

Nordlander, Jan och Rosen, Urban von. "En underground LP." *Svenska Dagbladet*. December 29, 1968.

Nordlander, Jan & Rosen, Urban von. "Pop-musikens James Dean bäddade för Doors' succé." *Svenska Dagbladet*. September 21, 1968.

Norlin, Arne. "Nu spelar Träd, Gräs & Stenar igen." *Aftonbladet*. May 19, 1980.

"Ny svensk pop." *Svenska Dagbladet*. March 8, 1971.

Nylén, Leif. "Aktioner, alternativ." *Paletten*. No. 4, 1968.

"Nytt om nöjen." *Dagens Nyheter*. October 7, 1969.

Olsson, Mats. "Slitna klyschor." *Arbetet*. August 13, 1971.

Oscar. "Ljudband genom Akademien blev happening för Edenman." *Dagens Nyheter*. November 26, 1966.

Otis. "Låt Harvester spela i skolan." *Sydsvenska Dagbladet*. February 25, 1969.

Otis. "Är Träd, Gräs och Stenar pop? - 'Den bästa beskrivningen vi hört'" *Sydsvenska Dagbladet*. December 15, 1969.

Persson, Benny. "Veckans skiva." *Upsala Nya Tidning*. April 15, 1972.

Persson, Bo Anders. "I köket." *Nutida Musik*. No. 3-4, 1968-69.

Persson, Bo Anders. "Joel Jansson och den möjliga svenskrocken: ett öppet brev." *Musikens Makt*. No. 6, 1974.

Persson, Bo Anders och Tidholm, Thomas. "Om Terry Riley och oss andra." *T'a 6*. No. 2, 1968.

Persson, Bo Anders. "Är det bara begåvade som får spela?" *Göteborgs-Posten*. August 12, 1972.

Pettersson, Jan-Åke. "Blir popen folkligare?" *Arbetet*. November 30, 1970.

"Popmusik borde tas upp i musiklärar-utbildningen." *Östersunds-Posten*. November 29, 1969.

"Pottor och regn första popdagen." *Dagens Nyheter*. June 13, 1970.

Rabe, Folke. "Göran Palm i ogjort väder." *Dagens Nyheter*. May 14, 1969.

Rander, Tommy. "Träd, gräs och Stenar på Hagahuset - Dom bjuder på mat, musik o. utställning." *Göteborgs-Tidningen*. February 20, 1972.

Rasmusson, Ludvig. "Blandad Pistolshow med International H." *Dagens Nyheter*. September 25, 1968.

Rasmusson, Ludvig. "Historien om ett popband." *Dagens Nyheter*. May 12, 1968.

Rasmusson, Ludvig. "International Harvester sjunger helst svenskt." *Dagens Nyheter*. August 25, 1968.

Rasmusson, Ludvig. "Popens entertain-ers." *Dagens Nyheter*. September 21, 1968.

Rasmusson, Ludvig. "Popmusiker spelar falskt." *Dagens Nyheter*. October 6, 1968.

Rasmusson, Ludvig. "Riktig svensk pop." *Dagens Nyheter*. February 12, 1969.

Rasmusson, Ludvig. "Sommaren - bra poptest." *Dagens Nyheter*. June 29, 1969.

Rasmusson, Ludvig. "Teenage Fair - ett ställe för dem ingen bryr sig om." *Dagens Nyheter*. November 5, 1968.

reit. "'Earthquake' - et positivt eksperiment." *Sjællanstidende*. May 10, 1971.

"Rock för kropp och själ - Träd, Gräs och Stenar." *Bohusläningen*. April 1, 1972.

Rosen, Urban von. "Pop för barn." *Svenska Dagbladet*. June 19, 1969.

"Runt Sergels torg." *Dagens Nyheter*. August 13, 1969.

Sallander, Henrik. "Spela hellre själva!" *Dagens Nyheter*. March 21, 1972.

Sandblad, Håkan. "Står vissen musik extra nära folket?" *Göteborgs handels- och Sjöfartstidning*. September 21, 1970.

Sjöberg, Mats. "Träd, Gräs och Stenar fick spela på asfalt." *Norrbottens-Kuriren*. July 29, 1971.

Sjögren, Kent. "Torsbyrock mot Chirac." *Värmlands folkblad*, August 7, 1995.

Sjögren, Klas. "Ömsint musik." *Gränslöst*. No. 3, 1998.

Svensson, Per. "Minns ni Träd, Gräs & Stenar." *Tonfallet*. No. 9, 1980.

Svensson, Torbjörn. "TRÄD, GRÄS OCH STENAR ett annat ord för människa." *Bergslagsposten*. October 20, 1971.

S-Å. "Våg av nyodlarglädje i norra Klarälvdalen." *Nya Wermlands-Tidningen*. August 23, 1971.

"Träd, Gräs och Stenar." *Aftonbladet*. December 27, 1972.

"Träd, gräs och stenar på Vindelälvens strand." *Västerbottens Folkblad*. August 2, 1971.

"Träd, gräs och stenar till Jönköping med musik och mat." *Smålands Folkblad*. March 21, 1972.

"Träd, gräs och stenar: 'Tillbaka till naturen'" *Norrskensflamman*. November 20, 1971.

"TV hos oss. Inga kanalkrockar - vi ser när vi hinner." *Dagens Nyheter*. December 28, 1969.

"TV, skiva och teater för Mecki Mark Men." *Dagens Nyheter*. August 12, 1967.

"Unga i gammal skola gör pop av folk-musik. *Söderhamns-Hälsinge-Kuriren*. September 26, 1970.

Vinterhed, Kerstin. "Kjartans psykiska ohälsa." *Dagens Nyheter*. December 21, 1969.

Woodbury, Jason P. "Psychedelic Arizonans The Myrrors reborn on Arena Negra." *Phoenix New Times*. February 10, 2015. http://www.phoenixnewtimes.com/ content/printView/6604633 (20180302)

Wykman, Henk. "Extrem popkonsert på fastande mage." *Göteborgs-Tidningen*. April 26, 1968.

"Vänlig odling." *Huvudbladet*. No. 2, 1972.

Åberg, Lars. "Den nya popen." *Aftonbla-det*. June 11, 1971.

About the Authors and Editors

Håkan Agnsäter
is a musician and writer from Stockholm. His book *Affischerna 1967-1979*, collecting posters from the Swedish alternative movement, was published in 2013. He was the drummer of the band Solen Skiner in the 1970s, and runs the site www.affischerna.se.

Mats Eriksson Dunér
is an artist from the city of Malmö. In 2018, his interview with Thomas Tidholm was published as part of the International Harvester box, and in 2019, he participated in the anthology *Ockuperat! Svenska husockupationer*, documenting the Swedish house-occupation movement. His latest film, *Aktivering Samtal* (Act Dialogue) was shown at the Tempo documentary festival in 2020.

Mark Iosifescu
is a writer and musician from New York City. He is the co-founder of Pleasure Editions, a small press publisher of avant-garde literature, poetry, trans-lation, and fine art, and he has been editor of Anthology Editions' line of music and culture books since 2017.

Linda McAllister
is a translator from Stockholm, Sweden. Her work spans many fields, from academic writing on art and theory to nursery rhymes, poetry, and literature. She is especially interested in strong voices, unique perspectives, humor, and tricky language.

Jakob Sjöholm
is a musician and photographer from Stockholm, and a member of Träd, Gräs och Stenar since December 1970. He previously worked as a math and crafts teacher at the Ekerö junior high school, and as a member of the Hot Boys and Jajja Band.

Jonas Stål
is a writer, editor, podcaster, and librarian from the city of Nyköping. His writing about Swedish music of the sixties can be found as part of the compilation *Stora Popbox: Svensk Pop 1964-1969*, and the book *Vi har ingenting att göra* (We Have Nothing to Do). He is the creator and editor of the literary podcast *Litteraturväven*.

Thanks to all the photographers, copywriters and artists who contributed to the book. A special thanks to everyone in and around the band who shared their memories.

Thanks to Yael and Naomi Gartz Feiler and Eva Göransson for all the help with access to Mera and Torbjörn's archive. Thanks also to Jon Edergren, who designed the original edition of the book.

This English language edition would not have been possible without the translation work of Linda McAllister, the design and cover by Martha Ormiston, the proofreading by Chris Peterson, and the combined efforts of Keith Abrahamsson, Jesse Pollock, Mark Iosifescu, Donna Allen, and Casey Whalen at Anthology Editions.

Last but not least, thanks to Tobias Barenthin Lindblad at Dokument Press, who helped us get the project off the ground.

Thank you!